TROPIC OF HOCKEY

TROPIC OF HOCKEY

MY SEARCH FOR THE GAME IN UNLIKELY PLACES

DAVE BIDINI

M&S

National Library of Canada Cataloguing in Publication Data

Bidini, Dave
   Tropic of hockey: my search for the game in unlikely places

ISBN 0-7710-1457-0 (bound).–ISBN 0-7710-1458-9 (pbk.)

I. Title.

GV847.B52 2000   796.962   C00-931678-7

We acknowledge the financial support of the Government of Canada through
the Book Publishing Industry Development Program for our publishing
activities. We further acknowledge the support of the Canada Council for the
Arts and the Ontario Arts Council for our publishing program.

Text design by Ingrid Paulson
Typeset in Janson by M&S, Toronto
Printed and bound in Canada

McClelland & Stewart Ltd.
The Canadian Publishers
481 University Avenue
Toronto, Ontario
M5G 2E9
www.mcclelland.com

2   3   4   5   05   04   03   02   01

For Janet

"Hockey is a road that you follow."

– Jane Siberry

CONTENTS

PROLOGUE

THE NIGHT OF THE GOALTENDER

It was 1986, just outside Athens, Georgia, when hockey found me. After an uneventful pilgrimage to the home of REM – rock 'n' roll's best band that year – my friend Tim Vesely and I left town in the falling blue-black of the Southern night. Soon the engine of our Olds was labouring across the sloping countryside, rattling and wheezing like a dog pulling on a leash. So, we turned off at the first exit and clanged into the nearest town, Clarksville.

We rolled into the town square, switched the engine off, and sat there clinging to that universal untruth: "Maybe it just needs to cool down a little." We waited, fired the engine, but there was neither a *prrrr*, nor a *clank*.

It was a gorgeous night. Soft. Warm. Insects sang. A police cruiser approached in our rear-view and pulled in behind us. I had visions of Cracker troopers and the Jackson County jail. We climbed out of our car and he climbed out of his. To my relief, he looked nothing like Warren Oates.

He spoke first. "So what are you guys doing in Clarksville in the middle of a Sunday night in a broken-down Olds with Ontario plates?" There was the long answer, of course, but we gave him the short one. And then he said:

"Well, there's no garage open now. You'd best wait until morning to get this looked at."

"What about hotels?" we asked.

"Motels. There's Harvey's place up the road. Let's see if old Harv's still awake."

We rode in the cruiser to the motel. It felt pretty cool getting to ride in the back seat of a Georgian copmobile without first having to bludgeon someone to death. We sat behind the steel mesh partition and watched the dark countryside roll past. The cop made small talk. He seemed like a decent fellow.

At the motel, we followed him to an open door that leaked the blue, winking light of a television. The cop called in, "Harv? Harv? You up?" An old man in his pyjamas came to the door. "Got a breakdown here," the cop told him. "Kids need a room until they can get their car fixed."

"All right," said Harv, rubbing his eyes. "The office." And we followed him.

Harv was a tall fellow with a dented face and ravaged skin.

"Where're you boys from?" he asked, in a voice like falling rocks.

"Toronto," said Tim.

"Toronto?" he echoed, scratching his head.

"You know it?" I asked.

"Know it? Christ, I'm from Oshawa."

It was then that I noticed the pictures on the office walls: goalie pictures. The wood panelling was covered with them, old photographs of Harvey standing in the net, his face young and smooth, his head topped with bristle-brush hair. He was wearing black pads and gloves that looked like oven mitts. An unvarnished stick was angled against his skates, which were old and wrinkled and leathery, a white number painted on the ankles. Underneath the glass countertop on which Harv had opened the motel's registry, there were two hockey cards: Harvey Bennett, Junior, Philadelphia Flyers, and Curt Bennett, Atlanta Flames.

"Who are they?" I asked.

"Two of my boys. Both of them in the National Hockey League."

Born in 1925 in Edington, Saskatchewan, Harvey had been a career minor-leaguer who was called up from the Boston Olympics to fill in during the wartime player shortage. His only big-league year was in 1944–45 with the Boston Bruins, when he played twenty-five games and went ten wins, twelve losses, two ties (4.20 goals-against average). Harvey's footnote to the story of hockey was that he was in the net on the night Rocket Richard scored his fiftieth goal. His profile in *Total Hockey* shows that he played for the Regina Abbotts, Providence Reds, Chatham Maroons, Trois-Rivières Lions and Washington Presidents, long-extinct teams. I imagined backwater rinks and cold bus rides. I could see every game carved into his face.

"Didn't wear masks then," said Harv, pointing to an old photo of himself.

"That must have been tough," I said.

"Tough? I took shots here, here, here, and here," he said, poking his face.

"Do you still watch hockey?" I asked.

"No. Not since the Flames left Atlanta. You know, a lot of people were sad when they took them away. You'd be surprised. There're good hockey fans down here. They were just starting to get to know the game, before they went . . ."

"Up to Calgary."

"Ya. Calgary."

The old goalie took our names and gave us a room where moths studded the walls like thumb-tacks. We turned on the TV and there was Dave Thomas of SCTV being interviewed by David Letterman. We turned off the lights, feeling like we'd been weirdly embraced by Canada. The next day, Harvey called a tow truck and drove us to the garage. He talked to the mechanic, who fixed our transmission and sent us home. Harvey was our guardian angel in pads and gloves, a messenger from beyond. It wasn't until we hit the open road that I realized how unlikely it had been to find this spectral figure from Canada's game in such a faraway place. And as the snow started to fall across Ohio, grew thick over Niagara County, and turned into a blizzard once we reached home, I hoped that one day I would look back and understand.

The first thing I did when I got back to Toronto was to start playing hockey. I figured it was the least I could do to acknowledge the hockey gods. I hadn't played competitively since I'd turned my back on the game as a teenager but, after asking around, I found a Sunday night skate of musicians in McCormick Arena in downtown Toronto. McCormick is nestled on a side street in a neighbourhood that's relatively sleepy, but every now and then, some stoner tire-irons a car and makes off with his weight in Thundermug and Neil Diamond cassettes, which shows you what crack will do to the mind. I played there once a week, struggling to find strength in my legs and learning how to shoot, and I got better with each game. Before I knew it, I'd fallen in love with hockey all over again.

Thirteen years later, I play four, sometimes five games a week. I can't get enough. It's reached the point where I measure everything else in my life by whether I have as much fun as I do playing hockey. I have driven countless miles at reckless speeds along dirt roads, over frozen lakes, and down icy highways; I've fought traffic jams, blizzards, heat waves, parades, funeral processions, and speed traps; I've backed out of family dinners, band rehearsals, and dates with friends – all to take an elevating whirl around the cold oval. When I am on tour (I play in the rock band Rheostatics), the worst part is not being able to play hockey. I once said this aloud to friends, only to have Janet punch me in the shoulder. Janet is my wife. Her punch hurt.

"What was that for?" I asked.

"The worst part, eh?"

I thought quickly. "Well, you know, besides being away from . . ."

"From who?"

"Okay: the second worst part."

"The worst part, eh?"

Did I miss hockey more than I missed her? That I even had to ask the question shows how my life is governed. Hockey has blinkered my perspective not only of the world at hand, but also of the world at large. My compulsion has even stopped me from travelling. In 1997, Janet spent the winter traipsing around the cinnamon trees and silk stalls of Southeast Asia, but I didn't go with her because it would have imperilled my recreational hockey schedule. Instead, I drove every night to the rink, my hockey bag stuffed in the trunk like a drugged antelope, and for two hours sucked in cold Zamboni fumes as if they were smoke from a magic hookah.

It wasn't until I met Richard Harrison, the talented Calgary poet, that I realized there might be a way to see the world *and* play hockey. On a trip to the Côte D'Ivoire, Richard had discovered hockey being played on a rink built for Scandinavian tourists in the 1950s. He'd been sitting in the lobby of the Hôtel D'Ivoire when one of the hotel employees strode across the floor decked out in a Chicago Black Hawks jersey. Fearful that this was the first stage of malarial dementia, Richard moved in for a closer look and found himself face to face with this tropical Magnuson. Richard pointed vigorously at the player's crest, and the fellow responded, "Bobby Hull."

Now, if you were to walk up to a stranger in a big North American city and gesture wordlessly at his midriff, chances are he'd snap your finger off. But luckily for Richard, the African Black Hawk was approachable, and he was able to get to the bottom of the mystery of hockey in the Ivory Coast. He learned that a tournament was staged once a year (the temperature and dust storms made it impossible to maintain ice the rest of the time) using players from neighbouring hotels, who'd learned the game using equipment the Scandinavians had donated.

At first glance, the story is unlikely. "Africans playing hockey? Pshaw!" you scoff. But sport, like dandelion seeds sown on the wind, has the tendency to settle where you least expect it. All it takes is one freak or more in love with a game, and presto, the Jamaican bobsled team. Igor Kuperman, the director of information of the Phoenix Coyotes, has written about a two-team Indian hockey league made up of players from cities on either side of a mountain range. He describes a rink in the shadows of the Himalayas and games that last for days whenever the fog is too thick for the visiting team's plane to leave.

Stories like this piqued my curiosity. What would the game be like so far from its home? If I were to travel to look for the game in distant lands, would I glimpse our game being born? Would I see it as it had existed at the dawn of the last century? See hockey as it was before it became complicated by economics, corporate lust, the ravages of progress; before the pro game had betrayed tradition for quick-buck teams and a style that relied more on chalkboard patterns than spontaneous, tongue-wagging, river play? Maybe I could find a bunch of kids who'd never heard of Alexei Yashin, who'd never been prompted by a scoreboard command. Maybe I could see hockey the way it was once played here: a game of passion, of the people.

I was given a final push to search abroad for the game by the National Hockey League, but it's not what you think. The determining factor for my trip came on the afternoon of June 13, 1998. Janet and I were sitting on the chesterfield, taking in the third game of the Stanley Cup finals between the Detroit Red Wings and Washington Capitals. Outside, the sun beat like a kick drum against the curtains, and men in undershirts watered their sidewalks. Kids hoofed around a whiffleball and played Soak the Cat. An ice cream truck dingled up the street.

"Who's winning?" asked Janet, flipping through a magazine.

I turned to her blankly.

"What's the score? Who's winning?"

"Oh, the score," I said. "Beats me."

I was not being disingenuous. I had no idea who was winning. It was a terrible revelation. Years ago, my face would have been pressed to the screen. I would have memorized vital statistics and scribbled down line combinations on a piece of paper. I would have studied the teams' home and away records, head-to-head season play, the dimensions of their arenas. I would have taped the games, bought imported newspapers, and read columnists who'd followed the teams all year. Not this year. Instead, I was listlessly gazing at the television, waiting for something stunning to happen.

"Where's the series stand?" Janet asked.

The play volleyed from blue line to blue line. Both the Red Wings and Capitals were employing the Trap, a form of hockey which is the athletic equivalent of playing Pong. "Hockey Night in Canada" announcers Bob Cole and Harry Neale, who had suffered through every playoff series of the post-season, sounded as if they were describing the action with their chins propped on their hands. Finally, two players I'd never heard of fenced for the puck and chipped it into the stands. The referee called a TV time out and both teams drifted, heads lowered, towards their benches.

I looked at Janet. She looked back. I didn't say anything. I had no idea who was winning. I flipped channels. A blonde woman stood at a kitchen counter, squeezing butterscotch over shortbread cookies. This was more interesting. And so I watched Martha Stewart instead of the Stanley Cup finals.

I had no choice but to leave.

PART ONE

China

I

KRIS KING LOOKS TERRIBLE

I am going to China.

We've all been asked "So, what's new?" many times in our lives, but it's almost never that you get to answer, "I am going to China." I am more likely to respond, "Frig all. It's not like I'm going to China or anything." So when I got the chance, I milked it. I was Marco Polo draped in robes, hand held aloft, eyes to the sky: "I am going . . . to *China!*" I liked saying it. I said it lots. I might as well have walked around town with a *Guy Who Is Going to China* sign around my neck.

Janet and I planned our trip based on the principle that, when we dropped the name of the country and stated our purpose, people would have to wobble on their heels in disbelief: "They play hockey there?" Of course, there were other factors. Janet suggested that we stay clear of war zones, active volcanoes, and places overrun by infestations or plague. I proposed that we limit ourselves to nations regarded for their flush toilets.

"Well, that rules out about half the world," she said.

"The toilets can't be that bad, can they?" I asked.

"Ah, no. You bring toilet paper; you're fine."

"You bring what?"

"You'll be fine. Don't be a baby."

My apprehension over toilets was not just infantilism. I believe that if most men were asked to draw up plans for their dream bathroom, it would be located about fifty feet underground and have a steel-reinforced door. Maybe a stack of *Mad* magazines. Most of us could live there.

I was such a greenhorn when it came to prolonged, distant travel that I found even the process of making perfunctory arrangements for our trip exciting. I hadn't wandered but a mile from home when I started to feel the tingle of high adventure. That was my visit to the Tropical Disease Clinic. There I was shot full of a magic serum, which provided protection against yellow fever, diphtheria, and typhoid. The sense of adventure was fleeting, however, for I soon grew melancholy that I could no longer be stricken by such terrible diseases. Had I developed one of these horrible strains, I imagined the conversation in one of the city's taverns.

"Did you hear about Dave?" they'd ask.

"No. What?"

"He went to China and got yellow fever."

"Man, he's really living!"

There was a poster in the doctor's office identifying parasites found in developing countries. I remembered the Redmond O'Hanlon story about the parasite that slinks into the body through the penis and umbrellas inside one's intestines. This reminded me not to go swimming in China – and perhaps not anywhere ever again. I felt secure in the knowledge that this bug would not get within a country mile of my penis until I was struck by a rather phobic thought: What if that little fellow managed to stand up on the bowl with his hands arrowed and leap off the edge, only to shoot into me like that tiny submarine in *The Fantastic Voyage*? I explained this fear to Janet. "Don't be ridiculous," she said. "There's no such thing as a toilet bowl in China."

While I wrestled with the riddle of how toilets could apparently exist without toilet bowls, I left Janet to prepare herself for the Far

East. My only pre-trip endeavour was to sort out my hockey bag. This was not the effortless job it may appear.

The challenge of lugging an equipment duffle around the world was daunting enough, let alone one sagging with wet socks, sweaty T-shirts, and used tape clods. As I cleaned it, I found the bottom to be too damp and malodorous to inflict upon the world; its foul stench could defeat all measures we'd take to comport ourselves like touring diplomats. I envisioned my gear being held at the border and searched by an unlucky customs official with a hanky pressed to his face, who would have no choice but to drag it out back against a wall and blast holes into its fetid body.

I bought a new hockey bag. It was the kind with pockets and flaps and a reinforced base that will not bow no matter how much swampy rink water you pour into it. I started packing it with a bar of soap, a pair of athletic underpants, and a shower towel. Janet had a good laugh at that one, as in all my years of recreational hockey, I have never once showered at the rink. If you understand anything about the leisure hockey community, you know that it is divided into those who shower and those who don't. For some, waving one's gherkin in front of other men is easy; they can tromp around naked in the company of others and not turn the slightest shade of red. But I find something disconcerting about a fellow who will stand unclothed in front of you and carry on a conversation as if he'd bumped into you at the frozen-food section of the supermarket. He could be Carl Sagan unveiling the secrets of the cosmos, yet I would absorb nothing. I find that the presence of one's dangling protuberance has the tendency to overshadow even the most profound thoughts. Perhaps this explains why dressing-room banter rarely touches upon science or mathematics. Really, it's hard enough to sell one's theory of the universe in a tweed suit, let alone with yer wanger hanging out.

In addition to hygiene products, I filled my bag with hockey tape, pucks, shoulder pads, pants, elbow pads, shin guards, helmet, skates, hockey socks, jockstrap, and garter belt. The bag bulged like a lumpy balloon, and looked as if a pinprick would send it flying. I had barely enough room in the side pocket to squeeze in my gummy, blue mouth guard, a recent purchase which, when fitted between my gums, made me feel like I was chewing on a child's bathtub toy. But I had a practical reason for bringing it. The last thing I wanted was to end up with a handful of my own teeth, strapped pale and bloodied into a dentist's chair in some fly-infested office in a strange land, although I must admit the notion of spending time in a foreign hospital seemed like the kind of episode that made one a true adventurer.

Janet's pre-trip preparation put me to shame: she signed up for Mandarin lessons. I was jealous until I realized I should be thankful that it had occurred to at least one of us that we'd be spending the next six weeks among people who spoke another language. She quickly mastered several key phrases, not the least significant being "My husband is a writer," which she repeated over and over, usually while staring into the toaster oven or riding her bike. This made me feel quite important until I learned that the word for writer was similar to those for table and chicken.

"You might have to get used to the fact that I'll be calling you a table chicken every now and then," Janet warned, before going on to say "My husband is a table chicken" over and over – perhaps with the intention of thrumming me into a catatonic state, making the phrase quite apt. I told her that it was fine to say, but hard to accept if you were the one being mistaken for either a table or a chicken.

"What if we order chicken in a restaurant and you use the word for writer by mistake?" I wondered.

"Maybe they'll bring us George Plimpton," she said.

I managed to learn one phrase in Mandarin: *Wo da bing xi*. In English, this means "I play ice hockey." Mandarin is a language based on tonal ups and downs that sound rather like a flautist running his fingers over the sound holes. While I am to linguistics what B.F. Skinner is to hip hop, still I found Mandarin fun to speak, and I understood why Janet was using it so much. After a while, *Wo da bing xi* was pretty much all I wanted to say, even though I realized the problem of knowing only one phrase in a land roughly three-quarters the size of Canada with, oh, forty times the people. For instance, should I have to tell an officer of the law of some kind

of danger – say, a baby trapped inside a burning building – I wouldn't
be much help if all I knew how to say was "I play ice hockey!"

"*Wo da bing xi! Wo da bing xi!*" I'd scream while gesturing at the
flaming door. The cops would have no choice but to subdue me with
a blunt club.

On the day we left for China – March 1, 1999 – I arrived at the
airport carrying my Winwell hockey bag and three Koho hockey
sticks. Even though my lapsed physique made me look more like a
Colonial League journeyman, armed with my own gear I still felt
like a pro. I noticed other travellers squinting at me across the floor,
trying to square my face with a hockey card. But it was an impossible composite, and I could hear them telling their friends later, "I
saw the Leafs at the airport today. Kris King looks terrible."

We made our way to the departure gate, my hockey bag strapped
to my back like a camel's hump. Janet was equipped with all the essen-
tials of international transport – visas, passports, tickets, traveller's
cheques, insurance, guide books, and toothpaste – and I with all the
tools of athletic combat, plus two blank scribblers and a tape recorder.

No matter how thoroughly I prepare before going abroad, I find
air travel hard. I enjoy it to an extent, but not without a deep-rooted
fear that by hopping that little half-foot gap between passenger chute
and airplane, I'm consigning myself to death at 30,000 feet. I could
probably trace this fear back to the time I saw *Airport '77* at the drive-
in. I still look for George Kennedy whenever I get on a plane, and if
I don't find him, I know I'm all right. Fortunately, no one who ever
travelled Air Korea looked anything like George Kennedy.

But the flight was uneventful, and we landed fifteen hours later
at Hong Kong's new international airport, where we were met by a
strange man in glasses. This wasn't quite the scene from a Bond
caper that it sounds, because the stranger was a man with whom I
was vaguely familiar. I'd written to Herb Shoveller – a journalist for
the *London Free Press* who was on sabbatical in Hong Kong with his

family – after reading his *National Post* article about hockey in
Mongolia. He'd visited Ulan Bator in December 1998 with a
Chinese expatriate team for a round-robin tourney against a local
Mongol club, and had talked about natural ice and players wearing
newspaper pads. He talked of sitting in his hotel room watching
CNN, then looking out his window to see men riding horses through
the snow.

I told Herb, by e-mail, that I was planning to visit his city for the
Hong Kong Fives' Hockey Tournament, which I'd read about while
researching Chinese hockey on the Internet, and he offered to
collect us on arrival.

We stayed with the Shovellers and their children, Aislin and Ben,
in Repulse Bay, one of the island's toniest neighbourhoods. Their
apartment complex – which included a Polo shop, a Japanese restaurant, and a café that sold a seventeen-dollar cup of coffee – was built
on a hillside. It was designed to look like an enormous flag rippling
in the wind, and it lorded over the bay. Remarkably, there was a
seven-storey rectangular gap in the middle of the building so that
the mythical Chinese dragon could pass through, should it decide
to slither down from the mountains. A product of *feng shui*, the gap
made the building look like a cyclops. Many Westerners who lived
in Repulse Bay shook their heads when they talked of how *feng shui*
had left the building with a divot the size of Peterborough, but this
design feature had practical use beyond serving as the dragon's
passageway. In a city of eight million, many of whom lived in grey
apartment cubes, there was only one Repulse Bay, and "the building
with the hole in it," was all you had to say for people to know exactly
where to find you.

The Bay was patrolled twenty-four hours a day by security staff
in white suits. They watched over the lush, manicured grounds
where newlyweds posed for photos in formal wear rented from a
nearby shop. Entire families could be found sitting tuxedoed and
bejewelled on the lawn, scrutinized by an impassive sentinel lest
someone pluck a clover. Jackie Chan had shot a film here; European
diplomats peopled the ritzy apartments; and ex-pats who'd been
shipped across the ocean by multinationals made it their home. This

was not a place where you'd find Megadeth blasting from behind a window draped with the Confederate flag. It was as exclusive and self-important as Beverly Hills, and as lovely. I liked to stand on the white stone terrace with my hand on the balustrade looking over the South China Sea, imagining I was John Barrymore in a scarf staring into an eternity of sky and water. The terrace felt like a starting point – the tip of a latitude, the mouth of a trade route – and, ignoring the sound of sentries describing my appearance into their walkie-talkies, I was almost at peace.

After a full day's rest, we headed into town to find SkyRink, the home of the tournament.

The thought crossed my mind that SkyRink might not be anything close to what its name suggested. I almost expected to be disappointed since, these days, arena names make little sense. For instance, not only does the National Car Rental Center, home of the Florida Panthers, promise little in the way of aesthetics, you can't even rent a car there. Same with the horseless Saddledome in Calgary. And despite the nation's affection for the old Maple Leaf Gardens, there's probably more foliage growing on the Hoover Dam. These erroneous names aren't reserved only for the pro ranks, either. In Toronto, new hockey complexes are being called Ice Gardens, Ice Land, and Ice Palace, names better suited to the American south, where the word "ice" is required so that people don't show up in shorts clutching frozen cappuccinos. But in Canada, what does one expect to find in an arena? Beach volleyball? The Antiques Roadshow? A name like Ice Land is proof of how insidious the American lexicon is in Canada's game. I prefer rinks to be named after dead people – Ted Reeve, Jimmy Simpson, Max Bell. The names suggest a persona, a link to the past, the warmth of someone's den.

Judging by the nature of other arenas with *Sky* in their name, SkyRink did not hold much promise. SkyDome, the home of the Toronto Blue Jays, is fine if you enjoy the perils of sitting in a place where slabs of concrete have been known to come crashing down. In Edmonton, the Skyreach Centre is now the home of the Edmonton Oilers. The building used to be called Northlands Coliseum – a name that evokes hoarfrost and mulled wine and poplar trees – but the name was changed to Skyreach – which evokes nothing – when the local telephone company tossed a few million at the club, aping a trend that has besmirched more than a few stadia. The acquisition of naming rights is one of the scourges of modern sport. Candlestick Park in San Francisco was renamed 3Com Park after a software company, Jack Murphy Stadium in San Diego became QUALCOMM Stadium (software again), and Joe Robbie Stadium in Miami became Pro Player Stadium (you guessed it: men's underwear). Perhaps the most extreme example is the STAPLES Center, the home of the LA Kings. Until I heard the name, I hadn't realized how much hockey reminded me of the fast-paced world of office supplies.

The road out of the Bay was trimmed with long-armed trees cupping orange and pink blossoms like altar boys holding candles. The flowers hung in bunches over the road and whipped against the flank of the bus, which rushed along the winding road gripping the edge of the cliff. The bus tilted and tipped as it fought corners and, with each turn, small vistas of the city were revealed: knots of blue and white high-rises; the shimmering green track of the Happy Valley raceway; a whitewashed mansion with guard dogs and gold gates; a regatta of iron ships floating in the bay; the stone shelves of an old terraced graveyard rising over the city; and, at the bottom of a street of Victorian homes, a procession of checker-skirted schoolgirls.

We drove under one overpass, then another, and suddenly the city was very loud. The first few moments entering a strange city are always stage-directed by your senses. They're so inflamed by the newness of the environment that you find yourself thinking things like, "My God! That exhaust smells so wonderful and strange!" or "That garbage over there is just so darned colourful!" even as the locals are making choking sounds. While abroad, the senses refuse to be burdened by the mundane. They're wearing sombreros and drinking umbrella drinks and carrying on.

The bus let us off on Cheung Sha Wan Road in Kowloon market, renowned throughout the world as the hub of the pirated electronics underground. The market rattled at full pelt. Stereo salesmen had dragged their tallest sound systems to the edge of the sidewalk and were blasting Canto-Pop at ear-splitting volumes. There was junk everywhere. An electronics boneyard littered the sidewalk with hacked-apart eight-tracks and CB radios – not to mention the obligatory box of used LPs with the same unloved Seals and Crofts albums you'd find at home – laid out on old newspapers and blankets. Fruit vendors came at me bearing weird-looking apples. In narrow alleyways, goat carcasses and pig heads and groupers the size of cricket bats hung under vinyl canopies. A corner apothecary offered boxes of Leung Chi See Dog Pills, Ping On Ointment, Essence of Deer, and Atomic Enema in its window; next door a young man sat, legs crossed behind a row of typewriters with flowers stemmed through their print bars; wholesale clothing depots flooded three city blocks – Fancy Fashion, Funny Fashion, Top and Top Fashion, Bukky Fashion and, of course, Fukky Fashion; shops tented in the middle of the street and lit by bare bulbs were festooned with cables, speaker wires, baskets of fuses, watches, and belt buckles; and a small pastry shop sold crates of sea prune, liquorice prune, and dried sour-cream prune, which young girls pressed into their mouths by the handful. The high clucking pitch of restaurant crowds filled the air.

I was in Parkdale no longer.

We stood in front of Dragon Centre mall, a huge building that loomed arms-crossed over the market. The entrance was filled with a circus of laughing children being scooped up by an escalator. We rode with them, upwards into the building behind a floor-to-ceiling glass façade. The ride was spectacular. We stared out at Kowloon across acres of high-rises pressed shoulder to shoulder, their sides thistled with television antennae. Laundry waved in a parade of coloured flags. Beyond that: smokestacks, the sea, the red horizon.

We floated higher.

Finally, on the eighth floor of the mall, I heard hockey – the honking of the score-clock, the bang of the puck against the boards, the referee's whistle, skates chopping snow. I smelled the chemicals of

the ice and the Zamboni diesel, and then I saw it: a rink small enough
to fit in your palm, a sprite's pond, a place for Tom Thumb, Gabby
Boudreau. To best describe it I have to use a word not often associ-
ated with the greatest sporting stadia of our time: cute.

It was a play rink.

It was one-fifth the size of an NHL oval – 18 metres by 42 metres,
to be exact. Perhaps a homesick architect from Trois-Rivières had
been left with a narrow concrete channel and decided to fill it with
ice. It was maybe the width of three bowling lanes. I suspected that
bigger puddles had been left by the monsoon. Every element of
SkyRink was odd. Since it was eight storeys up inside a glass tower,
you could look out and forecast the weather from the way the
clouds rolled in off the South China Sea. There was a mezzanine
with an arcade – pinball machines, toy cars, and robotic clowns –
that cantilevered over the rink and filled the air with the sound of
bells and horns and children crying out to each other. Between the
mezzanine and the rink was a yellow roller coaster that was close
enough to the ice that you could reach up with a hockey stick and
tap it. It was a flame-tongued, turquoise dragon that hurtled over
the ice at high speeds, a frightful spectacle for even the most steel-
nerved goaltender. It seemed that SkyRink had been designed with
the idea of marrying amusement-park folly to hockey, and while
hockey has experimented with this theme before – San Jose's shark
blimp and Anaheim's daredevil duck come to mind, as do the barrel
jumping and dogsled races that were part of intermissions in the
1920s – at least those novelties were kept at a safe distance from
the action. But at SkyRink, there was no barrier or railing to
prevent someone in the arcade from pelting the players with eggs
or worse, and it did nothing to allay my fears of being killed by a
large metal lizard.

At both ends of the ice, loose white netting was strung up behind
the goals. It reminded me of the mesh in those old Soviet rinks,
which Team Canada used to complain about. The SkyRink netting
served two purposes: to catch pucks and to act as a curtain for the
dressing area, which lay just behind the end boards. It did neither
job well. It whipped pucks back to the ice, and, like Cheryl Tiegs'

macramé tank top, if you looked closely enough, you could see everything. Behind the netting, players freely changed in and out of their clothes. The scene was like something out of a rogue health club: fellows in towels strode to and from the bathrooms, the odd player revealing his bare ass and hairy stomach (or bare, hairy ass). This abundance of flesh did little to ease my fear of being naked before strangers, and while not every player flashed skin – some used a series of towels like semaphore flags to guard their parts – many treated the area like a Roman bath. Exhibitionists would dig SkyRink. I thought of that brazen Canadian couple who were caught love-making in the windows of the SkyDome Hotel. Here, you could press ham before eight million people.

SkyRink had a Zamboni. It was old and dented and looked as if it had stood in the way of a Matthew Barnaby shitfit. It had South China Ice Hockey League written in Chinese and English on the side and was driven by a young Chinese man in yellow sweats who was far too slender to bring any credibility to his job.

SkyRink had other credibility problems. Frankly, it didn't smell bad enough. Let's face it: hockey stinks. It's a bloated, heavy odour that you can poke with your finger. The first time I set foot in a rink after years away from the game, I rushed a hockey sock to my face to guard myself from the stench. Of course, after a few weeks in my equipment bag, the sock was well stewed and I was forced to wrap something else around my mouth. When I ran out of socks, I had to embrace the game's feral miasma.

But SkyRink smelled like jasmine (I should have been grateful, I know). The source of this fragrance was Kathy K's Pro Shop, which was stocked with a surprising complement of top-of-the-line hockey gear. Unlike many skate-sharpening depots – which tend to smell of plugged plumbing and are operated by large, unshaven men – Kathy K's carried the scent of blossoms, and if that wasn't strange enough, Kathy thanked you for your business and offered a bowl of candies by the cash register, allowing you to take to the ice chewing a gumball and spitting rainbow trails of purple, blue, and red.

There was also the food problem. And again, it wasn't so much a problem as, well, a treat. There was no snack bar at SkyRink, unless you counted the Jack in the Box, which I only ever saw used by ex-pats teary-eyed for the taste of grease. Instead, there was a food court opposite the rink, where women with faces carved by time spooned sea snails the size of silver dollars and braised aubergine and double-cooked pork onto plastic plates, the aroma of garlic and soya and sesame oil scenting the air. There were kiosks selling blackened grouper, lemon chicken, bean curd seared in garlic and peppers, sushi, and hot soup with prawns – not your typical hockey cuisine.

The crowd at SkyRink was also its own. It was mostly seniors who had wandered over from the food court (proving that, no matter where you go in the world, you'll find the same people hanging out in malls). It was a rare treat to skate along the boards and exchange glances with a group of old men who could have been extras in *The Last Emperor*. After a few days, I discovered that they appreciated pratfalls and gaffes rather than athletic grace and beauty. If someone scored an end-to-end goal, they'd get little reaction, but if they tripped over the net or were slew-footed or got slashed in the eye, the old men would laugh and pantomime their fall. The less able you were on your skates the more you were liked by the gallery; before the tournament ended, there was a real chance that I'd be a star.

2

AHMED YELLED AT MOHAMMED

The full name of the tournament was The Sunday Ice Hockey Fives '99, Sunday being a communications company that was at war over the lucrative Hong Kong market. The telecommunications racket was cut-throat and companies were throwing sponsorships at anything that moved. Every second billboard around the city promoted Sunday, Orange, Distacom, and Nokia, and you were left out if you didn't carry a cellphone.

Tom Barnes loved his cellphone. He worked it tirelessly. Barnes was one of the organizers of the Fives and worked for Asiasports, a company that also helped organize hockey tournaments in Thailand and Manila. The Fives (named for the number of players allowed on the ice per side, one less than in typical hockey) was in its seventh year.

Other than Herb Shoveller, Tom Barnes was my main hockey contact in Hong Kong. He organized the Budweiser South China Ice Hockey League, a year-round recreational league with upwards of twelve teams, including all-Asian clubs. Barnes estimated that the league consisted of forty per cent Canadians, thirty per cent locals from Hong Kong, fifteen per cent Americans, and fifteen per cent Europeans. The fee to play in the Bud League was 1,800 HK dollars – about $350 Canadian – per season, a sum comparable to what you pay for recreational hockey in Toronto. There was also a junior league with upwards of ninety kids aged four to sixteen, and a women's division that grew more popular each year. In theory, Barnes was the most important man in HK hockey, which is a little like being the world's best country-and-western bass player. Barnes ran most facets of the tournament. At the rink, he operated the CD deck, supplied T-shirts and hats to the souvenir booth, refereed games, collected tournament fees, polished the trophies, and stocked water and ice and beer for competing clubs, all the while staying in touch with his very pregnant wife, who was expecting to drop Barnesy junior any day. A native of St. Louis, Barnes was the tourney's figurehead: a round-faced fellow with a goatee.

Barnes' goatee troubled me. I'd be lying if I said that it didn't distort my impression of the man. I believe that the goatee is to hockey what shoulder pads are to women's fashion: something that gives the impression of what the person is not, rather than what he is. That, and goatees look dumb. They are worn by two types of people: geeks who want to look tough and thugs who want to look cool. Now, if you are currently sporting a goatee and feel compelled to fling this book across the room, fine. But hear me out: the biggest jerks I've played against have worn goatees. "Goatee guy" describes someone prone to slashing you in the neck when you aren't looking and then turning away. Ever since goatees started showing up in beer ads, they've crept like a hairy rash across the face of recreational hockey (as bad as guys bellowing "Yeahhhh Baby!" after scoring). What's worse is that when goatee guys look at themselves in the mirror, they see a dude who is walking the knife's edge, even though their look was popularized by Adam Duritz and Darius Rucker.

"Who?" you might ask.

My point exactly.

One was in Counting Crows, the other in Hootie and the Blowfish. Along with Chris Chelios and Brendan Shanahan, goatee guys are also responsible for the death of the fu-manchu moustache, which the goatee sadly replaced. In the '70s, the fu ruled. It personified hockey's ass-kicking attitude. Wendel Clark of the Maple Leafs wore the last hockey fu. Before him: Dave Keon, Turk Sanderson, Bob Gassoff, Jack McIlhargey. Tough dudes. The fu was confrontational facial hair. I also long for the days of Mike Antonovich, Lou Nistico, Mike Marson, John Wensink, and Rick MacLeish; bleary-eyed wastoids whose lawless, greasy lids were one degree from dreadlocks. Their prototypes? Sly Stone and Brad Delp.

Friends, it ain't even close.

Barnes had followed in the path of James Robinson, one of the founding fathers of recreational hockey in China. Robinson was the person I'd turned to for background on hockey in Hong Kong. He told me that the region's original arena wasn't SkyRink, but the Lai Chi Kok Amusement Park rink, which Robinson remembers as "a small figure-skating rink shaped like the state of Oklahoma." He told me that it was a narrow rectangle with a small panhandle, without any sideboards at all, only a metal hand rail. Because of the panhandle, you could stand at one end of the rink and not actually see the other goal. Fog had been a serious problem in the spring and summer, and, because of the poor a/c system and condensation problems on the underside of the roof, each morning players would have to knock away stalagmites of ice that had frozen to the surface over the night.

Robinson, an architect born in Chicago, arrived in Hong Kong in 1979. It took him five years to find a game. He says, "Our first games were at seven every Sunday morning. I was the only American playing with a bunch of French Canadians, and we would scrimmage against local Chinese teams. Unless you spoke French or Cantonese, no one would pass to you." In 1983, Robinson put a notice up at the Canadian Club of Hong Kong to recruit new skaters. He got maybe fifteen responses. In a city of eight million. This group became the Can-Am Ice Hockey (Hong Kong) Association. Lack of local competition forced them to compete abroad, so they travelled to South Korea to play against the Korean National team, as well as US Army clubs, often on natural ice.

Robinson dreamed up the idea for an international tourney after playing a Japanese hockey club, who visited Hong Kong for the 1987 Rugby Sevens. In the first few years of the Fives, teams came from as far away as Bahrain and as nearby as Taiwan. Robinson had kept a scrapbook on the tournament's history, and when I thumbed through it certain newspaper accounts of earlier Fives leaped out at me. Alan Campbell wrote in *Discovery* magazine: "After storming the Thai net for three minutes, Hong Kong right winger Chung Wai Ting beat goalkeeper Parkpoom Thongaram with a low shot!" In another article that detailed the visit of Montreal Canadien great Jean Béliveau in 1984 (he was flown over by Can-Am for a clinic at Lai Chi Kok), writer Nicola Parkinson describes a puck as "a toughened rubber disc" and hockey as a game of "blinding speed and incredible patterns of colour."

The HK tournament was divided into two weekends. The first weekend featured international men's and kids' teams, while the second had domestic and North American men's and women's sides. The tourney had grown to include forty-four teams, making it unquestionably Asia's largest ice-hockey contest. In total, sixteen nationalities were represented. I would not see action with my adopted club – the Hong Kong Canadians – until the second Friday, so the beginning of my stay was spent watching teams from around the world. It was a club list to tingle the mind – Singapore Winter Flames, Japanese Tomy Monsters, St. Lucia Saints, United Arab Emirates Nationals, Bud Americans, Manila Knights, Dubai Mighty Camels, Al-Ma Pee Wees, Can Tai Dragons, and Bangkok Flying Farangs – names that belonged to a sports league of the future.

On the second day of the tournament we saw the Arabs play. They were the United Arab Emirates' first national team and the Sunday Fives was their inaugural world competition. They were the only government-funded team in the whole of the Middle East, and their players came from Sudan, Palestine, Al Ain, and Dubai. Janet and I had just settled into our seats when we noticed them coming up the escalator, their sticks tilted across their shoulders. They were dressed in full gear, and they wouldn't have been out of place at my neighbourhood rink, except for their thick beards, their sombre eyes, and the fact that they addressed each other in Arabic. Their dark faces reminded me of a team of John Tonellis, even though their jerseys were pink and white, which was something they'd have to find out about the hard way.

Before I arrived in Hong Kong, I had wondered whether an Arab team could really skate. One of the things that I had to put behind me was the notion of how preposterous it was for any player without Canadian lineage to be half-way decent at the game. It was this kind of attitude, I believe, that got Canadian hockey in trouble in the first place. But it wasn't easy to drop it. While I was growing up, whenever a European-born player like Ken Hodge, Owen Nolan, Juha Widing, or Stan Mikita made the NHL, it invariably turned out that they'd learned their craft in Canada. I had a major adjustment to make to be able to hear the name Mohammed Yousef Mohammed Darwish and think, not of dust storms and camels, but of blizzards, block heaters, and donuts.

The play of the Arabian team went a long way towards debunking those stereotypes. The UAE Nats' first game was against the Singapore Winter Flames, one of four competing teams from that small tropical island. By the time the referee waved the teams to their benches and blew into his whistle, it was obvious that the Nats could play. Barnes loaded a Chumbawamba CD as they stormed the ice. They chased the puck like hounds after a rabbit, doing all of the things that good hockey players are supposed to do: skating to the openings, clearing the puck up the boards, being aware of where their linemates were on the ice. The only skill they hadn't mastered was the slapshot, which they liked to fire with abandon and from as far back as their own blue line, using a follow-through that reminded me more of a woodsman chopping at the base of a tree than Squid MacInnis. But anyone who remembers their early days playing the game could hardly blame them for this: the slapshot is the broadest show of strength in a game without hitting or direct body contact. Still, despite their awkward delivery, more often than not the Nats hit the fat of the net and, after the first period, the Singapore goalie had touched more rubber than the Marquis de Sade.

The UAE team's first names were printed on the backs of their jerseys, as family names like Sulayem Al Nuaimi were simply too long to fit across their shoulders. Once I recognized this, I could follow along in the program and identify the players. Obaid, Turqi, Mohammed, Nasser, and Kareem made up the defence, and they had classic rearguard physiques: tall and lanky, with impressive reach. But they were also wobbly on their feet, though this was not without charm. I was particularly drawn to the slash-skating Mohammed, who stood six-feet tall and moved like a man running in swimming fins. He compensated for his slow-footedness by throwing his body in front of every shot and, because of the rink's small scale, he was rarely caught out of position. Mohammed was like Luds Ludwig. He would intercept passes by sliding his body flat against the ice, as if harbouring a secret desire to luge. He often did this at centre ice, the first time I'd ever seen a player block a shot so far up the rink. After a while, the forwards saw that what Mohammed was doing was effective, and so they started sliding too, at which point I realized that the UAE didn't play what you or I would call a traditional style.

They played Arab hockey.

The UAE's forwards were fast and smart. Ahmed was the team's centre and captain. He was also their leader. He struck me as the toughest and most determined of the Nats – a desert-league Yzerman – whose passing was as sharp as any I'd come across in the men's loop at home. He also played without a cage or visor, which immediately endeared him to me. You could see his eyes flare when he took the puck through the neutral zone, and his intensity was such that he often travelled around the Singapore defence as uncontested as a tiger at a garden party.

That said, Ahmed also played like someone who had just learned the game. He reminded me of my own days starting out, when the only thing I wanted was to have the puck. When you're new to the game, your mind isn't occupied with feeding the open man or plugging the checking lane or ringing the puck around the boards. Instead, you want control of the puck and, once in possession of it, you don't want to give it up. Because of the infancy of the UAE's game, their breakouts more or less consisted of the forwards attempting to skate through the other team. There was very little head-manning or dump and chase and, while ineffective, it was refreshing to watch; no matter how many times this produced a turnover or loss of possession, I was happy to find a hockey system that hadn't yet been poisoned by the Left-Wing Lock. Besides, I couldn't remember the last time I saw a big leaguer try to score a goal by skating through the other team, and it was this lack of regard for (or knowledge of) chalkboard etiquette that separated the Nats from many of the teams back home.

Omar and Juma were Ahmed's wingers. They were good skaters who knew how to do a thing or two with the puck. They wore full cages and had goal-scorer numbers: 9 and 99, respectively. Omar had a wild crop of black hair that spiked through his CCM helmet. He played with European zip and flair, and his feet looked like they were dancing when he moved through the middle of the ice – which may or may not have slowed him. His tongue wagged and he smiled a lot. Juma, on the other hand, moved confidently, his shoulders squared, and taking him down looked to be as much fun as checking a moving pool table. He policed Omar and sometimes worked in tandem with Khalifa, a rowdy sixteen-year-old with a moustache who wore a Philadelphia Flyers jersey off the ice, and whose game seemed inspired by old Broad Street Bullies assault reels.

The UAE coach – a Canadian fellow in blue and red sweats whom the players called Bear – called out to his players from the bench, which was almost beside the goal. The benches were so deep in the zone that once out of the gate, you were at the top of the faceoff circle, poised for a shot. They had large, heavy doors like you'd find on a stretch limousine, and were rimmed with the shiny metal railing that surrounded the ice. Along with the low tin roof, all that metal made the venue extremely loud. Every buzz and whistle was bright and harsh, to say nothing of the PA system, which Barnes kept poking: *"You're never gonna keep me down!"*

Hong Kong was my first exotic hockey port, and I was curious to find out whether the scourge of Hockey Rock had infected the rest of the world. If SkyRink was any indication, it did not look good. Barnes had a happy trigger finger, and with it came a bombardment of alt rock sludge – "Love Shack" and Third Eye Blind and that odious techno–country mutant "Cotton-Eyed Joe." Hockey Rock gives hockey a bad name, with songs like "Hurt So Good" and "Owner of a Lonely Heart." You'd think Andy Travis of WKRP was up there programming his eight-track. In olden days, Wurlitzer tunes would pass the seconds between faceoffs and intermissions, but modern arena music has become part of the corporate control of the sports environment: the same companies who own the teams own the record companies who supply the product. What Barnes had to gain by this, I don't know. Maybe he liked the stuff.

I blame the goatee.

Skating out to the sound of Pennywise, Singapore broke the scoreless tie. I'd been taken with the UAE team, but it was hard to cheer against Singapore. I racked my brain trying to think of some reason to dislike the Singaporean nation, but could not. No matter how hard I tried, I couldn't recall any Singaporean ever burned in effigy outside a foreign embassy, boycotts or trade embargoes imposed upon them, obnoxious Singaporean athletes, serial killers, prop comics, or MOR pop stars foisted upon the public. I'd forgotten it was a dictatorship, so the worst I could say about Singapore was that a girl-drink had been named after it.

A tasty gin splash, at that.

If that wasn't bad enough, organizers of the Singapore entry were so magnanimous that they even brought a taxi squad to China. According to the program, they were the only side with a backup goaltender, a boy who looked about twelve and whose jersey sported number o6. They also had the single greatest complement of players wearing glasses, and their best player, a fellow named Loeve, waved to his mother in the stands each time he faced off.

Daniel Teo played for another Singapore team. When he saw me scribbling in my book he asked, "What're ya writing?" When I told him that I was working on a book for M&S, he said, "Wow!

McClelland and Stewart? Really?" I almost smacked him right there for being a smartass, but was glad that I didn't. "I've seen their name on Amazon!" he exclaimed. The kid was all right, and he filled me in on the history of hockey in Singapore.

"Hockey first started out back in the 1970s, but those older rinks closed down out of neglect and now there are only two," he said. "One is situated in an area called Kallang. It's called Ice World Kallang. The other – the Fuji Ice Palace, which was opened by the Japanese – is way out west in Jurong.

"The rink in Kallang is about twenty-three by ten metres – one-quarter the size of SkyRink. It isn't even a hockey rink, not really; it's better suited to figure skating or leisure skating. We don't have fancy stuff like fibreglass boards; the boards there only go up to your waist, so it can be pretty dangerous. Jurong rink is a little bigger and has better facilities, but the price for a two-hour training session is three hundred dollars US. Many kids who take up the sport don't last, mostly because of the cost and lack of coaches."

Daniel got started in the game through in-line skating with his friends, and then moved to the ice. "All we did was fiddle around with the puck day after day, not knowing what we were supposed to do with it," he said. "We finally managed to get hold of an imported set of instructional videos, and only then did we learn the wrist shot and slapshot. Before that, we didn't even know you were supposed to raise the puck."

Singaporean hockey was comparable to the kind played in the rest of Southeast Asia. Kuala Lumpur, Jakarta, Saigon, Manila, and Bangkok all have rinks. There is an eleven-team league out of Bangkok, including the Thai national team, led by star player Vanchalerm "Top" Raltapong, a fashion model by day who'd not once skated outside Thailand. Top fell in love with hockey after he saw Mario Lemieux score four goals in the 1988–89 NHL all-star game. "From then on, I dreamed of playing in an all-star game," he told writer Steve Sandford. "Everyone said I was crazy, but it is still my dream."

The most popular ex-pat team in Bangkok are the Bangkok Flying Farangs, four-year veterans of the HK Fives. The Farangs hold an international charity tournament every November – the OK Cup, named after a Czech airline – with proceeds going to an inner-city relief shelter run by priest and hockey fan Father Joe Maieris. There is a banquet on the final night of the tourney featuring traditional Thai dancing and trophies awarded in the form of Thai deities. The rink – the Interworld Ice Skating Rink – is North American-sized, except for slightly wider corners, and sits on the fifth floor of the Imperial World Mall in Samrong. Todd Gilmore, a member of the Farangs, says, "The rink is like a wave pool: the puck jumps off the ice and skating backwards can be a little tricky. The heat also creates a mist, hiding the action from the fans. The ends of the rink have high nets instead of glass. Three years ago, a Dubai player named George Topolnyski took a slapshot, which was deflected, and it flew about twenty feet above the net, smashing a large picture of the King of Thailand, which was hanging on the wall. I remember that a terrible hush fell over the rink, because the King is greatly revered and loved. We were told afterwards that this was not a good omen. It may have been a coincidence, but the Thai economy fell to pieces itself after that."

In Indonesia, a pair of local teams staged that country's first ever competition in 1997 using players who wore a mix of roller and ice hockey equipment; in Taiwan, teams from Taipei, Taichung, and Kaohsiung recently formed a three-team league, but since the cities are such a great distance from one another, the team from Tai Pei has to fly, courtesy of the local airline, for games every Sunday morning; in Vietnam, there is a rink in Ho Chi Minh City which is used only sporadically, but once a year the Canadian Embassy organizes a weekend, roof-top street hockey tournament involving mostly ex-pats, although they have yet to take to the ice; while in India, the Simla Ice Skating Club, located approximately 1,300 feet above sea level in the Himalayas, and the Ladakh Ice Skating Club in Leh, which is near the Tibet border, play games occasionally, often featuring Buddhist monks in a combination of figure skates and army paraphernalia, with goals indicated by a judge behind the net waving a small red flag.

Hearing these stories about the grassroots of Asian hockey – a handful of rinks with great distances between them, no radio or television coverage of games, a dearth of coaching and equipment, not to mention of ice – reminded me of what I've learned about hockey at the turn of the last century. Knowing this, it was even more remarkable that some of the players I was seeing in Hong Kong were as adept at the game as they were. For instance, the Singapore Winter Flames' goalie, who wore number 01, was a revelation. He was the size of a small filing cabinet and favoured acrobatics in thwarting the shooter. He played like a soccer goalie – as if the net behind him was ten feet tall. Whenever a UAE player closed in, he showed him an open side as if he were a toreador waving his cape, only to lunge at the puck at the last second and make the save. The goalie's name was Marcus Tang Yze Meng and he kept the Flames in the game. While Singapore had a few good forwards, they were young and inexperienced and, more often than not, were happy to let Meng bail them out.

Singapore won the game 5–1. Meng's play sent the Arabs back to the bench in disgust. I saw Omar kick his skates at the boards after a missed chance. The UAE's goalie was notable too, but for all the wrong reasons. To achieve their goal of becoming the world's first all-Arab hockey team, the Nats had told their regular goaltender – a fellow from New Brunswick who lived in Dubai – to stay home. Instead, Mohammed Darwish learned the position in the months leading up to the tourney. He was not what one would call a natural at his position. Against Singapore, his lack of experience was glaring.

To be fair, Darwish was also improperly equipped for the position. When I showed pictures of him to a goalie friend back home, he noticed that Darwish's chest protector was the kind worn in lacrosse. The UAE skaters were equipped with CCM helmets and Easton sticks, but Darwish was about as protected as a canary in a mine shaft. That's not to say that he suffered any injuries while blocking shots during the game because, in truth, he didn't block many.

Darwish wore his equipment like a costume. Or, rather, the equipment wore him. Whenever a puck was lofted towards the net, he struggled like a person trying to fight off a swarm of bees. It was as if he was trying to deflect not one puck, but many. In his book *They Call Me Gump*, Gump Worsley likens playing goal to standing in a barrel; by the same token, Darwish looked encumbered, like a man strapped to a sandwich board. He also had trouble skating. Those who have never worn goalie skates imagine skating in them to be like sliding across the living room floor in your stocking feet, but they're wrong. Goalie skates are longer than normal skates and they grip more of the ice, and with the added weight of the pads hugging your legs, moving from side to side can be as much fun as kicking a brick wall. Darwish was so awkward on his skates that one of the team's defencemen had to scrape his crease for him at the beginning of each game.

The UAE team, realizing that Darwish was in trouble, spent the better part of their game flinging themselves along the ice to block the Singapore team's shots. Soon they were doing more sliding than skating and, after a while, the Flames adjusted accordingly. They shot from every part of the ice surface, peppering Darwish with rockets and lobs and bank-shots, every puck an adventure. At one point, Darwish stopped a shot with the top of his goalie helmet. It was a freak save, but the puck hiccupped to a Singapore winger who made an easy goal. Skating back to the bench, Ahmed yelled at Mohammed, who'd left the winger unmarked. Mohammed yelled at Turqi, his defence partner. Nasser yelled at Mohammed, who yelled back as they settled on the bench. It wasn't pretty.

But here was a team.

3

Ben Shoveller, whose bedroom I was inhabiting in Repulse Bay, played for the Nortel PeeWees, who skated out to face the Manila Angels in the game following UAE vs. Singapore. Ben glided past us during warm-up and we waved at him. He took off his glove and flipped up his thumb, smiling like a muggins. I liked hanging around with Ben because he reminded me of what it was like to be a twelve-year-old obsessed with sports. He'd collected the entire set of Screech Owls books, a handful of *Sports Illustrated for Kids* (one issue had a cover photo of Ken Griffey Jr. presenting his father with the gift of a rotten fish), and kept clippings and notices of his games pasted on the fridge. He also read stories with titles like "Touchdown Hero Fire Fighter" or "The Curveball That Saved Pittsburgh" (though I found no "Son of Flubber") – hyperbolic sporting tales that feed the minds of kids for whom winning is the true manifestation of heroism.

Ben's love of sports took me back to that sweet pink smell of the flat broken bubblegum stick that came in a hockey-card pack filled with pictures of Andy Brown's glove coming at you like a cobra's hood or Gilles Marotte with his Black Hawks crest inked out or Guy Charron with plastic hair. His books reminded me of the ones my parents gave me for Christmas – *The Ice Men, This Is Hockey, The Burly Bruins, Brian MacFarlane's Hockey Annual, Bobby Orr: My Game*; and magazines like *Hockey Pictorial, Hockey Illustrated,* and *Hockey Digest*, which ran stories like "Skip Krake Hopes He's Here to Stay" and "Kirkland Lake Is Still the Cradle of Hockey" and "The Overnight Success of Mike Laughton" and ads featuring John Ferguson's Power Knits, Bobby Hull's Golden Jet Candy Bar, Norm Ullman for Mr. Mort Clothiers, Bobby Orr for Bobby Orr's Pizza Parlour, and Jim McKenny for Bahr Auto Sales. I used to cut them out and paste them into my Hilroy scrapbook while trying to stay awake listening to games from the coast. In the morning I'd open my eyes to the winter light, and ask, "Did the Leafs win?" and bolt down the hallway for the *Globe* or *Star* or *Telegram* if they had.

Watching Ben skate reminded me of my beginnings as a player: my feet screaming inside the prison of my boots with my toes bent against their cruel tips, the nut of my helmet digging like a finger-nail into the side of my head, my gloves unmalleable shells, my cup pinching my thighs and balls, and my teammates scuttling up the rink like baby turtles across a beach.

My first goal came at Centennial Arena in Etobicoke, a double rink constructed in the shadow of Centennial Hill, which was built back in the days when grassing over landfill to create recreational grounds seemed like a good idea. I was loitering around the net when the puck appeared out of nowhere and fell flat against my blade. Terrified with excitement, I pushed it with all the determination of a man trying to tip a bus. I fell on the ice and watched the puck move through a thicket of sticks and bodies, studying it like a curling skip. I followed it along the ice as it disappeared underneath the goalie's pads. My teammates jumped on me and started pounding my head. We spun around on the ice in a tangle of arms and feet. I remember looking up and seeing my mother in her kerchief, my dad in his overcoat. They were younger than I am today.

It wasn't until a few years later that I experienced a second glory: I was named Player of the Week. Player of the Week was a

The author at
Centennial Hill

distinction to which every house-league player aspired. Most often, it was won by the league's top scorers, rarely by its scrubs. I played out of Pine Point arena, a small rink nestled in an old suburb. The arena's lobby was our community's heart, and Saturday morning drew a busy neighbourhood congress: cars pulling tired through the dawn into the parking lot, fathers in plaid fedoras and white curling sweaters carrying sagging gear bags for their yawning children. I remember the puff of steam from their coffee cups, the Coke sign that hung above the snack bar, its snap-on letters – POGO 80¢ – the black and yellow zigzag of toques, the flecked fur of banana-toed mukluks, the sparkle of lip gloss on the mouths of teenage girls, the spray of orange slices, and the blue-grey smoke of Rothman's, Peter Jackson, and Export "A" unfiltered as it fogged the windows.

The goal that earned me Player of the Week came on a breakaway. I think it was the first time I'd ever been alone behind the defence. I felt I'd been hurled into space, a sensation of wonder and amazement and freedom combined with great fear and uncertainty.

To have a clear-cut breakaway also meant that I was unbound by the rink's geometry; although the two-line pass and the offside were rules that had been drilled into our heads by our coaches, they mattered not at all, for the only things that stood before me were an expanse of white ice and the goalie, standing like a knight guarding a drawbridge. I crossed the blue line and glided towards him, leaning into my shot. The puck flew into the air, and I landed on my side on the ice as I watched it rise into the top corner of the net. It was glorious. The next week, I found my photo clipped to a piece of white Bristol board set up on a stand in the middle of the lobby, "Player of the Week: David Bidini" written in black marker.

I stared at it in disbelief. It was the best moment of my hockey life. Being immortalized in a colour photograph made me feel closer to the NHL players whose pictures were taped to my locker at school and on my bedroom walls at home. It was the greatest achievement I could imagine. Parents at the rink congratulated my father. Kids talked about my goal at school and around the neighbourhood. For the first time in my hockey career, I was the envy of my teammates. I had entered hockey's inner circle.

Of course, I could not stay there. Being Player of the Week also scared the shit out of me. It should have spurred me on to greater athletic achievements, but instead, the burden of being singled out was too much to bear. If I could go back in time and right a few things, I would kiss Margaret Nakamura while standing beside her on the riverbank in grade six instead of throwing a rock at her head, and I would play like a star on the rise after winning that recognition. But instead, I developed a terrible suspicion that people were watching me and thinking to themselves, "Another rush and no goal." My behaviour on the ice changed. I turned away from the play and took myself off the ice. "Don't screw up," became my mantra. Not only was I no longer just an average player, but I was less than I'd been before.

In my last year of hockey, I was selected by a team in the early rounds, but the pressure was too much. I responded to the challenge by playing my worst hockey ever. I quit the game feeling distressed and confused. When you're that age, you ask yourself questions like,

What is God? and Will I go to heaven? But there was another question that troubled me, and I still have no answer: How could feeling so good make me feel so bad?

Mr. Ramirez of the Philippines stood behind the goal wailing, his hands entwined in the netting. He pressed his face into the mesh and cried *"Dada! Dada!"* as if calling for a lost dog. He was flush-faced, and he jumped up and down whenever the play came near the net. We made our way towards him.

"Hello," we said.

"Hallo," he replied.

He had a wide, beatific face and he was sweating.

"Your team?" we asked, pointing to the Manila Angels' bench.

"Yes. My son!" he said, smiling.

"Which one?" we asked.

"Here. Here!" he said, gesturing to the goal.

"The goalie?" I asked.

"Dada," he said.

"He's good!" I said.

"He will lose!" he replied.

"No. He's very tal-ent-ed."

"They will lose!" he said, sounding excited.

"What does it say on his mask?" I asked.

It was painted yellow and black, with feathers of white along the sides.

"It says 'Dada,'" said Mr. Ramirez.

"Why Dada?" asked Janet.

"It is his name!" he said. "I called him Darwin, but none of the kids on his team could say that word. They said 'Dada' over and over, and then it became his hockey name."

I wanted to say, "Just like Geddy Lee of Rush!" but did not (the name Geddy morphed out of Gary, which Lee's grandmother could not pronounce). If ever there was a suspicion that hockey in the tropics lacked credibility, Darwin's hockey name dispelled it. Like

Doggie Kuhn, King Kwong, Newsy Lalonde, hockey players in the far reaches of the world were also taking nicknames. They were reviving a tradition that has become almost extinct. Nicknames have always been great fodder for hockey lore. Newsy Lalonde worked in a print shop in his youth; Frank McCool was called Ulcers after his fondness for drinking milk before games; Squee Allen was named for the sound of his voice; Count Grosso because he looked like Dracula; Taffy Abel had a sweet tooth; Thomas B. O'Neill was nicknamed Windy by a priest after refusing to concede a point during a school debate; and players such as Dit Clapper, Bep Guidolin, and Teeder Kennedy were, like Darwin, named by friends or relatives who mispronounced their names.

"My son's friend painted his mask," said Mr. Ramirez, proudly.

"It's beautiful," said Janet.

"Yes. The white represents the wings of an angel. It is the one and only."

"It is historic," I said.

"The score? It is three to one."

Janet shot me a look. I'm not very good when it comes to communicating with people who speak another language. I tend to speak slowly and deliberately, and inevitably come off sounding like a Sesame Street character, saying things like, "You have good food," and "It is beautiful day." This habit can even corrupt conversation with English speakers. Already, I was asking the Shovellers, "We go out now?"

Janet, on the other hand, communicated easily with the locals. It's an innate skill that she must have acquired when this sort of thing was handed out. I was both jealous and deeply grateful. When I raised the matter with her, she humbled me with one of what was becoming a series of fabulous tales about how, while in India, she overcame great odds in dangerous places to find food and abode. It was a polite way of suggesting that I leave the small talk to her. She was right, but that didn't make it any easier. So whenever she gave me that look of pity, as if to say, "Nice try, but let me take it from here," I looked back at her with affection, and blundered on.

"No. His-tor-ic. Legendary. Legend-ary. Leg-end-"

Janet cut me off. "How long has your son played goal?"

"He has played forever," said Mr. Ramirez. "He stays up until one o'clock in the morning even though he has school at five-thirty, just to watch hockey on ESPN. He always looks for Gretzky. And sometimes Hasek."

I wanted to ask Mr. Ramirez a few questions about hockey in the Philippines, but remembered my gag order. Luckily, they were answered a few days later by Oggie Benitez, a skating instructor from Manila who'd helped organize the fifty-six person contingent from the island, and who made me wonder whether everybody in Filipino hockey had a name like a Muppet.

Hockey in the Philippines was a mystery to me. There was no entry in *Total Hockey*, nor was there any record of international competition, not even among Asian countries. Oggie explained that the game was a mere infant in the Philippines. There were only three rinks in Manila, all of them in shopping malls. One of them had a post in the middle of it. Oggie said that Filipinos hadn't seen ice until 1992, when the first rink opened.

"It doesn't get cold in the Philippines, or snow, but Filipinos are thrill-seekers, and they love to skate. They see hockey as a fast-moving adventure sport, and with the game now broadcast on cable, kids see it and they want to play. It is new to them. It is exciting, and a number of Filipinos have gone to the US and excelled in ice skating. But even in Jamaica, where it's so hot, they have the bobsled team, right? People shouldn't be so surprised."

Despite the infancy of the Filipino program – if you could call it a program – it had produced teams like the all-girl Manila Mega Wingers, who had a chance to win the women's division of the Hong Kong Fives. I know that doesn't sound like much but, since the Mega Wingers were the first Filipino team, I figured that their players had written themselves into hockey history simply by showing up. They played in the Inter-Mall league in Manila, in the Philippines' first women's hockey division. I asked one of the players what her friends at school thought about her playing hockey and she pointed to her teammates and said: "These are my friends." I should have known. Not only did the Mega Wingers ice a fairly competitive team, but they also had some of the best names I've ever seen written on a score-sheet. I know it's hard to improve on Zarley Zalapski, Per Jus, or Eddie Beers, but the Mega Wingers could ice a forward line with Regina Fermin centring Precious and Jewel Rabena. Their captain was Anabell MacCaw – a name dusted in grit if I'd ever heard one – and if that wasn't enough, their goalie went by the singular name Pia.

The Filipino fans packed an entire side of the SkyRink bleachers. Their voices had all the warmth and softness of the Macbeth witches. Whenever one of their players got the puck – even if it was to throw it away in desperation – they shrieked and waved purses and clanged bells and shook bags of candies. They chanted "*Go Manila!*" and "*Pasa!*" and "*Pasok!*" (*pasa* meaning pass and *pasok* goal in Tagalog) and were urged forward by a stout woman from Quezon City named Arlene Llanes, who moved around the stands like an apple on Benzedrine. The first time I met her, she stood on her heels and spoke rapidly and with great fervour about hockey in her country, shoving her face at mine while she talked. When I told her that I had considered playing hockey in Manila and writing about it, she grabbed my arm and pulled me close, saying: "If you don't come play in Manila, I will kill you." Arlene and the rest of the Filipino fans had no problem stabbing you in the sternum with their elbows to emphasize a point. After the game, I was set upon by a group of their children who saw me produce a handful of souvenir Leafs pins, which the club had given me to dole out on my travels. They wrapped their arms around my legs, and those who could grabbed at my fingers. I felt like Gulliver set upon by Lilliputians.

We watched with Mr. Ramirez as the Nortel PeeWees took a 4–1 lead over the Angels. The Angels' number 99 was a boy named Del Rosario, who towered over the shorter Nortel team. Were I a scout (and that's how I sometimes felt jotting down phrases like "good size" and "quick hands" in my notebook), I would have dropped a dime and called the parent team. Del Rosario's speed and size allowed him to carry the puck through the North American peewees, and by the middle of the second period, he'd evened the game 4–4. He knew how to execute a neat little inside-out move that brought the Nortel goalie to the ice every time, the way a person might trick a cat onto its stomach by teasing it with just the right length of wool. The irony of Del Rosario's play was not lost on me. There I was watching Hong Kong's privileged North American peewees with their Nike skates, yet the player who'd drawn my attention was this big Filipino kid. It wouldn't be the last time I'd see something like this.

"He is a strong boy," Mr. Ramirez said of Del Rosario. "He, like the other kids, wants to be better. My son takes ballet lessons because he wants to be better. He says he wants to do this because it will make him more flexible. I encourage him. He found out that one of the players drafted in the third round by Washington was from the Philippines. This gives him hope, and so my other son and I teach him from a book about goaltending."

"He looks strong on his skates," I said.

"He's getting better each time he plays. My son, you know, he had fifteen shots from number seven and he stopped them all. Fifteen breakaways!"

"Like in a shootout," I said.

"Yes. No goals. A shutout?" he stated.

"No. Like a shootout."

"Yes. No goals. A shootout?"

"Yes. Um. No. You're right. A shutout."

"A shu-ootout?"

Mr. Ramirez stood behind the goal and cried as Dada sprawled across the crease to make a save. The old man jumped up and down and grabbed our arms and shoulders, shouting "*Dada! Dada!*" A few seconds later, one of the Nortel players picked the puck up in the crease and flipped it over his son, who lay on his back like a snow angel, staring up at the ceiling. Mr. Ramirez buried his face in his shoulder, throwing one arm over his head.

"Oh, well," he conceded. "We will lose."

"Winning is overrated," I said to him, evoking another look of confusion.

"Dada, get up!" he yelled to his son.

Dada lay there.

"Dada! Get up!"

The ref skated over and told the young Filipino to get to his feet. "Stand up, Dada!"

Dada rose slowly, squeezing his father's voice from his head.

In the third period, with the Nortel team finally neutralizing Del Rosario, Ben Shoveller scored on Dada. He threw his hands and stick into the air and embraced his linemates, who shuffled off with him in ecstasy to the bench. I looked around to see Herb's reaction. He was standing at the end of the bench with the other hockey fathers, waving video cameras and cellphones. Herb was beaming. His job as a hockey dad was a twenty-four hour commitment, and here was one of the rewards. It made me feel a trifle guilty about my past.

During my house league swoon, my dad would say to me in the car on the way home: "You should carry the puck more. Really, you're good when you carry the puck." It was sound advice delivered sensitively, but it made me feel worse. And when those instructions gave way to shouts of "Two hands on the stick!" or "Stick on the ice!" raining down from the stands, it made it harder to play the game. Had I known how much my playing hockey soaked up my dad's time and energy, I might not have behaved the way I did. Really, he deserved a few more pats on the back from the other fathers, maybe another Player of the Week notice to add to our name. In the end, I probably wasted all those hours he'd spent dressing me and getting me to the rink in the blue hours of the morning after slugging it out in the office all week. His effort resulted not in a strong-willed competitor, but a coward who'd turned away from success. When I thought of this, I felt like shit.

My selfishness became obvious to me after spending two weeks in the Shoveller home. Much of Herb's time was spent getting Ben to school or a game. On top of that, he and his wife, Joanne, who also had a career, tended to their daughter, Aislin, who was nine. To further complicate matters, Herb had planned a trip to Vietnam and it looked like he would miss Ben's final game if his team advanced.

"I'm all chewed up about it," he told me one morning. "Ben's not saying anything, but I think it hurts him. He's conscious of the fact that I won't be there."

This became clear after the Manila game. The PeeWees won, but Ben skated off the ice looking sad. We found him sitting in his uniform on the bench.

"Great game," we told him.

"How about that Del Rosario guy?" I asked.

Ben stared at the floor.

"You scored a nice goal though."

He reached down to unlace a skate.

"What's the matter, Ben?" asked Herb, standing beside us.

Ben removed his skate.

"Let's take the rest of this stuff off, buddy," said Herb.

We left the Shovellers and made our way out of the rink. But before we could, we ran into Mr. Ramirez. Janet asked if she could take his picture with his son.

"Yes, of course!" he cried, delighted.

We found Dada and took their picture. There's Mr. Ramirez, looking proud of his young goaltender, and there's his son, wishing the old man would disappear.

4

WENDEL AND THE BELLS

The next morning I sat on the patio of the Repulse Bay cake and tea shop and read the *South China Morning Post*. A three-inch paragraph hidden in the corner of the sports section set my mind travelling: "In Montreal, the Tampa Bay Lightning improved to 2–0 since they were sold to William Davidson with a 6–1 victory against the Canadiens behind Wendel Clark's hat trick."

The sports pages of the *Hong Kong Standard* and the *South China Morning Post* covered every kind of game: tennis, rugby, golf, basketball, field hockey, football, swimming, soccer, cricket, and hockey. On my first day in China, I opened a paper to find a quarter-page photo of Turner Stevenson levelling Dainius Zubrus with a check: CANADIENS STAGE LATE BLITZ. There were Reuters game reports, which I studied in detail. I'd convinced myself on the plane that being away from trade gossip, scoring leaders, and front-office player poker would be the only way I could return to the game feeling revitalized, but there was no getting away from hockey. Nor did I want to be totally isolated, not when the news concerned Wendel Clark.

The report of Wendel's hat trick read like a koan. Millions of Chinese would rise that morning, sip their tea, eat breakfast, and pass their eyes over those words, but few would be as moved by them as I. The paragraph aroused a multitude of thoughts on life, home, and the power of hockey.

Over the years, the athlete who has most affected my life has been Wendel Clark. While my ideal hockey player would be someone who possesses Borje Salming's liquid skating style, Doug Gilmour's fanged intensity, Boxcar Glennie's citizen hustle, and Johnny Bower's slapstick genius, no one symbolized hope and happiness the way Wendel did when he came along in 1985, the same year I was reborn a hockey fan.

Before Wendel, I despised sports. I realize that's an inauspicious thing to put in a book about hockey but, during my teenage years, I viewed sports fans as dull-witted, chick-baiting dickheads. There's simply no other way of putting it. I formed this impression after attending countless Argonaut football games at Exhibition Stadium with my father. They were often miserable days. I wore Mod clothes – porkpie hat, black shoes, white shirt, skinny black tie, and trench coat with target buttons running up and down the lapels – and was invariably ridiculed by skags in dark-blue Argo jerseys with boxes of hot dogs propped on their stomachs. I considered it an act of defiance to sit there and absorb their rousting.

During one game, my father and I were sitting in front of a group of these louts, their testosterone musk roiling high on the air, who were belching *"Fucking suck"* at the players, even though their voices were within earshot of children. Sometime in the first quarter, one of them started whipping the side of my head with his scarf, and laughing. After a few minutes, I turned my head sideways, and he stopped. Then he started up again. This pathetic cat-and-mouse game lasted until halftime. I pictured my tormentor stump-necked with arms the size of Pacific salmon. I was too freaked out to know what to do.

In the third quarter, the head goon and his crew started tossing around a baseball hat, which eventually tumbled into our row. It fell straight into my father's lap. My initial reaction was to take it and

fling it away but, before I could, the guy grabbed my dad's arm. I
stood up, turned around, pointed at him, and screamed the scream
of a thousand angry fishmongers:

"*You are a fucking asshole!*"

He had a face like a mouse, with teeny eyes and a moustache that
fanned out under his nose. He swiped at me with his fist, but missed.
I stood rigid before my seat, my heart thumping in my chest. My
uncle, who was sitting three seats down from us, yelled, "Leave the
kid alone!" and there was shouting and the sound of seats clapping
back. Pretty soon people started yelling "Kick 'em out!" and, as the
cops raced down the stairs and pulled those louts from their seats, it
struck me that it was the first time in my life that I'd ever stood up
to anyone. It was also the last time, I thought, that I'd ever care
about sports again.

Racquetball, darts, steeplechase, aquatics, toy-boat regattas, the
Australian dwarf toss – I despised them in equal measure. Even the
sight of old people reading those illustrated fitness booklets they
give out free at pharmacies upset me. In high school, kids who liked
sports moved with confidence and in packs and, as a teenager
searching for a place to fit in, my anger smouldered. Sports became
antithetical to the free-minded and rebellious tint of my years, which
was better represented in the kind of music I liked. While I'd spent
my childhood dreaming of playing for the Leafs, after I was smitten
by the Ramones, sports was just a ball to be kicked away.

In the fall of 1984, my attitude changed. Ironically, it was music
that pulled me back in. I was going to school at York University, in
Toronto's northern suburbs, where I was music director of the
college radio station. My main responsibility was to make sure that
our Coke machine – acquired by way of some bogus sponsorship
deal – was filled with Molson Extra Old Stock, received in trade for
radio spots that never aired. One night, I was sitting around with
my friend, Robbie Sheffman, who was promising to produce a two-
four and other delights back at his apartment if I let him borrow an
album from the record library.

"Have you heard 'The Bells' by Lou Reed?" he asked.

I told him that I hadn't.

"Come on over, check it out. There's a game on, too. Canada versus Russia."

Everything about that scenario appealed to me except the game. Robbie lived about a ten-minute drive from the campus, so we got toasted for the ride. It was a lovely September evening. On my way there, I searched for something on the car radio and happened upon a broadcast of the game. It was the first time in years that I'd listened to hockey on the radio, and I was gripped. My ear was drawn to the sound of announcer Joe Bowen's coarse voice as it scratched across the AM. He seemed to be calling the action the way a reporter in the '60s might have described a street riot, his words escaping from his throat as if something astonishing was happening with each play. As I drove past the scarecrow trees and dead-brown grounds of the campus, I felt the broadcast could have been an eerie transmission from a passing Sputnik. Bowen's voice trembled as he reported, "You have to wonder just how long the Canadians can keep this up . . ." I felt a shiver run like a fingernail up my spine.

As soon as we got to Sheff's apartment, he flicked on the game. Then he put on Lou Reed and lowered the volume. I can't say that Lou is my favourite artist of all time, but sometimes he's just the thing to hear. The tension in the music supported what was being shown on the screen, and the game, tied 2–2, sucked me in. The contest was fraught with drama. Every player's face was clenched. Loose pucks were met by a frenzy of arms and legs, and whenever a player managed to peel free from the pack, he would be caught by another. In spite of this, there were many chances on net. Close-ups of the goaltenders' masks showed streams of water spilling from their chins. The players' eyes were glazed over with the grim knowledge that destiny was upon them. I imagined some greater being writing feverishly on parchment as the play moved around the ice.

For the first time, I saw these athletes as citizens vulnerable to the world. They had spent their lives learning and perfecting their craft and were now being tested in full view of their countrymen. Since the game also carried the weight of East versus West, I watched as one might have watched the flight of the Hindenburg, or the Apollo moon landing, or Trudeau's War Measures address, conscious that history was being born. During a faceoff, the camera zoomed in from the stands and I saw the names Gretzky, Bossy, Krutov, and Makarov sewn across their jerseys, and I thought to myself, *Here. Here is where I join them on their journey.*

Lou was singing, "Oh, here come the bells." The game moved into overtime. The hockey was hard, desperate, fast. Finally, John Tonelli stood behind the net flanked by two Russian defencemen, their eyes trained on the puck in front of them. Tonelli looked to his left, to his right, then wrapped both players in headlocks, all three falling to the ice. They lay together like sidewalk drunks. Tonelli put his palms to the ice and was the first to rise. He gathered the apple and whipped it along the boards to the blue line, then collapsed against the glass. Paul Coffey stopped the puck with his stick and fired high. Mike Bossy deflected it, and Canada won, 3–2.

I surprised myself by how loudly I cheered. And mine was just a single voice in a vast choir. We walked out to Sheff's balcony, which faced two other apartment towers. The balconies of all three buildings were crammed with people waving pennants and toasting each other with beer. Someone tried singing the national anthem. The buildings looked like three cruise ships on New Year's Eve, passing at the stroke of midnight. People were laughing and calling out to each other across the chasm. Sheff rolled a smoke, fitted it between his teeth, and asked, "So what did you think of that album?"

My eyes told the whole story.

I had heard the bells.

1985 was my first full season back with the NHL, so to speak, and Wendel Clark was the first player to grab my imagination. His debut game, goal, and fight felt like my own. He wore number 17 – which numerologists say represents immortality – and played with a reckless drive not seen since Tiger Williams, belying the pugilist stereotype with a touch like crushed velvet and a wrist shot that flew at the net with the grace of a sylph riding the air. When I first watched him play, he struck me as the consummate hockey player:

depending on his mood, he could beat you with either wild force or sublime artistry. Wendel had cross-generational appeal, too. Veteran fans liked him because he looked cut from granite and reminded them of Syl Apps, Ted Kennedy, Tim Horton – players from a distant era who did their job with a quiet and strong-willed intensity. Cynical cranks, their hearts crushed by owner Harold Ballard's systematic devastation of the mid-1970s Leafs, viewed Wendel as a portent of hope, a player immune to the new Leafs tradition of bad hockey, whose effort suggested expulsion from darkness. Kids drawn to the modern game were thrilled by highlights of Wendel's bone-mashing hits and bloody punch-ups with villains like Basil McRae, Tim Hunter, and Bob Probert. In Quebec, they gave him a name that sounded like a C.S. Lewis character: Wonder Clark. Fans from small-town Canada saw in him a soft-spoken farm kid who charmed the big city on his own terms, the same way they once viewed Gordie Howe and the Bentleys. And when he lost the 1986 Calder Trophy to Gary Suter, an American, his reputation in Canada only grew larger. This was also the year of Free Trade. Wendel reflected our lives in more ways than one.

After graduating from university, Sheff landed a job at TSN, where he produced a show hosted by veteran broadcaster Pat Marsden, a bulbous man with a croaking voice whose face was like an onion steeped in brine. I had written a song about Wendel which Sheff mixed into a highlight reel, and one night, with Clark as the show's guest, Marsden played the video live on the air. When they came back, Wendel was drumming his fingers on the table.

"So what did you think of the tune, Wendel?" asked Marsden.

"I thought it was pretty good," he declared. "How about you?"

"Well, I don't think it'll ever go to number one . . ."

Writing a chart-topper wasn't the point (though I suppose it wasn't *not* the point), but I was thrilled that Wendel had heard my tribute. "The Ballad of Wendel Clark (Parts 1 and 2)" inspired the most prolific and successful songwriting period of my life, and Wendel was my muse. I know that's a role more often filled by loved ones, but artists drawing inspiration from sport are not as rare as you might think. Geddy Lee, for instance, plans his summer tours around the major-league baseball season. Alice Cooper does likewise with tee-off times. George Thorogood will not tour in the summer if it conflicts with his softball team's schedule. Jazz flautist Herbie Mann was a devoted New York Rangers fan who would often compose during intermissions, while author David Gowdey has suggested that painter (and Rangers devotee) Joan Miró developed his circling style after watching skaters move around the ice. Famed Hollywood hoofer Gene Kelly, whose father was Canadian, used to skate on a backyard rink in Pittsburgh and, when asked about his dancing technique, once said, "I played a lot of ice hockey as a kid. Some of my steps come right out of that game – wide open and close to the ground."

It works the other way, too. Hockey broadcasting legend Dave Hodge is a record collector of the highest order. I once asked him what his all-time favourite concert was, and he told me, "It depends. Maybe Phil Ochs at the Riverboat. But I was also there the night an unknown comic named Woody Allen opened up for Bob Dylan in the Village in '65." Hall of Famer Bobby Hull used to be a regular at The Moustache, the old '6os rock club adjacent to the Montreal Forum, while his son, Brett Hull, when asked by a reporter about his intensity on the ice, replied, "Intensity? The last time I felt intense was when I went to see Neil Young."

I once came across Hull the younger standing outside Team USA's dressing room during the 1991 Canada Cup, so I took the opportunity to ask him what his favourite Neil Young album was. He thought about it for a second, then said, "*Decade*," before walking away. It struck me as an odd choice, and Brett must have thought so too, because a few minutes later, I felt a tap on my arm.

"*Reactor*," he said with certainty.

I never met Wendel Clark, although it's not as if I didn't have the chance. A few times a year, I'd get calls from friends encountering him on the town.

"Hey, man. Guess who's at the bar?"

"Who?"

"WENDEL!"

"Cool."

"Whaddya mean 'cool?' Get down here!"

"Naw, naw. That's okay."

"*Okay?* It's friggin' *Wendel Clark!*"

I was wary of meeting Wendel for several reasons. Joyce Carol Oates tells a story about being introduced to Muhammad Ali in a restaurant. She was brought to Ali's table, took one look at him, and broke down in tears. My concern was the opposite; I was certain that if I started telling Wendel how much I liked the way he played, I would not have known where to stop. It's possible that I would have done everything short of professing brotherly love, and frankly, the idea of eating food through a straw for the rest of my life didn't appeal to me. True, I sometimes fantasized that Wendel, like the players who read Artaud in Brian Fawcett's "My Career With The Leafs," would be more enlightened than the average jock, but it was more likely he was every bit the beer-slamming babe hunter that you'd expect a pro hockey player to be. There is a bond between fan and athlete that is close to love – if it isn't love itself – but to explain this to Wendel would have been to risk my looks. I'm sure he wouldn't have understood.

Wendel was my favourite. Even though thousands of fans across Canada felt a similar attachment, I believed my relationship with him was singular. After the 1993 playoffs, I was certain that my life and Wendel's were cosmically linked. The parallels, I thought, were eerie. Clark's fortunes with the Leafs turned at the same time as the Rheostatics'. We'd both toiled in luckless artistic vacuums until '93, when Wendel captained the Toronto Maple Leafs to their first post-season in three years just as the Rheos inked our first (and only) big US record deal. We were both at our creative heights, playing to greater crowds and garnering more media attention than ever before. I saw Wendel as a brilliant young player who would one day lead the Leafs to the Stanley Cup in the same way that I saw myself as a musician who would make records that would give the nation its musical identity. At the time, all of this seemed possible.

Spring 1993 has been blazed into my memory. The Leafs extended their series against both the Red Wings and the St. Louis Blues to seven games, taking them both in the deciding match. They scraped into the playoffs as underdogs, which made their subsequent romp all the more sudden and dramatic. With this unexpected success, shy, trepidatious Toronto exploded in a pageant of blue paint. The Leafs' playoff run was the kind of event where even those who had never been to a game before were heading down to Maple Leaf Gardens to soak in the joy and fervour of the scene. Leafs fans were standing atop cars, hanging off signposts, and waving flags and pennants as they choked off Carlton Street, drawing the nation's eyes to a building that at one time represented the heartbeat of Canadian social life. Kids stood outside the rink colouring salad bowls, which they wore over their heads to look like Mike Foligno. Two hosers who lived down the street from me worked through the playoffs Simonizing their Buick for the purpose of painting GO LEAFS GO! across the doors. They spent their evenings kneeling on the street in their overalls spraying the body white and, once they'd done that, they painted the letters in blue along the side. I came across them circling Maple Leaf Gardens before one of the games, honking their horn and waving at the fans, their dog sitting upright in the passenger seat. The Leafs made artists out of commonfolk. Short of high-school art or adult re-entry classes, there are few places where people are encouraged to, say, sculpt human figures, even if they are of rival players bleeding from the head and swinging from gallows. During that spring run, there were lots of fans who painted signs and built little foil Stanley Cups, and who asked themselves the same question upon leaving their house for the game: "Geez. When's the last time I did this?"

During a show at the El Mocambo, a fan passed a lifesized cutout of Wendel Clark to me across the crowd. I walked home and waved it drunkenly at motorists, who hollered "*Wendel!*" out their car windows. At another show, a fellow came backstage to show us a hockey stick autographed by all twenty members of the 1967 team, the last Leafs group to win a Stanley Cup. During game seven against St. Louis, we were onstage during the third period. We ended the show with a long low note that sustained for a few minutes and, just as it faded, a kid who'd been listening to the game on his transistor radio couldn't contain himself any longer. "*Six nothing final!*" he boomed. The crowd cheered wildly.

Number 17 (Graig Abel)

If the Leafs could defeat their next opponent – the Los Angeles Kings – they would advance to meet the Montreal Canadiens. Leafs–Kings was a contest soaked with irony. Los Angeles was led by Wayne Gretzky, Canada's athlete of the half-century. The series placed him in the awkward position – one he ultimately relished – of standing in the way of a head-to-head match between Canada's two most storied sports teams. Montreal–Toronto would be a dream series for a nation of hockey fans who were feeling the game slip through their hands. It wouldn't be the first time Gretzky had troubled the system that had produced him. His impact on hockey in the States would make it possible for Phoenix and Colorado to harbour Winnipeg and Quebec's teams, and draw tycoons like Wayne Huizenga and Michael Eisner to the game, creating a market boom that helped the NHL become a desirable broadcasting entity. This would hasten Fox television's courtship, which yielded the blue puck, ruminations on four periods and the removal of the red line, all reactionary measures tabled by a crude, detached interest.

Gretzky had become the symbol of the free-market NHL, but Wendel Clark, by contrast, was cast as the defender of Canadian hockey. He and the Great One were a study in opposites. Ever since he scored 378 goals as a ten-year-old, 99's youth had been documented, while the one story of Clark's boyhood that slipped through was of a local tryout at which he'd arrived without a cage for his helmet, so his father fashioned him one using fence wire and tinfoil. As a twenty-something superstar, Gretzky had been sponsored by Easton aluminum sticks, Post cereal, McDonald's and Coca-Cola, while Wendel popped up every now and then on television to sell Chunky Soup. Gretzky had played for the egomaniacal Peter Pocklington, and had led his team to a string of Stanley Cup victories, while Wendel also toiled for a tyrannical owner – Harold Ballard – who commandeered the Leafs through their darkest decade ever. At his peak, Gretzky performed relatively injury-free alongside Mark Messier and others, while Wendel suffered multiple back and knee ailments while carrying Maple Leafs teams burdened with the likes of Paul Lawless. And if their career paths weren't dissimilar enough, it was during the 1987 Canada Cup – Gretzky's defining moment as a national hockey hero – that Wendel first injured his back, making him an early cut from the team and ending his chance to compete against the world's best.

With home and country glued to their television sets in 1993, it was no surprise that both players played the greatest hockey of their lives. The series was described by announcer Ron MacLean as one that you felt with your heart and your stomach. On game days, you could feel the pace of Toronto streets quicken as start time approached, and once the puck was dropped, city life was on pause. Our emotions hung on every rush, every faceoff won and lost. The result was a bellwether for the mood of the city on the day after the game.

In game two, Wendel Clark answered a hit on Doug Gilmour by challenging Kings defenceman Marty McSorley to a fight. The bout was vicious. They threw punches at each other from way behind their ears, a riotous melee of fist, blood, and muscle. When finally separated, both players skated wearily to the penalty box, heads lowered. A friend told me that he was at a singles hangout near the Gardens later that night when the Kings and Leafs teams walked through the door. They camped out at the bar, Clark and Gilmour standing at one end, Gretzky and McSorley at the other. He watched them glower at each other across the room, drilling holes with their eyes. By last call, neither team had moved. No one wanted to be the first to leave. They were at war off the ice, too.

The series was by turns beautiful and horrible. Game six was the most transcendent of them all. It was played in Los Angeles and was almost too much to bear for anyone who'd suffered through fifteen years of bad hockey, as Leafs fans had. It had been so long since we'd had our hearts twisted and wrenched this way that we comforted each other like earthquake victims, huddling in groups and refusing to watch alone. Friends joined us at our apartment for the game, which we watched on tenterhooks. We were so nervous you could have grated carrots on our gooseflesh. We were drunk by the start. I felt like a soldier about to be shipped overseas, terrified of his destiny. We got drunker and more rowdy with each period, and when the Kings established an early lead, we poured more booze and screamed louder. We prayed for the Leafs to lift themselves off the mat, but when the second period passed without event, it looked as if they would not. We drank more.

And then, out of nowhere came Wendel. His face was hard and determined, and his body swayed like a cobra. When he skated into the Kings' zone, he looked as if he wanted to scrape his opponent's heart from its cavity and fling it into the crowd. This was a performance to put the Kings on the defensive, and it worked, for Wendel weaved around them, his shoulders tipping side to side as if they were wings guiding a small plane. Twice he jumped off the bench to finish a hat trick with a goal that tied the game and sent it into overtime. For the most vital ten minutes of his hockey life, and with his team behind, Clark out-played the greatest player ever to lace on a pair of skates.

He made Gretzky eat shit.

During the intermission, my body felt bruised, as if it had been thrown repeatedly against a brick wall. I was exhausted. There are many who believe that one cannot truly know a sport without actually playing it, but watching certain games can be an intense physical experience. Some fans have never set foot on ice, but when your body lunges at the TV set, blood pumping furiously, teeth grinding, ass clamped, the veins rising out of your skin and spittle flying, the physicality of the game is shared by fan and player. With the exception of sex and heavy manual labour, we rarely use our bodies so completely.

Kerry Fraser dropped the puck to begin overtime. We coddled our hopes and watched. Then Gretzky scored. It was over quickly. Number 99 picked the puck up in the goalmouth and flicked it over Felix Potvin's shoulder with all the breeziness of a kid swiping at a crabapple. He did his little running-skating celebration and spun around a few times before being mobbed by his black and silver teammates. Canada was in paroxysms of despair, and there was Gretzky, jitterbugging. I've always felt that someone with so much talent should simply bow his head and let the applause spill over him like a tenor in the footlights, but I suppose his enthusiasm made the Great One who he was. The camera panned to Bruce

McNall, chortling from his seat. Sly Stallone loved it, Goldie Hawn, too. I imagined John Candy leaning against the wall of the rink, sick of it all.

We carried our pain into the night like a head impaled on a pike. At my place we continued drinking past the naming of the three stars, the national news, and the late movie. Janet escaped to bed. She told me that when she got up briefly near dawn, she found me reading Thomas Boswell's "Why Time Begins on Opening Day" to my friends. Apparently, I looked like Gregory Peck in *The Omen*, standing outside the cemetery in the driving rain, waving his bible and babbling feverishly. Hours later, I crawled into bed and shook her awake.

"We almost did it. Wendel almost did it," I sputtered.

"Dave?"

Alarmed, she pushed my body away. I leaned over the edge of the bed and vomited.

The series returned to Toronto, where the Kings won 5–4. Gretzky has called it his greatest game in the NHL. I have a tape of it in my closet, but can't bring myself to watch it. I was in Montreal playing a gig that night and missed the entire third period. We saw the first two in our dressing room, but were called to the stage with the game tied. After a few songs, we couldn't stand the suspense, so we asked a teenage fan to come up on stage and describe the last minute of play into the microphone from his transistor radio, which he listened to through an earplug. He stood alone on the stage at Club Soda, and then finally he shook his head.

His voice broke: "No."

After the show, I wandered to the Main, where I put my head down and cried.

The Leafs made the semi-finals again the next year, but suffered from management changes and a loss of direction. Wendel eventually left Toronto a shadow of his former self. I heard news of his trade to Quebec while walking down Bloor Street. A fellow I didn't know leaned out the window of his car and said, "Hey, Bidini! Did ya hear they traded Wendel Clark?"

I rushed home to the television.

They had.

A year later, the Rheostatics were dropped by our US label, and a few years after that Leafs moved into the Canadiens' division, forever ending the possibility that they would meet in the Stanley Cup final again. Wendel kicked around the league and returned to the team a few years later as part of an ill-conceived deal for Swedish defenceman Kenny Jonsson, but was left unprotected after the 1998 season. The league itself changed. New teams in Atlanta, Nashville, and Columbus, among others, were added, players' salaries escalated into the tens of millions, training-camp holdouts grew in numbers, Team Canada was unseated twice on the world stage (first by the United States, and then by the Czech Republic), old arenas like Chicago Stadium and the Montreal Forum and Memorial Auditorium were abandoned or demolished, and the Leafs moved out of Maple Leaf Gardens, their final game concluding with a funeral march from one end of the rink to the other by former players coming together at centre ice. Wendel Clark didn't attend. He had a game in Tampa Bay that night.

As I closed the *South China Morning Post* and drained my tea, I thought of how much of my life as a hockey fan, and my awakening as a person, had moved through Wendel's years as a Leaf. Once, I had explored the game and understood it and articulated my feelings towards it by means of his career. And there he was, in small type between the cricket results and tennis scores.

Somehow my hero had found me, miles from home.

5

THE FALL OF DARWISH

Abdullah was the chairman of the UAE Ice Hockey Committee. He looked like a Muslim Bill Derlago. He opened and closed the door at the end of the bench and was seen cupping his hands around his mouth shouting either encouragements or death threats at the players; it was hard to tell from the sober intensity of his glare. Whenever the UAE scored, he raised his arms above his head and, like the fans of South Philly, he could intimidate teams with his leonine roar.

You couldn't miss Colonel Abdullah Hashmi. He dwarfed the athletes he'd helped assemble into the United Arab Emirates' first national hockey team. He had built the team and took every loss personally. Abdullah had been one of the desert's first hockey players. He cannot remember how or why he started playing. He just remembers that he did. "When you're a kid, you want to try everything," he told me. "I was good at skating and then one day there were sticks. I took to the game easily, but I don't skate anymore: I fly instead."

Abdullah was a fighter pilot in the UAE army. Bear and Bill Upton were flight instructors whom Abdullah had recruited to coach the team. When he first happened upon his players, they were part of a figure-skating club from Al Ain, a desert city near an archaeological dig into one of the world's oldest ruins. Abdullah saw that the figure skaters were skilled enough in the game's foundation to make them competitive, and set out to secure equipment. Thus a hockey culture was born. I've often wondered how someone like Kurt Browning – who once skated the national anthem before an Oilers playoff game – would have performed were he fattened with creatine and taught the finer points of stickhandling and shooting. I imagined salchows buzz-sawing through the Left-Wing Lock, double Lutzes casting shadows over the heads of bewildered defencemen. The Arab players were the closest anyone had come to trying this experiment.

By the time the playoffs rolled around, the UAE Nats were the tournament's darlings. During their semi-final at SkyRink against the Empire Hotel All-Stars, the crowd was with them every play. The Nats packed the rink too, something that assured them a return trip next year. It was the Emirates' first international playoff game, and they out-played the All-Stars, whose goalie stood on his head to keep the contest close going into the final period. The score was 2–1 in the Arabs' favour when a penalty shot was called against them. Abdullah would tell me later: "I knew that that play would forever change the face of hockey in the UAE. If our goalie stops it, we prevail. If he does not, then *pffft*, it's over." The whole team knew this. They leaned against their bench looking terrified. The Empire Hotel team, a collection of Chinese and Hong Kong–born Westerners, sent out their captain to take the shot, who eyed the Arab goalie the way a fox might eye a crippled hen. Darwish stood rooted in his crease. It would be his first ever penalty shot, and almost certainly his last.

Darwish spanked his pads with his stick the way he'd seen the other goalies do, but the force of the blow rocked him back on his feet and he nearly fell over before grabbing the crossbar in time. Abdullah covered his face in disgust. The Empire player – Michael

Cheng – picked up the puck at centre ice, laughed, and moved in on the young Arab goalie.

In his novella "Goalie's Anxiety at the Penalty Kick," Peter Handke suggests that when a goaltender tries to guess what the shooter will do, he has as much chance of getting it right as someone trying to pry open a door with a straw. Goalies can over-guess in this situation, and one of the rules of the penalty shot is to not think too much. In this sense, Darwish's witlessness might have worked in his favour. He couldn't guess what the shooter would do because he'd never been in this position before, nor did he have a reference point; it's not as if he'd seen hundreds of penalty shots on television. He probably hadn't even watched a hundred games.

Cheng, on the other hand, had infinite options. His best play would have been to step over the blue line and fire a shot at the net (which is what Frank Mahovlich did on Tony Esposito in the 1971 Stanley Cup playoffs), for Darwish had all the lateral quickness of a tractor. But here, psychology favoured the UAE greenhorn, because Cheng's pride would not allow such brutish play. Instead, he folded in on Darwish and deked. This gave the Arab goalie a better chance to stop the puck, if for no other reason than that he was closer to it than he'd been at the outset. But Cheng's move was swift and sure, and once he'd pulled the puck to his backhand, he could have re-enacted the last scene of *Casablanca* in the time he had to slip the puck into the net.

Darwish, however, was more accomplished in falling to the ice than most goalies. It's not something that is practised very often, but the Arab netminder had a lot of experience falling on the ice. So when Cheng deked, Darwish dropped expertly. Many other games have been decided on stranger twists of fate – a thimble of snow, the wonky angle of a board slat, a delinquent clod of tape – and this was Darwish's one strength: the creative mishap.

Cheng flipped the puck at the net. Darwish sprawled on the ice and trapped it beneath his shoulder. He lay there like a drunk who's woken in a ditch with his keys pinned under him. The Chinese captain looked back at the net and slammed his stick along the

Darwish in victory

boards as the Arab kids rushed towards their goalie. You could tell from their visible relief that they would not now lose the game. The UAE scored immediately and shortly added another goal to ice their victory. Darwish brimmed with newfound confidence. Later in the game, the Chinese team positioned a player on the goaltenders' doorstep in hopes of getting a deflection. He remained there for ten, twenty seconds before Darwish cross-checked him in the back, Billy Smith style. The Chinese player looked around with indignation, but the crowd loved it. He moved in on Darwish, but the Arab goalie pushed him hard and the player fell over in the crease. The old men in the crowd grabbed their sides in delight. Abdullah slapped one player on the shoulder with such force that he lifted him off the ground, shooting him along the boards about three feet to his left.

I must confess a weakness for small goalies who play beyond their size. Before backstops of the 1980s like Patrick Roy and Ron Hextall turned goaltending into a large man's position, netminders

Popcorn in Don Mills, Ontario (Ken Elliott, Canadian Weekend Magazine)

like Mike Palmateer flourished in the National Hockey League. I mention him because he is responsible for one of my favourite saves of all time.

Mike Palmateer's best years with the Leafs were in the mid-to-late 1970s. He was a mop-headed imp from the Toronto suburb of Don Mills. Mike had a liking for pre-game popcorn: two bags atop his dressing-room stall, hot. He was once profiled in the *Toronto Star Weekend* magazine in a photographic essay showing him playing road hockey with a bunch of local scamps. He wasn't much bigger than the kids themselves, and his unrefined style appeared to be the product of countless hours freelancing in front of his mom's grey apartment complex. When kids saw Popcorn play, they saw themselves. Ken Dryden's size and Tony Esposito's butterfly style made mimicry difficult, but Popcorn's frame suited a child's moves. He was a figure straight from a Scott Young novel: a hero to his small fans. When he arrived from the Dallas farm team for his first pro game, he told reporters, "Toronto's goaltending troubles are over!"

Popcorn made saves in a flurry of arms, hands, and feet. He reacted to shots like a juggler in mid-routine who is suddenly thrown a ball from the crowd. He moved as if trying to distract the puck from entering the net. He confessed to a habit of calling play-by-play during games in the voice of Foster Hewitt, often referring to himself in the third person – "Palmateer makes the save!" – something that anyone who has ever played street hockey has done. He would tell the press, "Well, if I get killed, I get killed," sounding like Indiana Jones entering the Temple of Doom. Then he'd wink at the reporters.

His defining moment came in game seven of the 1978 quarter-final against the New York Islanders, series tied 3–3, Nassau County Coliseum, New York. It was a save that happened so fast not even television replays captured Popcorn's entire goalmouth flight. The play came with Islander centre Bryan Trottier standing alone at the side of the net, the puck nestled on his stick. The camera picked up Popcorn in mid-stretch as he dived head-first from one edge of the net to the other, as if suddenly lengthening his body at either end. Fully extended, he touched the very tip of his stick to the puck and deflected it over the boards. Trottier dropped his arms and looked to the roof. Popcorn had been faster moving across the crease than the puck had been leaving Trottier's stick. If you did the math, you would harumph at the figures. I remember sprawling across the rug in our basement with each replay, my face buried in the plush. In overtime, the Leafs won the game on Lanny McDonald's breakaway goal, arguably the most important Leafs marker of the post-expansion era. But Popcorn and company could not subdue their next opponent, the infallible Montreal Canadiens, and a few years later, Palmateer was traded to Washington. After he retired, an article in the paper showed him flipping patties in a Markham burger joint, his career finished by a bad left knee that would require twenty-two operations. For Popcorn, it was as if playing in the NHL had been a kid's wild charade. He was the lucky scrub among us who somehow snuck through.

With their victory, the Arabs advanced to the division final against the Singapore Winter Flames, the team who had beaten them in the round robin. The game was to take place at the Glacier in Festival Walk mall, a much newer rink in the upscale neighbourhood of Kowloon Tong. You'd find no goat heads or buckets of offal at Festival Walk, only boutiques selling perfume and lingerie, maybe books. I liked Kowloon Tong for the simple reason that its name sounded like a villain from the old days of Maple Leaf Wrestling ("Kowloon Tong is poised on the ropes to deliver his Sabian Slam! Oh, the humanity!"). I found that most Hong Kong names possessed a poetic cadence. Whenever I heard "Sham Sui Po" or "Tsim Sha Tsui" spoken in public, it sounded like two people whispering to one another. The stops on the Metro had evocative names – Lai Chi Cok, Tseun Wan, Shek Kip Mei, Kwun Tong, and Mong Kok – which might have served as the punchline to a bawdy limerick. And "Repulse Bay" conjured up images of a sleazy, forbidding place, which, considering the well-heeled status of its residents, made its name all the more cunning.

Hong Kong was a wonderland in other ways, too. I was dazzled by how well it worked. Never before had I been in a city so dense, yet not once did I feel part of an oppressive crush. There was an Anglo orderliness to Hong Kong that reminded me of parts of London, and its thoroughfares and markets were remarkably clean even though millions of people streamed through them daily. The city possessed a kind of urban equilibrium. I was sitting outside the Dragon Centre when a woman emerged from her clothes shop and threw into the air a thicket of plastic strapping. As it hit the pavement, a pauper appeared pulling a dolly of garbage bags filled with this very binding. He scooped it up, stuffed it into one of his bags, and moved on.

Another time, we were at a temple in Wan Chai, where red candles and great smoking hoops of incense were strung from the ceiling, casting a glow on the dark wooden posts and wainscotting. I was careful not to linger too long in front of any of the enshrined Buddhas for fear of being caught praying or showing disrespect, but just then, an old man in a white dress shirt appeared and walked slowly towards us. I assumed we were about to be upbraided for loitering in a place of worship, but instead he passed a bored glance over our faces, craned his neck, and lit a smoke with the flame of the holy candle.

We spent the afternoon of the Arab-Singapore final on Cheung Chau Island, one of a handful of settlements in the Hong Kong archipelago. The ferry journey back into Hong Kong was a dream. We made the trip just before nightfall. The faint lights of the city speckled the horizon as the ferry chugged across the dark waters. Day gave way to evening as we passed freighters and old drilling boats lit up like Christmas trees floating in the cool sea. Once the edge of the cityscape appeared, Hong Kong's shoreline sparkled like a bejewelled aquarium. The time passed like a slow cinematic reel of silver and gold. There was a harmonic madness to the jumble of apartments and office towers that suggested the city had been planned by a draughtsman who had drawn one design over the last, rather than start a new blueprint.

We docked and rode the Metro to Festival Walk. We were both wearing knapsacks, which we'd used to carry supplies for our trip to the island. Whenever I strapped mine on, I felt like I might as well have written "nerd tourist" across my forehead. Touring distant lands is not the ideal circumstance for a fashion statement (in fact, I believe that it cancels out any time you've ever looked good or stylish), but it wasn't easy having to spend six weeks looking like Don Knotts next to the hyper-hip young Chinese. I'd lobbied Janet for the permission to bring something other than a knapsack, but she stressed practicality and comfort over appearance. This was fine for someone whose northern Italian visage allowed her such a digression, but hard for me, who looked as stylish as a chess club president.

The Glacier, where the Arab-Singapore final was being played, was double the size of SkyRink. At the front of the arena, a stack of large styrofoam cubes were wrapped in white plastic fluff to look like a snowbank. The ice wasn't NHL size, and it had square corners, but it was easily the length of most local rinks in Canada. The Glacier had three levels of seating: the top was a restaurant and bar; the second was part of the shopping mezzanine; and the ice level had two sets of bleachers on one side, and the players' dressing room and timekeeper's area on the other. It seemed cooler than at SkyRink, and from the smell I could tell that the ice would be harder and faster.

I almost didn't recognize Abdullah when I saw him sitting at the café across from the rink. He was dressed in traditional Arab robes, dishdasha and al galfeyah. He looked like a desert prince. Sam, the UAE hockey committee's travelling photographer and media emissary, was in traditional dress as well. If it wasn't already obvious that this was the most important game in Arab hockey history, their formal wear drove the point home.

"Singapore . . . ," said Abdullah, touching his throat. He couldn't speak. He'd lost his voice from shouting too hard in the last game, so his words were few. Instead, he used arm ballet to communicate his thoughts, cutting a swath behind him and clearing a four-foot radius on either side of his table.

"Singapore . . . ," he continued, stabbing his temple with his finger. "They know us; we know them."

"Meng's in net," I said.

Abdullah pulled me close. "He can be beaten," he rasped. "That's not what worries me. Our goalie. You know the one," he said, his throat constricted with worry.

"But Darwish stopped that penalty shot," I reminded him.

Abdullah leaned back in his chair and snorted. The Arabs were more nervous than I'd seen them all tournament. Abdullah's foot was constantly tapping the floor. Sam could barely drink his coffee. He said a few words, and then got up and apologized: "I cannot stand this. Sorry, but I must leave. I have to be with the boys."

There were about 700 people at the Glacier. Janet and I sat with a group of Asian kids who cheered as soon as the Arab team touched the ice. It was a wonderful thing to see (I later learned that they were members of a rival Singapore team who wanted their countrymen to lose), and when Tom Barnes played Cornershop's "Brimful of Asha" – a modern masala of Western and Eastern pop – over the rink's sound system, I felt a rare global synergy created by Canada's sporting gift to the world.

Barnes introduced the starting lineups. He used a sentence which I never thought I'd hear spoken in a hockey rink: "At right defence, number twenty: Obaid Al Dharmaki." The Arabs were tight, but focussed. When I asked Abdullah what the team had done earlier that day, he said gravely, "Nothing." I'd wondered how a group of young Muslim kids would behave loosed in a Western-style city pulsing with life and activity (and girls, girls, girls), but Nasser told me a few weeks later: "The day after the first playoff win, I slept fourteen hours. I had nothing but an orange juice. I didn't leave my hotel room. I just lay there and thought about the game."

For all their anxiety and anticipation, the Arabs played their best hockey of the tournament, and the result of the game was never in doubt. Once again, Abdullah worked the door to the players' bench, where his robes billowed as he screamed silently at his players, as if mere expression could convey his point (it did). Omar and Ahmed skated together like wingbacks sweeping the ball back and forth, producing chance after chance. Omar scored early against Meng, which seemed to disconcert the goalie. The standard theory is that if you give quality goaltenders the opportunity to build confidence, they will get stronger, more impregnable as the game progresses. But if you can get to them early, especially in a pressure-packed game, there's a chance that the hint of self-doubt will throw their athletic alchemy out of whack. This is what happened to Meng after Omar's early goal. And the bigger ice surface – which benefited the stronger UAE – meant that the little goalie never really had a chance to regain his confidence. The Glacier was unkind to all of the Winter Flames, whose strategy – to put the puck on Darwish at every chance – was less successful than it had been at SkyRink, where all you had to do was step over the blue line to be in range of the goalie.

Darwish, for his part, was not terrible. He even stopped a rising slapshot from the blue line with his blocker, which made Abdullah hold his head and laugh, for he knew by the beginning of the last period that fate would smile on his desert Nats. The final score was 3–2 in favour of the Arabs. Omar scored a hat trick, guaranteeing that his name would appear the next day in both the *South China Morning Post* and the *Hong Kong Standard*, neither of which he could read. After the game, Barnes skidded out on the ice and gave Abdullah his trophy. He kissed it and raised it above his head and shouted soundlessly like King Kong. Barnes told the crowd that the HK Fives was the first international tournament that the Arab team had played in, and that they'd become champions a mere four months after holding their first practice as a team. Once every member of the Arab team had touched the cup, they skated the perimeter of the ice, crouching behind one another in a crazy speeding train. They moved faster and faster around the ice, their bodies caterpillaring like a midway ride, fifteen bearded faces aglow with victory.

After they broke formation, the UAE players transformed into Disney on Ice. The sight of a lithe Ukrainian beanpole covered in rhinestones doing twirls and jumps to the theme from *The King and I* is weird enough, but when these moves are done by young Arabs wearing shoulder pads and square helmets, you can only shake your head. I'd never seen anything like it in my life. Imagine Tie Domi raking his stick across Tim Hunter's face one minute, then spinning around like a tiddlywink the next. Think of Eric Lindros being announced as the game's first star, but instead of skating bored to centre ice, crossing his arms over his chest and rotating like a drill bit. The UAE team flung their bodies around the rink. They leaped and spun. Sam ran around the perimeter of the Glacier and threw UAE pennants to the cheering crowd. Abdullah hugged Bear; Bear hugged Bill Upton. Obaid skated to centre ice and cast his body into the air. He spun once, twice. He was not yet aware that hockey players do not do this kind of thing. Or do not do them yet.

A few days later, the UAE Nats touched down in Dubai, and for the first time ever, the national media showed up to greet an Arabian hockey team.

It was a start.

6

Look, it's Gordie Howe.

The last person I expected to run into in Hong Kong was Mr. Hockey. Okay, maybe not the last – Don Cherry was the last – but Gordie was certainly up there. So when I entered the Empire Hotel and saw him, I gave my head a good, eye-rattling shake before deciding that the silver Buddha sitting in the lobby was not merely a homesick invention of my subconscious, but, in fact, the legend of Floral, Saskatchewan. After asking a scrum of people who seemed stricken with the same disbelief, I found out that Gordie had been flown to Hong Kong by Tom Barnes to promote the HK Fives tourney. To my mind, this was a little like getting Pavarotti to sell opera in the Yukon, but at least it brought together every ex-pat in the city who'd ever seen a hockey game. Once word spread that Gordie was in town, they congregated daily in the hotel in hopes of getting Mr. Hockey's famous scribble. Along with meeting his fans, Gordie was also spending his time chatting up the Hong Kong press. While it's true that the flyhalf of the Fijian rugby team would probably have drawn more attention, the press were curious about Gordie in a "So, apparently you're worshipped as a god?" kind of way. However, this isn't to say that he could simply stroll down the streets with impunity.

"I've been recognized five times," he told me proudly. "And all by Chinese."

The Howe legend involves many tales featuring varying degrees of physical violence, making any encounter with him slightly unnerving. I have my favourites. Once, a WHA rookie found himself lining up against Gordie in his first pro game. The kid blinked worse than Gordie himself (Howe developed his physical tic after colliding with Leafs centre Teeder Kennedy in a 1950 playoff game, requiring emergency surgery. Sid Abel noted that, "They opened up Gordie's skull to remove pressure on his brain and the blood shot to the ceiling like a geyser") and so Gordie thought that the kid was mocking him. The puck dropped, Gordie threw off his gloves and, with two blows, put him in the hospital. When Howe got back to the bench, one of his teammates pulled him aside and asked, "Gordie, what the heck did you do that for?" Gordie told him, "Because that little snot-nosed brat was making fun of me." "Fun of you?" he said. "Didn't you know? That kid's got it twice as bad as you!"

Howe was hard on rookies. He once squared off with another poindexter, telling him, "Listen, son, in this league, we only clutch and grab at sweaters. We don't really go at it. They pay us too much money to get hurt." The kid took him at his word and Howe pummelled him. In his article "Howe Incredible," Mordecai Richler wrote that "when Donnie Marshall was with the Rangers, he was asked what it was like to play against Howe. In reply, he lifted his shirt to reveal a foot-long angry welt across his rib cage. 'Second period,' he said." John Ferguson was once cut by Howe for nine stitches. On the tongue. Trent Frayne recalls the time Howe, a rookie himself, was knocked down twice by Myles Lane, only to get up a third time and take him out. But perhaps the most telling tale of Howe's ferocity came at the expense of Lou Fontinato. They fought briefly in New York in 1959. It was brief because, in a matter of seconds, Howe broke Fontinato's nose, cracked his cheekbone, and knocked out several teeth. It took a team of plastic surgeons to make Fontinato look half-way right again.

Gordie's image has softened over the last few years. His wife, Colleen, probably has something to do with that. Howe is one of the few NHLers to acknowledge in public the influence of his wife on his life and career. This is rare in a male-dominated sport, where athletes are known more for booty call than marital fidelity. Colleen has a reputation for being a ball-breaking negotiator, but I could never tell how much of that was misogyny and how much of it truth. But no matter what is written or said about Colleen, Howe is rarely seen without her. They've even collaborated on a book about players and their wives and life after hockey. They make promotional appearances together and run Howe Enterprises as a team.

While I talked with Gordie, Janet talked with Colleen (at one point, Colleen interrupted us and said, "Gordie! Dave and Janet are writing a book together too!"). Talking to Gordie was easy. It's often the case with retired players. They're impressive storytellers and need little prompting. All you have to do is buy the coffee and turn on the tape recorder.

"In the early days of playing, most of my skating was down by what they called the Hudson Bay slough," said Gordie, leaning over the table, his enormous shoulders thrusting forward. "The city was rundown at the lower end and we'd get early snow or early rain and then all of that would freeze. I could skate twelve miles from downtown Saskatoon out to the airport. Almost as long as the Rideau, but not quite. Before that, of course, I had to get skates, which wasn't easy. My mother once gave a couple of dollars to a lady who was trying to feed her family, which was in desperate need of food. She was very grateful and so she came back a short while later with a gunnysack. There was a doily in it, a few other things, but then an old pair of skates fell out. And when they hit the floor, my sister immediately grabbed one and I grabbed the other. We went outside. Every house had a potato patch, and there was all this excess water, so when the snow came you automatically had a rink. So we went out there. After a while, my sister got cold, so she came in and took off her skate. I grabbed it. They were too big for me, but I didn't care. I skated twelve hours a day, every day. I had immense fun out there. I played for five teams and I played every position.

"I got my first big break when a kid, Frankie Shedden, went through the ice. He was in to about his armpits before we finally got him out. He had the only nickel-plated skates I'd ever seen and the blades were really nice. After he went through, we rushed him home. We had about two-and-a-half blocks to walk, so when we got there he was ice cold and his pants were stiff, the whole works. Frankie ended up getting really sick; so sick that he couldn't play hockey. One day, Mr. Shedden asked me if I was going to try out for peewee, and I said 'Well, I don't have skates.' And he said 'You do now.' He let me use Frankie's skates, and that's how I made the peewee team."

There were so many things that I wanted to ask Mr. Hockey, not the least being why he had a trademark pocking the Y above his sobriquet. It adorned the cover of the tournament program; an odd sight, to say the least. It suggested that Gordie was worried that some other celebrity might start calling himself Mr. Hockey, perhaps the Artist Once Again Known As Prince. I'm not implying that the name didn't befit a player of Howe's stature, but it made it look like the name of a cereal brand or detergent (which may have been the idea all along). Besides, Hong Kong already had a Mr. Hockey. He was a fellow named Jim Chiu Chi On who, at one time, owned and operated the only ice-hockey shop in Kowloon. His other distinction was of scoring four goals in the opening game of the 1995 HK Fives tournament, leading the HK Chinese to a 6–3 win, the first time that an Asian team defeated a squad of expatriates.

Jim once told a local paper: "I sometimes feel like a missionary promoting the game to the Hong Kong community. I find myself cast in the role of a teacher. I go around town and I ask Chinese people if they like ice hockey, and then I teach them. With so many young kids in Hong Kong now playing hockey, a victory in the Fives by an all-Chinese team is going to happen. It's inevitable."

Mr. Hockey, indeed.

But while Mr. Chiu's stats were impressive for Chinese hockey, Gordie's were astonishing for anything anyone has ever done with a puck and stick. At the time of our conversation, Gordie was still the all-time pro-hockey goal-scoring leader, with a total number of goals that combined both his WHA and NHL records. When I left Canada, Wayne Gretzky was tied with Gordie, but was out with an injury. I pointed this out to Gordie.

"Well, it's only a matter of time before he bags one," he sighed.

While Howe and I talked, members of the young Filipino team gathered behind us in the lobby. Here were three revolutions of the life cycle of hockey. Howe's was the first. He would put on a clinic a few days later for the kids, but would not play with them. He'd instruct and skate a little, but full-on competition was beyond him; both his kneecaps had been replaced and it hurt him to skate. Mr. Hockey was in pain. Colleen told Janet that he had been out cold for four days in the hospital recovering from the operation. He winced when he moved and grimaced when reaching for his coffee. It was no longer possible to picture Howe ramming his stick down John Ferguson's throat, or fighting Mike Walton in the all-star game. I couldn't imagine him yelling at anyone, not even in a stern, grandfatherly way. He looked more like a teacher in the way that he leaned back in his chair and expounded on his life. He was wise and rumpled and spoke gently, Northrop Frye in Tacks. A few days later, when he was signing autographs at the Glacier, a young Chinese woman came up to Janet and asked, "Could you please tell me who that old man is?" Janet told her. A few minutes later the woman asked to borrow a pen. "I want to get the autograph of Papa Howe!" she exclaimed.

With Howe's ascent to the cycle's summit and a place beside Phantom Joe Malone and Cyclone Taylor and Howie Morenz, there would be room for Gretzky where Howe had been. The wheel spun. Gretzky would pass into Howe's aura. He would assume the mantle for a generation of fans for whom he defined the game, and then one day, he would be sitting in a chair talking about the first time he ever held an aluminum stick or about some kid trying to break his record or about Gordie Howe, after whom he patterned his game. Wayne's dad once told him: "You just watch and do everything that Gordie does and you'll be okay." I'd seen the two of them together in the dressing room at Rendez-Vous '87 (the international hockey summit in Quebec City). Gordie was walking around the floor shouting "Where's Wiener?" until Wayne's head popped out from the entrance to the showers. He was so thin and small compared to the rest of the players. He wore blue long underwear that looked like pyjamas. "I'll be out in a second, Gordie," said Wayne. Howe jammed his hands in his jacket pockets, furrowed his brow, and shot Gretzky a prefect's look of dissatisfaction. Then he turned away and smiled.

Ninety-nine was the most-worn number in the tournament (one Singapore team even had two), from Filipino boys to Japanese girls, each of them emulating Gretzky, who took his number because he couldn't wear 9, Gordie's number. When Gretzky entered the Hall of Fame in 1999, he said two things that stayed with me. One was: "I felt like a kid every single game I played." The other: "There's some kid out there who's learning the game and who one day will come out and break my records." The wheel moves, and does not spare even the best. Gretzky understood that there's a fecundity to hockey as there is to life. Stars must die in order for others to be born. Another thing that Gretzky said: "Every time I go out there, that's one less chance to play."

When we finished the interview, Arlene Lanes grabbed Mr. Hockey and pulled him to her son, a fat kid with a face like a ripe tomato, who'd been sitting with his teammates. The wheel spun a third time.

"Will you sign my son's jersey?" asked Arlene.

"Oh, sure," said Mr. Hockey, pulling a felt marker from his trouser pocket.

"Turn around," said Arlene to her son. He would not.

"*Turn around!*" she wailed.

He still would not.

"Don't you want an autograph?" asked Gordie.

The kid scowled.

"*Eh!*" shouted Arlene, cuffing him on the head.

"That's all right," said Gordie. "Would it help if I told him that I know Wayne Gretzky?"

"This man, Mr. Howe, is Gretzky's friend!" Arlene snarled.

The kid looked up.

"Yes," said Howe, gently. "Wayne says that I am his hero."

"Ya?" said the kid

"*Turn around!*" screamed Arlene.

"Oh yes, he does," replied Gordie.

The kid turned around.

"Great. We'll put 'er right there," said Mr. Hockey, bending forward and signing off.

7

THE EYES OF SAM WONG

It was my turn to skate.

The tournament moved into its second half, when men's teams made up of ex-pats and international women's clubs took to the ice. My team was called the Hong Kong Canadians. As most pro franchises these days are named after weather systems or animals (or, in the case of the Columbus Blue Jackets, bugs), our name had the ring of a club that might have competed in an amateur tournament one hundred years ago. It was the first time I would be representing my country abroad.

The Canadians' first official game was at the Glacier. I made my way to Kowloon Tong with my hockey bag slung on my back like a fin, which swung behind me as I parted the waves of pedestrians making their way through the city. I must have looked like a shark wandering through a school of fish; as soon as I created my wake, it was filled by bodies. People pushed and elbowed and ducked under the bag and nobody said a thing. When I got on the subway, it lay in front of me like a big sleeping dog. Considering the time it would later spend stuffed in the trunk of my car, my hockey bag never had it better.

I arrived early for the game. All my adult hockey life, I've liked to sit alone and settle my head before playing. I've never meditated, but I find that whenever I enter a rink I pass into a zone of calm and tranquility. When empty, there's a peace to hockey rinks that divorces one from the outside world. I dropped my hockey bag to the floor and laid my skates in front of me like a zen master readying his incense and *zabuton*. I placed a fresh T-shirt on top of my running shoes under the bench, and put my stick on a rack over my head, all of this in an attempt to fuse with the aura of the rink: the cold of the ice pressing on my face like a flat mountain rock, the echo of the crowds, the still-life of the beer cans and hockey tape and gum wrappers strewn about the room, the silence of the benches, the ice machine thrumming.

I settled on a bench in the dressing room and started to change. As a kid, it was hard learning how to fasten all of that equipment onto my body, but these days when I wear it, I feel giddy and free. I draw enormous pleasure, for instance, from strapping the garter belt around my glutinous midriff. It tickles me that a garment so feminine is so vital to the hockey player's ensemble. Some say that hockey is, by nature, a macho sport, but the wearing of dangly underthings helps to debunk that theory. Similarly, the idea of fitting a plastic protective cup around one's nether regions strikes me as not being very macho at all; were hockey truly a manly game, we would have done away with the cup years ago. But I'm glad that we didn't, because there's something oddly thrilling about competing against people who actually want to damage your tender parts. I also admire the boldness of a sport that allows your groin to expand in public without shame or fear of reprisal. And I know that there's not one male hockey player out there who hasn't rapped his knuckles over his perforated shell and secretly proclaimed, "Call me Plasto-Dick! King of Mankind!" while pretending to secure the disc in its sleeve.

Once the cup and garter are in place, the shin pads are fitted, then promptly covered up by striped stockings clipped high on your leg. At this stage of undress, one looks as much like Marlene Dietrich as Dmitri Khristich. I relish that at one time in hockey's history, some fop decided to ink circles around the legs of the uniform, giving even the most battle-ravaged hockey player the fanciful look of a butterfly collector. We've all known tough hockey players who are surprisingly mild-mannered off the ice (enforcer Stu Grimson comes to mind – a fighter who thumps goons at night and writes children's fables by day) and perhaps those whimsical stockings have something to do with this. There was once a backlash against hockey socks in the 1980s, which resulted in the creation of Cooperalls, long pants with shin guards sewn into them. They replaced the hockey sock for a winter or two, but a serious design flaw – they were bell-bottoms – limited their appeal, and since the '70s revival hadn't yet hit, they eventually went the way of coaches shouting "By Crimminy!"

Skates are the most traditional part of a hockey player's ensemble, and the most important. In his book *Soccer in Sun and Shadow*, Eduardo Galeano suggests that the soccer ball is feminine in the way players treat it, and while I wouldn't say the same about the asexual puck, I believe that we care for our skates the way we might pamper a loved one. Players are forever coddling their blades: rubbing them down with a stone, protecting them with cotton sleeves, wiping off snow, drying them with a towel, rewarding the tongue with new laces, replacing or tightening rivets, and, most tellingly, entrusting them to expert hands to make them sharp and true before important games. No other piece of equipment is as loved and laboured over. Even the way we hold our skates – our fingers curved around the blade and housing – is tender. Elbow pads and socks are merely flung into hockey bags, but the skate is carefully tucked in. Some bags even come with a special compartment for them. Skates are also the one piece of equipment that players brag to each other about. It's dressing room news whenever someone gets a new pair because an investment in blades suggests that the player is serious about the game. I've been to the Hall of Fame and seen hundreds of sticks. But skates are the only other piece of equipment kept under glass there.

The sweater principle is pretty important, too. I'm the kind of fellow who dresses in public according to what's not in the laundry basket, but picking out a jersey for a game is a matter for deliberation. I'm like Liberace in this regard: "Hmmm. Am I feeling royal blue or garnet today? Perhaps a subtle mauve? What about black or a continental yellow?" The colour of your pants or socks is inconsequential, but jerseys make the player. Those who wear light colours play differently from those who wear black. Draping black over your body requires a conscious decision, because against the backdrop of the ice you almost always look bigger in dark colours. It sends a message about your style of play. No one thinks, "Tonight, I'm gonna crack skulls!" and then gets dressed in lavender.

The sweater also allows the rec player to display support for a favourite team. Skates, gloves, and pants often look the same, but the jersey is a mode of self-expression. This may explain why musicians such as Tiny Tim, Mike Levine, Snoop Doggy Dogg, and Coolio started wearing hockey jerseys. It's become almost a cliché for touring musicians to don the colours of the local sports club in an attempt to curry favour with the audience. I know a fellow by the name of Lou Klein who, while working at a rock festival a few years ago, heard that Robert Smith, lead singer of the Cure, wanted a Toronto Maple Leafs jersey for his show. The idea of Smith in a hockey sweater is an absurd thought. This is a man who has inspired legions of teenagers to dye their hair black, tease it into a sort of mussed bird's nest, ring black circles around their eyes over a patina of white pancake makeup, dress in long overcoats, and apply great gobs of lipstick to their mouths. There was a better chance that Bob Marley was into hockey.

The concert was being held a few hours outside of Toronto. Lou drove through the midday summer heat to the nearest town – Barrie – but couldn't find a Leafs jersey anywhere. He drove east to Peterborough, where he had the same result. He called his superiors, but they told him, "Robert must have his jersey!"

Lou sped to Toronto. He finally found one. The highway back was jammed with people driving to the concert, so he sat in the stifling heat of his car getting angrier with Robert Smith by the second. He finally made his way back to the site, where he stormed through the artist's compound, burst into the Cure's dressing room and flung the jersey across the trailer at Smith, who was reclining on a couch.

"Here's your jersey," said Lou. "I hope you like it, even though I know you'll never fuckin' wear it again."

Lou slammed the door and was fired on the spot. But he'd made his point. Robert Smith wore the jersey for the rest of his North American tour.

The last vital piece of equipment is the helmet. Don Cherry has theorized that helmets and face guards are largely responsible for the nastiness of the NHL game – vicious high sticks and slashes and chin-high chops. I agree with the Plaid One in this regard. One of the plagues of modern hockey is the number of players who get conked out of the game because of concussions and other cranial injuries. You'd have thought that as soon as the league made head-gear mandatory, the number of injuries would decrease, but it hasn't been the case. From a rec leaguer's point of view, there have been times when I've found my stick waving in the air and myself think-ing: "No worries. Just a little bonk off the old plastic." Players in cages or visors are more likely to throw their bodies in front of shots or passes. They are feeling invulnerable behind all that plastic. Protective headgear has resulted in a kind of football style of hockey, which has created a whole new way of getting hurt. I don't wear a visor, but the times I've tried one on, it felt like I was wearing an aquarium on my head. Things look and sound different, and it makes for a more interior, self-absorbed approach to the game.

There's a stigma attached to players who wear visors and cages. They're inevitably chippier than maskless players. That's not to say that players who don't wear them aren't chippy. It's just that those whose mugs are enmeshed in steel are a little more inclined to whap you in the face than players with a bare visage. Cage-wearers can hit and not fear reprisal. Taking a punch on the cage is like getting a beach ball bounced off your face. I have no problem with skaters who wear face masks and play an honourable game, but negligent visor-wearers, like goatee guys, should be drummed from the game. Then there's the visor-wearing goatee guy. Don't get me started.

The helmet is sometimes a canvas, an art-thing. Players sticker them with team crests, numbers, band decals, bumper stickers, Dole fruit emblems, and the like. Some paint them, others scrape away the colours. Some wear bubble helmets to look like Jammy Jagr or Mike Foligno; Jofas to look like Gretz or Jari Kurri; SKIOs to ape Butch Goring; or the classic CCM to look like Doug Gilmour or Kirk Muller or Bryan Trottier. Shopping for a helmet is like looking for a bed – it's something that you know you'll be spending a lot of time in for years to come.

Once this hulking costume is assembled, you walk out of the changing area feeling fifty pounds heavier, five inches wider, and at least a half-foot taller. Taking that first step onto the ice makes you feel like an actor entering the stage from the wings. It is here that you become your hockey self. Your language changes. Your words become gnarled and peppered with invective. You shout more excitedly than you ever would in your office, home, or yoga class. You make every excuse to use the word *fuck* because the explosive sound of it gets you into the game. It doesn't take much to trigger the F word. One game, I was jockeying my parts, which weren't sitting right in my cup.

"*Fuck!*" I screamed, as if I'd been bitten by a monkey.

"You okay, man?" asked one of my teammates.

"Just my fuckin' balls."

"Squared?"

"No. They're not sitting right."

"Fuck, I hate that."

"Ya, fuck."

"Still fucked up?"

"Ah, that's fuckin' better," I said, my hands plunged into my pants.

"Fuckin' eh."

Brad Niblock, our captain, and Mark Sigson, our goaltender, were the first of the Hong Kong Canadians to show up at the rink. Mark arrived with his dad, Keith, who'd come over from Winnipeg to visit and help coach the team. Keith was a dead ringer for hockey writer Scott Young. The first thing I said to him was: "Hey, you look exactly like Scott Young!"

"Who?" he asked, turning his ear.

"Scott Young! Neil's dad."

"Neil who?"

"Neil Young."

"Who?"

I took this as an early sign that our team was in trouble. The rest of the players soon followed, among them Yanic Canteini, a French-Canadian gadabout who worked for Mercedes-Benz. Yanic gave my international hockey experience a pan-Canadian feel – not only was this the first time I'd be taking to the ice in Asia against players from different parts of the globe, it was also the first time I'd be playing on the same team as a French Canadian.

Once suited up, I stepped out on the ice and saw that there were a few hundred people scattered among the stands. Here was another first: strangers watching me play hockey. The surface of the Glacier was hard and fast even though it lay in the subtropics. My skates nipped the ice, spraying shavings when I stopped, and it felt good to shake the last bit of jet lag from my legs. We lobbed shots at Mark and got a feel for the rink, and when the referee blew his whistle and dropped the puck to start the game, I was thrilled to be finally playing hockey, and determined to make an impression on my teammates.

But the game demanded more skating than I'd bargained for. After a few shifts, my legs and lungs felt the burden of having spent the better part of the week navigating a smoggy city on foot. While huffing on the bench, I asked myself why I hadn't chosen to document the evolution of lawn bowling around the world. But even if I'd been in peak form, our opponents on Team World skated better and were more skilled than any of us. Team World combined Dutch, German, Japanese, French, and British players – an unlikely mix which I'd assumed would work in our favour – and we lost by six goals. They were captained by a handsome young Dutchman named Nils Bakker, who wore neither a cage nor a visor, not because he was a fan of old-time hockey, but because he considered himself something of a playboy on skates. He looked like Spider Savage. He had long blond hair and skated dashingly, the prototypical European player. He scored twice and strode off the rink into the arms of a rapier-thin girl dressed in a chic black sweater and boots. She was beautiful. The Dutchman had groupies, too. Young women lined the rink and called out to him. Our cheering section, by contrast, consisted of Janet in jeans and backpack, and a Rheostatics nerd named Jason and his girl-friend, whom we'd met in a market in Causeway Bay. Not a glint of vogue on the three of them, god bless their hearts.

Team World's best player was a British defenceman who beat Mark for three goals. There's something I find troubling about hearing a British accent in the rink. It suits a soccer or cricket pitch fine, but in a rink, it bends my ear most unpleasantly. The vintage hockey accent, with all those gnarled *errrs* and *tthhbss*, has made me suspicious of someone who can't shout, "*Hey, ref, yer a friggin' hosebag!*" and sound like they mean it. A British accent makes hockey players sound just a little too smart. Were he a Cockney or a Scot, I might not have minded, but the fellow sounded like Jeremy friggin' Irons. So as his team laid their beating on us, I skated over to him and jibed: "Hey, bud, ya friggin' hosebag."

"Fak off," he replied. Then he flew past me and scored another goal.

After the buzzer sounded, our coach, Keith, looked hurt. During the game he'd changed lines, run a fifth defenceman through the roster, and opened and closed the bench door. He'd kept things pos-itive, too. Whenever a line came off that hadn't been scored on, Keith shouted: "We're playing our game!" Whenever one of our defencemen iced the puck, Keith yelled out to him: "We're playing our game!" And afterwards, when we gathered together in the dress-ing room and peeled off our wet gear, Keith sat down and decided, "Well, boys, we just didn't play our game." Yanic stood up and said, "We do better next time, right?" I didn't know whether he was issuing a consoling thought or a threat, but when he said it, two other players – Dirk and Pat – looked pissed off and I took this as a good sign. Don, for his part, said dryly, "Maybe it had something to do with our pre-game chant." He was right. *"Let's have fun!"* just didn't have the stuff to inspire us to play beyond our means.

Our next game was the following morning at SkyRink, but I never made it (we lost 2–1 to an ex-pat team from Singapore, who scored in the last minute). After the Team World game, Janet and I had wandered through Wan Chai and had each bought a fruit shake. Mine was watermelon. It tasted great, but within minutes, my heart and stomach were being squeezed. On the bus ride home to Repulse Bay, I felt as if cement had been poured down my guts. I gulped Pepto-Bismol and tried to fart or burp or do whatever it took to relieve the pressure, but all I could produce after long bouts were pathetic tweeps, the kind of sounds that would get you thrown out of a flatulence club. So when the alarm sounded for me to drag myself down to SkyRink to play Singapore, I could not. I spent the morning forcing bubbling liquids down my hatch until the tweeps sounded a little more like gasps of air being expelled from a balloon. I was determined to not spend my day sweating on the toilet. And really, it wouldn't have made for a very good book.

I managed to get myself up and out of the house for the afternoon game, even though I nearly yorked on the ride to SkyRink. The bus roared down Repulse Bay Road shaking like a white-water raft, but lucky for me, not even the lurching of the double-decker could shake the molten rock that had hardened inside my body.

The first thing I did when I took to the ice at SkyRink was look for the roller coaster. My eyes followed the track all the way around to the bay where, to my relief, two men wearing work-belts and yellow overalls were pinging its front wheel repeatedly with a small hammer. The pinging was loud and bright, and after a while, the workmen gave up. I lifted my stick into the air and touched the track. The dragon slept on. I played without fear of death from above.

SkyRink looked even smaller once I was on it. It only took three strides from behind the net to get to centre ice. You could stand at

one end of the rink, shoot the puck down the ice, and watch it ric-
ochet to your skates. It was like a being trapped in a game of
Rebound. Once the ice filled up with players, you couldn't take a
couple of strides without being knocked into another skater. After
a few shifts, I thought I could tell where the skaters were going
to be, but it was still impossible to tell what the puck was going to
do. Patches of concrete showed through where the boards met the
ice and a padded billboard that read Budweiser South China Ice
Hockey League was strung up below the railing. Upon hitting the
billboard, the puck bounced like a murder ball in whatever direction it pleased, and when it made contact with the boards – which
weren't really boards at all, but squares of Plexiglas – it made the
unpleasant sound of a jackboot kicking a door, before spinning
madly up the ice.

It made no sense but, despite being sick, I played well in our 12–1
drubbing of the South East Asian Express (then again, if I hadn't
played well in beating the other team by eleven goals, I shouldn't
have been playing at all). Before the match, Mark suggested that we
chant "*Beer!*" to bring our team luck. So we gathered in a little scrum
around our goalie, put our hands in a bundle, and shouted in a
parody of Canadian hosers set loose in Hong Kong. Feeling that he
had not raised the stakes high enough, Mark promised a beer for
anyone who scored a goal. His idea worked and the fellows ran up
the score. After the game, Keith produced a bag of beers and the
team destroyed them. "We played our game, fellows! Our game!"
he trumpeted in the change area.

I felt bad for the Express. It was awful to watch some of their
younger players skate in defeat towards their families, who were
leaning against the mesh with their cameras cocked. But in international hockey, big losses have to be put into perspective. I don't
know if it would have made the Express feel any better, but during
the 1998 D-Pool World Championships in Perth, Australia, the
New Zealand team was beaten 58–0 by the home team. And 58–0
seems like a sister-kisser next to the 92–0 score – the most lopsided
hockey total on record – that the diabolical South Koreans pasted

on Thailand that year at the D-Pool World Junior Championships.

But scoring a few goals made my teammates feel a little better going into our game that evening against Bud Gold at the Glacier. Bud Gold (which sounded more like the name of an NFL coach than a hockey team) were made up of CBCs – Canadian-born Chinese. They wore yellow jerseys blazed with the red Budweiser logo. I'd seen them play earlier: they were fast and tough, and I knew it would be a good game.

Because there was only an hour between games, there was no point changing into my street clothes. So I left my hockey gear on and strolled through the Kowloon market to catch a taxi to Festival Walk. At this time of night, Cheung Sha Wan Road was swirling with colour. Neon signs hung over the street from an electric latticework, illuminating the market in a jubilee of light. I took in the streetscape holding my hockey stick like a staff, but most of the Chinese were merely nonplussed. A few vendors laughed at me, but I might as well have been wearing a funny hat for their muted reaction. I even stickhandled a melon rind between stalls: nothing. It wasn't until I visited the mainland that I realized that it takes a lot more than a hoser with a Koho to stand out in China.

When we showed up at the Glacier, Gordie Howe was on the ice, swarmed by two hundred kids. Gordie towered over them like a white pine. Ben was there with Herb, Joanne, and Aislin. It was like hockey Christmas and Gordie was Santa. The stands were jammed with people watching the silver-haired legend show their sons and daughters how to take a shot. Gordie would pull some kid out of the crowd and stand them three feet away from the boards with the puck. He'd shoot against the wall a few times and then the kid would try. Gordie would wait patiently until the puck was lifted off the ice, then he'd put his hands over the kid's grip, and show her where to place her weight. Gordie had a gentle way, and someday that girl or boy would grow up and say: "When I lived in China, I was taught how to take a wrist shot by Mr. Hockey." It was a fine thing for the Howes to do, and watching Gordie move around out there eased my nerves before the big game.

Gordie Howe in Hong Kong

Keith arrived at the Glacier wearing a checkered blazer, which he'd been saving for an important game. "Your lucky jacket?" I asked, tugging the fabric on his arm.

"We'll see," he said, chewing a fingernail.

Keith wanted to move me up to forward. His plan made sense. Against Bud Gold, we needed more speed up front, and though I'm not a fast skater, we had too many defensive types on offence. Keith's idea was to spread the talent around, and it was fine with me. I believe that every defenceman harbours a secret desire to be a forward, anyway. Backliners are saddled with the thankless task of having to clear the front of the net, chase loose pucks around the boards, get bodychecked in the corners, take shots off the toe, knee, foot and ankle, suffer checking wingers, and cover up for the forward's defensive lapses. Wingers and centremen just float around and collect the glory. In many ways, defencemen are like bass players – they stand at the back of the play, creating the rhythm and the tempo of the game so that those leading the attack can sing the songs, score the goals, have solo careers, get endorsement deals, do between-period interviews, date beautiful women, crash expensive cars, and suffer the occasional beating at the hands of a jealous bass player.

Mark led us onto the ice. He kneeled in his crease and stretched. It hurt to watch him. He leaned back until the top of his helmet was touching his skates, a genuflection in reverse. He held this contortion for a few seconds, then slipped from the butterfly and stretched his body across one leg and then the other, before springing to his feet and spinning his arms around at his side. He called out to us to shoot at him from the blue line, instructing us to move in a few feet each time. One by one we wound up and threw everything we had at our goalie. After a flurry of shots, he waved us away. I went for one last skate around the rink and smiled at Janet in the stands. The wind licked my face and my legs felt loose, my body relaxed. Then Mark spanked his stick on the ice, the signal for us to gather around him in the crease.

"*Beer!*"

I skated to the bench.

"Just play our game!" shouted Keith nervously.

The game started with a flurry. The Bud Gold players were smaller than us, but they had faster forwards. Their defence, however, was porous, and I thought it was a weakness we could exploit. Off the whistle, Dirk stormed the net and ran over the Bud Gold goalie. It was a nasty thing to do, and I felt bad because I knew that goalie. A few days earlier, I'd seen him sitting in the stands at SkyRink wearing a Toronto Maple Leafs jersey, so I'd approached him and said, "Do you like the Toronto Maple Leafs?" expecting a response in Cantonese. But Sam Wong was from Mississauga, Ontario. He'd moved to Hong Kong after graduating from university. During the warm-up, I tapped him on the pads and wished him luck, but like most goalies trying to cool their heads before the big game, he looked up at me and said nothing.

We changed lines and I skated out with Yanic. I played the left side. We kept the puck in the Bud zone for long stretches, ringing it around to the point then skating in front of the net, hoping for a rebound or a deflection. The corners at the Glacier were wide and square, so you had a bit more time to collect the puck and figure out what to do with it. Bud Gold's strategy was to freeze the disc whenever they got the chance, but this backfired when Yanic won a draw and sent it to Mark Irwin, our best defencemen, who fired it from the point. The shot missed, but the puck came spinning out to the slot, where I slashed at it like a golfer hacking at a ball in the rough. The puck skidded to a Bud Gold defencemen, who tried to tamp it with his stick. Yanic skated towards the puck and so did the rest of the Bud Gold team. The next thing I knew, Sam Wong was looking into his net where, to borrow a phrase from poet John B. Lee, the puck was moving around in the mesh like a hard black fish darting of its own accord.

I couldn't tell who had scored the goal and neither could the score-keeper. But it didn't matter. We were mobbed by our teammates. It felt great: our bodies scrumming together like a single moving organism. Tom Barnes, for his part, thumbed the CD player as if he had a nervous tic. Though I'd had to suffer through bits of the Offspring for the better part of two weeks, it was great to skate off the ice and see Keith waving his fist in the air while Geddy Lee sang "The Spirit of Radio":

"Invisible airwaves crackle with life!"

A Toronto song for a Toronto goal. I was thrilled that Rush had followed me to the Glacier. It made me feel like I was skating on my neighbourhood rink.

Yanic punched me in the shoulder: "Ya, man, ya!"

"Way to work, man," I said.

"Our game! Our game!" howled Keith.

"Okay. We go to the net, okay?" said Yanic, panting breathlessly. "We go there again. We mess them up that way and we get in there fast. I go fast and you hang back and I look," he said, pointing to his eyes. "I look and you go, okay?"

"Okay!"

"OUR GAME!"

We laid back after going up 1–0. It's a habit of all truant teams to coast on a lead. As a result, we paid the inevitable price. Brad took a penalty for dumping one of their players in front of the net and Bud Gold scored while I was killing the penalty. Both Yanic and I had a great shift, moving around the ice like waterbugs, dashing from point to point and swiping at the puck. We even managed to get a shot on goal. But just as the penalty was coming to an end, I lost one of their wingers along the boards. He cut in past me and made a clever move off the wing. Mark dived and poke-checked the puck away, but it ended up on the stick of a Bud Gold forward, who wristed it high into Mark's chest. The puck ricocheted off him and bounced in the slot, where a player I should have been checking flipped it into the empty net. It lay there like a frozen turd. The crowd whooped. The stands were jammed with friends and relatives of Bud Gold who'd spent the day in the mall then come to the game at night. The Bud Gold players swarmed the scorer and he shook his fist at the crowd. Joy blossomed throughout the stands. I wasn't unhappy for him.

Before the game, I'd wondered whether a partisan crowd would get the better of us, but I think there's something about large crowds who wish you ill that gives your angst a focus. It's the same in music as in athletics. Hostile crowds are usually moronic and reflect poorly on the team you're playing. Perhaps I would have been worried had the Bud fans burned effigies of Keith in the stands, but the last thing I felt was intimidated. A crowd who loves you and demands that you perform well: now that's intimidating.

The first half ended tied 1–1 and we got a two-minute rest. Keith gave us a pep talk, which more or less involved him pacing up and down the bench punching his fist into his hand and repeating you-know-what. Mark Sigson said, "We're all over these guys. Keep it up and we'll be fine." It was nice hearing that from our goalie. When a goalie is relaxed enough to sound encouraging, you know you're all right. Most of the time they just pour water over their heads and try not to vomit.

In the second period, both teams found their rhythm. The hockey was free and confident. We punched and counterpunched like two fighters in mid-round. If you were watching from above, you might have sensed a lull in the play, but at ice-level, it was a rush. My brain and feet were racing. Neither team gave the puck away and both tried to create measured chances rather than foolish dashes deep into the zone. The hockey was less creative, but it was harder to play.

Five minutes into the period, Yanic took the puck from one of our defencemen and skated out of the zone. I followed on my off-wing. We moved up the ice on a two-on-two against the Bud Gold defence. Yanic put his head down and skated hard. He looked up briefly, and with a flick of the wrists, sent the puck across to me. I had little time to consider the possibilities while the puck was on its way. I'm sure that the best players have already planned their next four moves during that time, but the best I could do was think, "Oh, fuck." The puck was wobbling on its end like a runaway tire, but I corralled it neatly on my backhand. If I'd accepted the pass on the forehand, I might have cut to the middle, but instead I went outside. Being a defenceman, I knew that it was harder to defend outside speed than inside, although I won't deceive you: I came to that realization well after this play. But when you're in the body of the moment, your reactions are instinctive, and much of the beauty of a move lies in the fact that it is impulsive. It's not as if some coach had diagrammed the play on the chalkboard; heck, Keith didn't even own a piece of chalk. Instead, the play came from a place within myself, where physical harmony met my imagination. As I skated around the defenceman, he huffed, did a half-turn and swiped at my feet. He missed. I broke free and moved in on Sam Wong.

Eric Nesterenko once told Studs Terkel, "I haven't kept many pictures of myself, but I found one where I'm in full flight. I'm leaning into a turn. You pick up the centrifugal force and you lay in it. For a few seconds, like a gyroscope, it supports you. I'm in full flight and my head is turned. I'm concentrating on something and I'm grinning. That's the way I like to picture myself . . . I'm on another level of existence, just being in pure motion."

As I bore in on the goalie, I felt caught in the ripple of something strong and alive. It was one of the great revelatory moments that sports promises; the jewel every athlete looks for but rarely finds, rather, it finds you.

I'll always remember this play as if seeing it from a distance. It's no wonder; my mind seemed to levitate above my body, as if it were a boat riding the crest of a wave. To the person in the stands, the high pitch of the game, the din of voices rising to meet the climax of the moment, may have dominated the scene, but on the ice I felt like an action-film hero who hears only the sound of blood pounding in his ears. Solitude. A *chi* of energy and light. I was alone before the goaltender, a four-inch hole peeking through his battered armour as if it were an eye winking at me. I had skated into a place so calm that I'd lost myself, propelled by physical music. I looked into Sam Wong's eyes.

I shot.

A goal in Hong Kong.

The team collapsed upon me. They shouted into my face and slugged my chest and helmet and shook my body. It felt great. When I got to the bench, Keith came over and whacked me in the shoulder, his blazer swinging open.

"No one told me we had a ringer!" he said, his face as bright as a pumpkin.

"Ringer! Ringer!" shouted Yanic. The others joined in.

I shouted back at them.

"We're playing our game!"

8

THE FOXES OF PEA PACK

Two days later, we left Hong Kong for Beijing. The game against Bud Gold had been our finest hour – a 3–1 victory – but the next day we lost by three goals to Distacom. They were just too motivated for us. There were a few teams in the tourney who were determined to win. The Nortel entry had conducted an exhaustive player search throughout their offices in Canada to find the best available athletes, many of whom had flown in for the event. Their games against some of the lesser clubs had all the competition of a man clubbing a hamster with a baseball bat. Once the international teams left the scene, the HK Fives devolved into a typical North American hockey event with ill-tempered coaches and unruly players with goatees. It became more about winning than playing. It wasn't the kind of hockey that I'd flown half-way around the world to play or write about. We left before the final game, won by Tom Barnes and the Bud Americans.

Booking our tickets on the train had not been easy. Somewhere in my past, I must have been taken with the idea of riding a train in elegance across the Orient. It probably came after watching some mystery movie starring Peter Ustinov. I imagined myself sitting, legs crossed on a leather bench, smoking a Sweet Cap through a long silver filter, a book open on my lap, staring out a lightly misted window at the Szechuan landscape. Possibly I'd be wearing a monocle, very possibly I'd be in the company of a beautiful woman who had descended from deposed Russian royalty, her sloped face and smooth legs angled in shadows.

I didn't reveal this fantasy to my wife. I merely demanded sulkingly that we get a soft sleeper. Janet was appalled. "How do you expect to meet people if you just stay in your compartment for the entire trip? You know, when I was in India, Taz and I . . ."

Taz was Janet's friend with whom she'd travelled in India. She was starting to appear in Janet's stories as the ultimate symbol of high adventure. Whenever Janet wanted to shame me into feeling that I wasn't allowing myself to experience fully the world in which I was travelling, she described something she'd done with Taz. I started to resent the woman. I was also starting to resent Paul Theroux. Janet and I were both reading *Riding the Iron Rooster*, his account of crossing China by train, and Janet, defending the idea of travelling second or third class, argued, "Theroux travelled like that, and look at all the great stories that he collected, all the people he met . . ."

"So you say my book is gonna be no good unless . . ."

"No. I'm not saying that."

"Well, I want a soft sleeper."

"I'm just saying . . ."

"A soft sleeper."

"Fine. But when Taz and I . . ."

And so it went. But I won, and as the train trundled towards mainland China, I was in my movie. The compartment had turquoise drapes and antimacassars and, on the table, a vase with a single plastic rose. But outside the window, there was only the grey Chinese cityscape. Guangzhou appeared as a wall of belching factories, the buildings smeared with a heavy black dust as if someone had emptied an ashtray over the town. Plastic bags littered the railway tracks as we rode beside slumping city walls where, every now and then, a face would peer through the checkerboard holes left in the brick, eyes locked on the train moving people to any-where but here. As the city slumped to an end, the dusty outskirts of town gave way to low, sponge-toffee cliffs. The setting now looked prehistoric. There were caves at the bottom of the cliffs, where doors had been jammed into the rock. I half expected to see a shaggy-vested hunter astride a mastodon out of the corner of my eye. We were passing across thousands of years. Just two hours out of town, all the glitter and sparkle of Hong Kong had given way to a country of stone and dust and the scrabblings of life, as neglected as the crumbs of an eraser that has rubbed out centuries of progress.

I spiked my elbows on the linen tablecloth and opened my note-book. Traditional Chinese music played over a speaker above the window, and every now and then a voice would say something in Mandarin, causing Janet to riffle through her phrase book. The sleeper was relatively new – the car had been added only a few years earlier – but the ride was of another age: the purr of metal, the frosty glint of the window, the fading turquoise of the blankets, the black ink of the *China Daily News*. I half expected the door to open, reveal-ing Claude Rains in a white tunic.

We pulled into Beijing just after nightfall to the tune of "Auld Lang Syne" squeaking over the speakers. I pulled the hockey bag down from the luggage rack and hauled it across my shoulders, then planted my feet and tromped through the dark train station in search of a taxi. Janet had learned a word to help us get to where we wanted to go: *fang ya'an*, hotel. We showed our driver the guidebook, which had the name of the hotel printed in Chinese characters. There was a Plexiglas barrier between him and us, which struck me as odd given how little crime there was in Beijing. So we had to speak through a tiny hole and at great volume when we conversed. The driver addressed us in Chinese and we responded with cries of "*Fang ya'an! Fang ya'an!*" To his credit, he never gave us the "these tourists are fuckin' nuts" stare. He only jabbered on in Chinese and expected us to understand.

It was dark and cold and the streets were lit with tree lights, lanterns, and other decorations left over from the Chinese New Year. The driver navigated down tiny alleys looking for our hotel. He stopped in front of one place with two large red doors, the kind you might find at the front of a stable. He pointed at them and said, "*Fang ya'an! Fang ya'an!*" I looked at Janet and told her, "Wait here." Then I realized that, were I in a Ustinov murder mystery, she almost certainly would have been abducted and held for a ransom of emeralds and sapphires.

I opened the gates and stepped into an old courtyard. The hotel office was to the left. Inside were a man and a woman – the woman in a red wool sweater, the man in a black suit – with the heat cranked to the high thirties.

"*Fang ya'an?*"

They spoke to me in Chinese.

I produced the guide book and the fellow waved his hand in front of his face. He grabbed me by the arm and brought me to the door. He pointed out the window down the street and made curving motions with his fingers.

"*Fang ya'an,*" he finished.

We had the wrong hotel.

I thanked him, but before I left, the woman said "Ah!" and came across the room with her card. I asked, "How much? Dollars?" but before she could answer, the man grunted and pulled me out the door. It was not good business practice, but it was courteous.

We found the right *fang ya'an* farther on. We gave our passports to two mean-looking women at the front desk who showed us to our room: a dark chamber that smelled of old cabbage. It was hot and dry and there were huge divots in the walls. It was listed as mid-range accommodation in the guide book.

That night, I worked the phones. After spending an hour figuring out how to dial the operator, I was finally able to get hold of Ray Plummer, a six-foot-five, three-hundred-pound Canadian who helps run the ex-pat Beijing team that trains regularly at the Capital Arena. I tracked down Plummer in a bar, where he was drinking with a team of Russian hockey players. I asked if I could come and meet him. He made me write down his itinerary for the evening, an elaborate plan involving five different bars. There was a rugby game on television, so Plummer had to work it so that he not only hit the

British pub for the satellite feed of the game, but entertained his hard-drinking Russian friends as well.

I told Plummer I'd see him on one of his stops and briefed Janet.

"Sounds like fun," she said, raising her eyebrows.

"Let's just lie down for a second and we'll see."

We hit the lights and were out cold.

I awoke at seven a.m.

Our plans for our time in Beijing were sketchy. My friend Steven Chiu, whom I hadn't been in touch with for years, had spotted my name on a "Hockey in Asia" Internet mailing list. He told me that a woman named Helen Schley, with whom he played rec hockey, knew a team from America that would be in China at the same time as us. He said that they were travelling around the country playing hockey.

Helen got word to Steve that the team was leaving for Harbin in northern China the next morning, and were to play three games against the local senior and junior clubs. I was thrilled with the possibility of finding kindred spirits on my nomadic road. The next day, I called Ray Plummer to get hold of Helen. He was in the middle of a party with the Americans. I told him about my eagerness to go north, and he passed the phone to Reeve Schley III, the American team's captain and Helen's father.

"Where do ya play?" he asked me over the phone.

"Toronto," I said.

"No. No. Where on the ice?"

"Left wing. Or defence," I told him.

"All right. You can come."

"Great."

"Ya. Well, we need a winger. It'll give us three lines and four defencemen. We're leaving tomorrow. Can you make it?"

"I'll meet you at the airport," I said.

"How will I recognize you?"

"I'll have my hockey stick."

"Ya. Of course."

"And you?"

"Sticks. Sticks and bags and old people."

There were twenty, maybe thirty of them. Old, yes. Their spouses in tow, they straggled through the airport with their hockey bags and sticks and luggage stacked on airline push carts. Before they arrived, I approached every Westerner I saw at the airport and asked them a question that must have sounded to them like some strange sort of espionage code: "Do you know Reeve Schley?"

"Weave shway?"

"Real who?"

"Please what?"

But no one else could have passed for Reeve. He was a large man in a down jacket and a Tilley hat. He had thick glasses and appeared to be shepherding his charges with all the focus and intensity of a stoned llama. Every now and then, Reeve would turn around, scratch his head and call out loud: "Where the heck's Elizabeth?" When I introduced myself, he looked down at me from under his glasses, said, "Ya, well, hello," and then hollered, "Where's Dick? I mean, Christ, anybody seen Dick?"

Reeve was the consummate American. He was very friendly, as well as loud and broad-mannered. Put Americans in any country and they'll not hesitate to wander around hollering at the top of their voices; it's the best and worst thing about them. The Foxes were a movable mass of big jackets and toques, and had they not flashed Eastons and Titans, I might have mistaken them for a hunting party. Next to the Chinese, they looked enormous, their faces pink and blotched, patches of white hair mottled on their chins. All eyes were on them as they checked their bags.

Janet and I were booked on an earlier flight, so I told Reeve that we'd see him on the other end. "*Wang lu*," he said to me as we parted ways.

"No, *wang lu*," I offered, perplexed.

Then he scratched his head and shouted some more.

Our flight on Northern Swan Airlines carried us over a vast white plain, a desert of ice that stretched forever. When we landed on the tarmac, the cold air stung my face – it felt good – and when I sucked in the cold, it frosted my chest. I could see my breath against the icy blue sky.

Hockey weather.

There are certain things you notice about people that you rarely mention aloud for fear of generalizing them, but I have no choice but to write that, when we landed in Harbin, it seemed everyone had an enormous head. Giant apple crates. Zenith television sets. People there were built solid waist to neck, like they'd been raised on grain and milk. Having spent two weeks among the small-featured Cantonese of the south, I was amazed at how different the northerners looked. I immediately thought to myself that these heads were ideal for hockey. These people could take a few bonks on the ice and still get up for more.

The airport gift shop displayed stuffed deer heads and fur pelts: more northern collectibles than you'd find at a way station on the Prairies. We were set upon by a few local cabbies – I expected them to offer to drive us into town for an inflated tourist rate, but instead, they wanted to try out my stick. I pulled a puck out of my hockey bag and we patted it around, right there in the airport. There were already more people taken by the sight of my hockey gear than had shown any interest in Hong Kong. This boded well.

"*Wo da bing xi,*" I said to them.

"*Ah, bing xi!*" they responded

"*Bing xi* is . . . great!" I said.

"*Bing xi!* Okay!"

I was thrilled to be having a conversation about hockey with a bunch of cab drivers in Northern China. Granted, it loses a little in the translation:

"I play ice hockey."

"Ah, ice hockey!"

"Ice hockey is . . . great!"

"Ice hockey! Okay!"

During our scrum, we were approached by a fellow who spoke broken English. He held out his arms, smiled and made whippy wrist shots with an invisible stick. His name, as printed on the business card he thrust at me, was Jickey Jar. He was a skinny man with wispy hair who reminded me of Bob Denver. He laughed and said, "Like this? Yes?" poking at the imaginary puck, and I said, "Yes!" and told him that I was here to play hockey.

"Oh, hockey. You must be very strong!"

"Oh, no," I said.

"Oh, yes," he said, touching my arm.

"Well, I guess I'm pretty strong."

Janet looked at me.

"Well, you know, not like the pros," I corrected.

But Jickey would have none of it. He said, "You must be very important to be here playing hockey. Listen, you can write me if you want, any time! Or perhaps you can e-mail me! You have e-mail?"

I told him that I did.

"These were printed for me! My address is here," he said, pointing to the card. But whoever had chosen Jickey's e-mail account had played a terrible joke. Jickey's address was @pubic.hr.com. I don't think he ever knew.

Jickey spoke excitedly about his job – he was the local rep for Carlsberg beer – and relished the opportunity to speak English. Little did we know that he would be one of the last Chinese we'd be able to do this with in Harbin. He excused himself when the people he was meeting walked through the double doors. They were followed soon after by Reeve and his group: twenty large Americans, striding like big ugly geese through the airport.

Reeve's team, I learned, were called the Essex Hunt Club Foxes. They hailed from Pea Pack, New Jersey, a name that sounded borrowed from a Sherwood Anderson novel. Reeve was the eldest Fox. He was sixty-seven, but Dick Whiting, Dick Sanford, Jim Cummins, and Frank Nelson were closing fast. It took me a while to figure out their names because the elder Foxes shared a look and style. They all had snowy hair, were rumpled and well-spoken. Three of them had Roman numerals after their names. They'd come together through their fathers' fraternity, which had competed in a league at St. Paul's College, the birthplace of hockey in the USA and the school that American sporting hero Hobey Baker had attended. The Foxes' younger set – Elizabeth, Mike, Dave, and Reeve Junior – were all in their mid-twenties and represented the next generation of globe-trotting hockey aristocrats.

Wang Lu turned out to be our guide, not a mysterious incantation, and she herded us onto the tour bus. She sat next to the driver and talked into a wireless microphone that honked terrible, Townshendian feedback every hundred words or so. Lu was young and beatific. Her face was as bright as the moon. Even though her head was not terribly big, I still liked her.

One of the first things Wang Lu told us over the crackling speakers was that Harbin's sister city was Edmonton, Alberta. It came as no surprise, since the road to Harbin had all the charm and pizzazz of a stretch of Albertan highway: furrows dusted with snow, rows of conifers, the cold sun sinking in the white sky. But it warmed my heart to think that a region so far from home was linked to Canada. When Paul Theroux called Harbin a "Chinese hinterland," he must have been thinking of its wild emptiness: acres of frozen dirt dotted with the odd abandoned tractor, a bouquet of birds tossed into the sky, the dipping sun turning the land into the meringue atop a lemon pie. When Wang Lu told us that Harbin ranked number one in China among exporters of wheat, I thought that it looked exactly like such a place: hard, unyielding terrain worked by leather-skinned farm hands whose faces were sculpted by the wind. Harbin was the perfect place for a Tim Horton's.

I drifted in and out of Wang Lu's speech, perking up at the sentence: "It is a place where you can find many beautiful girls in high-heeled boots." Jim Cummins rubbed his hands together. Wang Lu asked if there were any questions.

"Where are the girls?" shouted Jim, a fifty-year-old antiquarian bookseller from New York.

"That is not . . . on the program," said Wang Lu, rather embarrassed.

"Why not?!?"

"Because you must play hockey!" replied Wang Lu.

"How do you say 'Where's the bathroom?'" asked Reeve.

"What about 'Leave me alone?'"

"'I don't have any!'"

"'How much is the soup?'"

"'Where is the hotel?'"

"'Don't bother me!'"

I asked Lu how to call for a pass in Chinese. I figured this would come in handy for our game later that night, but the Foxes weren't interested.

"Never mind that," said Cummins. "How about 'Where's the beer?'"

We pulled up at the Hotel Singapore. Wang Lu and the rest of the Harbinians were quite proud of this building. It was an enormous grey structure built on the fringes of the city, and Wang Lu told us many times that it was a certified five-star hotel, Harbin's first. Janet and I were as impressed as anyone. There was a grand piano off the lobby where a young man in tails was playing the theme from *Doctor Zhivago*. He was accompanied by a long-armed violinist in a black evening dress who strolled through the adjoining bar while she played. Behind the piano was a long staircase that wound towards the dining room above the lobby. A team of sharp-suited girls who were waiting to check us in stood around a semicircle of marble, which served as the hotel's front desk. Arriving at the Hotel Singapore was a little like finding the Helmsley Central Park in the middle of Baie-Comeau. It was a palace of opulence, a glittering beacon on the gaping plain.

Janet and I knew at first glance that we could not afford to stay at the Hotel Singapore. We admitted this to Wang Lu, who took the concierge aside and tried to square us a deal. It worked. We got the Foxes' group rate and then some. After we were sorted out, Lu gathered the team around and instructed us, "Now, at five-thirty, you will meet here for the bus, which will take you to the rink for your game against the old-boys team. You will play for one-and-a-half hours and then you will go to dinner. If you do not want to go to dinner, we will bring you back to the hotel and you will eat here. Some of you would like to rest. Okay?"

And with that, we inherited a team. We took the elevator to our room, starfished on the king-sized bed and turned on the television. The screen blinked and there was Dominik Hasek flat on his back in the crease. Then he was gone. A graphic flashed: New Jersey 1, Buffalo 1. A female sportscaster spoke and I listened closely for "*bing xi*" but her voice was a crazy stream of words and phrases.

"Shit," I said.

"What?"

"Just missed the hockey highlights."

"There'll be more," said Janet.

"*Wo da bing xi*," I whispered to the television, hoping that Hasek would come back.

But he never did.

9

BOBBY CLARKE'S TEETH

Before coming to China, I researched Asian sport at the Toronto Reference Library, where I pored over many volumes before finding any reference to hockey. Most of my reading was usurped by scholarly tracts about Mao's obsession with calisthenics, which had spread throughout the land. Apparently, once word got around of the big guy's exercising habits, thousands of citizens took to parks and fields as if suddenly possessed by the ghost of Ed Ames. In photographs, they appeared altogether too happy to be doing this, which leads me to believe that despite China's cultural independence and astonishingly long history, their love of stretching is what truly separates them from us.

The Chinese sport scholars wrote endlessly about the Asian infatuation with health through exercise, and in *Sport in China*, professor W. H. Freeman said that traditional Chinese sport was characterized by four features: health improvement as their common purpose; movements mimicking those of living things; embodying the philosophical concepts of research value; reflecting society.

Since there was nothing in there like "clubbing one's opponent on the head while standing on ice holding a wooden cudgel," I gave up hope that I would ever find out anything about Chinese hockey. But then, on page 103, Freeman wrote that "other national sports traditional in the culture of China have continued to this day. They include boyikuo, a game resembling modern hockey, which is popular among the Daur People of northeastern China."

The Daur People. They sounded like a goth band from the 1980s, or maybe the name of a low-budget horror film. *The Coming of the Daurs. The Attack of the Daur People. The Night of the Living Daurs.* But the Daur, it turned out, were an ethnic minority who once lived along the Nenjiang River in the coldest part of northern China. It was here that they invented boyikuo, which they've been playing since 600 AD. Freeman revealed nothing about the nature of this game, only that it was played outdoors on ice. However, he did go on the describe how, once the Daur were assimilated into the northern town of Harbin, they excelled at hockey. It was no accident that ninety per cent of the Chinese women's national team players came from here. They were the fourth-ranked team in the world and had produced the world's best female goaltender, Hong Guo.

The Daur originally settled near a neighbouring ethnic minority – the Hezhen – known to the Chinese as "the fish tribe" for their penchant for making clothes out of fish skin. The fish were gutted, then dried and tanned, at which point the skins were sewn together to make light, waterproof outdoor wear. The Hezhens made fish-skin pants, hats, shoes, and jackets, so it only stood to reason that fish-skin jocks, gloves, and goalie pads were within their creative realm. I imagined the Hezhens and the Daurs as the Oilers and Flames chasing a frozen bearpaw downriver, wearing fish-skin helmets, and waving sticks made from giant deer antlers.

I asked Wang Lu if she could tell me where to find the Daurs.

"The who?" she said.

"The Daur people. They play hockey."

"Daur?"

"Ya, you know: Daur."

"Well, you will go to your first game tonight against the Harbin team!"

"Yes. I know. But I have to find the Daur."

"The who?"

After an hour snoozing in the hotel, we piled into the tour bus with the Foxes for our first trip to the rink. We took to the streets on the cusp of day and night. The city was suspended in blue light, fringed with a dreamy black glow. I'd only seen this colour once before, in the Northwest Territories. It was the colour of cold. Our journey to the arena was eerie. Cars and buses drifted like spectres through the streets. Very few of them used their headlights, a throwback to the Maoist ways of frugality. You never saw a car coming at you until it emerged from the exhaust expelled by the vehicle in front of it. I was astonished that there weren't more car wrecks or nasty pile-ups, but there were no horns sounded, no angry fists shaken. Instead, motorists just lowered their heads and moved on. We passed city buses full of children coming home from school, their faces pressed against the glass, their breath making pools of water. I saw in those faces the features of Harbin's ancestry: Russian, Japanese, Mongol, Chinese. One child had pink cheeks, a sharp Russian nose, and velvety Chinese eyes that locked onto mine. I'll always remember his face. It was the face of cold. His eyes widened and his mouth dropped. He raised his hands to the window, so I waved at him. But he wasn't waving back. He was simply looking, his eyes locked on mine, as if observing a strange animal.

The city looked roughed-up and rubbled. Walls were collapsing, the streets were sooty and unswept, and the roads were ravaged with potholes and craters. I sensed that only the cold had kept the city from imploding, the ice and frost gluing the buildings to the ground. We passed shaggy horses pulling buggies driven by men in great fur hats, hauling coal and wood and bricks and hunks of con-crete. They smoked and wore the look of those for whom a hard life has been hardened even more by the weather. People sat at little tables on the sidewalk wrapped in blankets and ate bowls of noodles. Someone poured oil into a wok and a cloud of steam mushroomed. Women in folding chairs watched over old blankets with trinkets laid across them. Chestnut vendors. Seed merchants. Hawkers of hawthorn berries. They wore fur boots and kerchiefs, gloves, and long coats, and stood in front of houses with turrets sagging under the darkening sky.

We left the heart of the city and passed through the gates of a sporting grounds. A bunch of kids in parkas were kicking around a volleyball on a concrete pitch dusted with snow. The arena stood at the far end of the grounds. It was part of a larger square where the gymnasium, swimming pool, and athletes' residence were located. The arena's exterior was white with bright blue tiles, and the steel gridwork laid flat above the entrance – it may or may not have been art – made the arena's facade look like the meeting of waves. The word "constructivist" came to mind, though I'm not sure that's what it was. There was a twenty-foot metallic squiggle in front of the arena that I think was meant to look like a flame. The Asian Games had been staged here in 1983, and were the reason the arena was built.

Inside, the lobby of the rink was dark and still. There was a silver wall sculpture of figure skaters, speed skaters, and hockey players, set against wood panelling. The figures were positioned around a gold and silver sun with flames like deadly saw blades. Gold birds flew between the skaters. With their rigid lines and acute angles, they could have been drawn by geometrists; but, in their own way, they were quite beautiful. I couldn't remember the last time I'd walked into a rink and seen art.

On the opposite wall was a glass trophy case. But instead of trophies and medals awarded to local athletes, it was filled with black and white photographs of policemen in action: policemen subduing miscreants, policemen pouring tea for the elderly, and, in one strange shot, policemen playing the accordion in an old cottage. When I asked Lu what the deal was, she turned her palms up and made a face. A few days later, she quizzed one of the rink employees, who said, "Don't you know? We've had the best police force in China for thirty years."

Past the trophy case was a room where a round man in an old grey suit sat in a chair. Steam billowed from a kettle that wheezed beside him on a hot plate. Reeve stuck his head in: "Which way to the rink?" he asked. The man smiled and waved.

"Lu?" said Reeve, looking behind him.

"*Bing xi*," I said to the man.

He sipped his tea and nodded.

"Where's Lu?"

We gathered outside his room to wait for Lu, who was busy talking to the bus driver. We turned back to the man. "Ha! Ha!" he said, suddenly, as if trying to frighten a cat. He pointed at a wall, and since there was nothing on it but wood panelling, we took this as a suggestion to move on. We wandered down the hall. The lights were dim and we could see nothing. The hallway was empty. The Foxes were timid, so I led the way.

Apart from the faint smell of hockey – there was no jasmine or incense to sweeten it – there was only darkness. I walked on trying to sense my way to the ice, which is to say that, after a few turns, I was lost.

"Where the hell's Lu?"

"Maybe we should go back."

"It's dark."

"I'm cold."

"It stinks in here."

There was nothing to distinguish the hallways other than a few signs in Chinese. One of them said "Smoking Harm to Health. No Smoking. Disobeyer Will Be Fined." The walls were old and sooty and the floor tiles had been torn and scuffed by many skates and shuffling crowds. The rink grew colder. I was about to suggest that we camp out and wait for Lu to find us when a figure emerged from a room at the end of a hallway. He moved towards us. He looked like a man without a head: a headless rink attendant. But as he grew closer, I realized he was a very small man whose back was hunched. Behind him, steam shot out of another room where tea was brewing. You could smell it: the smell of China. As he emerged from the fog, I saw that he was carrying a ring of keys. He held them up and they glinted

Bobby Clarke's teeth

in the dark, swinging off the ring like gold teeth. He dangled them as if trying to coax us forward. Finally, I saw his face. He was sunken-cheeked and small-featured. He wore a blue Mao jacket and cap.

"*Bing xi?*" I asked him.

He opened his mouth.

Bobby Clarke's teeth.

We followed him down the murky hallway to a staircase leading to the ice, where we were enveloped in warm arena light. The rink was filled with players, not one of them moving. They were staring at us. I stared back. We must have been quite a sight: the elderly Foxes in their down jackets, hiking boots, and toques; Wang Lu dashing up from behind; Janet with her camera; and me, smiling like a frigging idiot. I stopped on the top stair and looked down at them: a panoply of thirty men, maybe forty, many of them even older than the Foxes. Their faces were hard and flat and scribbled with age. They had the distant look of northern exiles, of lives lived behind a wall. Some were missing teeth, and, of course, they had big heads. Some were paunch-bellied and their elbows protruded from moth-eaten sweaters. Others wore no padding at all. Jofa helmets sat like red flower pots on their heads, their sticks were gnarled with feathered tape, their feet laced into wrinkled leather skates that looked like they'd been pilfered from a hockey museum. Their jerseys reminded me of the Soviet Red Army's, only the names on the back were in Chinese characters. Some wore baseball caps instead of helmets. Some, I learned, had carried their equipment in large shopping bags.

The old custodian waved his arm in a scooping motion to get us to follow him, but I couldn't stop looking at the men on the ice. Most of the players grinned, a few did not. Some rubbed their chins with old leather gloves and spat. Others pointed and gestured with their sticks and smiled, high-wattage smiles on enormous, open faces, laughing at a joke that only elderly Chinese hockey players tell each other. It probably goes something like: "Did you hear the one about the American hockey team who came half-way around the world only to get their asses kicked by old fuckers twice their age?" I flashed them the V sign. They spanked their sticks on the ice and laughed even harder.

We followed the custodian around the end of the rink to our dressing room. The players' heads turned and followed us. Green army-issue crash pads were stacked behind the net, the foam stuffing showing at the seams, the result of countless speed-skating spills. The seats in the arena – 5,000 of them – were plastic orange buckets, the kind you might find in a bus station or lunch counter. There was a blank pixelboard the size of a Jumbotron at one end of the rink with Hotel Inter-continental Harbin written below. The Foxes wondered what the pixelboard was used for, but Wang Lu was uncertain. "Must be a big video screen," said Frank Nelson, but I didn't think so, too unlikely a technology for a rink so cold and dark. A few weeks later, I watched a televised basketball game in Shanghai where there was a screen like this one. All it did was project the score of the game in three-storey-high gold pixels, the numbers towering over the players, soaking the stands in a pale glow.

The custodian did not move quickly, so it took some time to get us to our dressing room. It was the coldest I have ever been in. It reminded me of a rank change room in a high-school gymnasium, with little wooden compartments for each player and rusted hooks overhead. There were frosted windows on one side and an old card table on the other. There appeared to be a boiler of some kind in the corner, which the old man worked on with a long steel rod. I assumed this device had something to do with generating heat, but I never did find out, for it generated none.

We changed into our equipment. Reeve gave me a red Foxes jersey to wear. He'd designed it himself (Reeve was a portrait artist for a Manhattan art gallery) and it had a drawing on it of a small furry thing with black stripes.

"Nice jersey," I lied.

"Foxes," said Mike Moran, raising his eyebrows. Foxes that could leave the team mistaken for the Hunt Club Wombats or Artichokes. I assumed that Reeve was better at drawing people.

We filed out of the room and hit the ice. At one end, the Chinese National Team Oldtimers were firing shots on their goalie with pucks lined up along their blue line. The youngest member of the club was forty-one. The oldest, Mr. Guo, wore tinted bottle glasses, and was so old he could have been Stan Mikita's babysitter. The goaltender had spiky white hair and frosty eyebrows, and was the shape of a shrunken turnip, yet he sprung up and down in his crease like a jack-in-the-box. I got a clear look at him and wondered whether he might have played goal in the maskless era, for his face was pocked and creviced. His wasn't the only one. The forwards were soft and fat, yet they moved like rippling silk and were steady on their feet. They gave the impression that a rink-length rush would leave them exhausted, if not dead, but once they started moving the puck around, I was reminded again of the Russians: economy of motion, quick bursts of speed, precision passing.

I should have known not to write the old boys off as over-the-hill. I'd been deceived once before by an old player, the Leafs great Norm Ullman. It happened in a celebrity game against the Leafs Oldtimers. Ullman had a great crest of white hair and moved with all the suddenness of a park bench. He was the Buddy Ebsen of hockey, creaking and sawing when he moved. I spent most of the game trying not to run into him, cautious of his fragility, so when he carried the puck across the blue line against my defence, I saw not a Hall of Famer, but Grandpa Simpson. I skated backwards casually, staying a few feet away from the old smoothie. He never looked at me, not once. Finally, when he got within shooting distance of our goalie, I reached out with my stick to take the puck away. Zip. He was past me in a flash. He went *through* me. I ended up sprawled on the ice as he moved in and beat our goalie, top shelf, to a great ovation. I now consider it an honour to have been humiliated by the old hockey pro who, in that split second, showed me why he was so highly regarded in the heyday of his career.

The Oldtimers fed us our Affluent North American Hockey Tour of Asia '99 on a platter, only letting up long enough to give us the odd shot on goal and scoring chance. *Snap!* went their passes. *Crack!* went their shots. Their skates kissed the ice and they moved fluidly, beautifully. The Foxes were frustrated and did not take well to being out-matched.

"Christ. We're paying for this?" said Reeve, on the bench.

"What's wrong?" I asked.

"These guys are good!" he said.

"Ya. So?"

"They're too good!"

I took my first shift on a line with Reeve and Elizabeth Lewis. Thus, my centreman was a sixty-seven-year-old portrait artist from New Jersey and my right winger was a small woman from New England who'd captained the Colgate women's team.

It was the first time I'd ever skated on an Olympic-sized ice surface; at times it felt like skating on an ocean. I looked across to Elizabeth, but she seemed no bigger than a dragonfly. On the horizon were the boards, the end of the rink was a coastline thinning in the distance. I was amazed at how much ice there was, and how long it took me to get to an errant puck. Since the Chinese were so able on their skates, invariably they got to it sooner, and too often I chased down the puck to find only the shavings of a defencemen who'd got there before me. I can only imagine how it must have been for Team Canada in 1972 in the Soviet Union after playing in the bandboxes of the NHL. They must have felt like men overboard, adrift in a frosty sea.

Once I understood the challenges of the big surface, I realized I'd have to move twice as fast. As soon as my body understood this, it could adjust, sort of. I'm not the type whose skills are supported by long stretches of skating. I'd just as soon the puck come to me as race after it. But it felt good to make long, cross-ice passes tape-to-tape. You had to whip the puck the way you'd muscle a hard wrist shot, with a little extra torque. And when I carried the puck through the neutral zone – which was twice as big as in a normal rink – I gained velocity. I was really moving.

The Chinese Oldtimers were good at all aspects of the game. Whenever they set up in our zone, they passed the puck as if they were drawing a pentangle: point to point to point, each pass threading through our skates and sticks too quickly for our eyes. Ironically, it was the Harbin junior team's goalie, hired by the Foxes for the game, who kept us alive. Otherwise, it would have been brutal slaughter.

After ten minutes, I finally got near the net after taking a pass from Elizabeth, who whipped the puck to me in the slot from the corner. Reeve had started the play by sending Elizabeth over the blue line on a nice cross-ice pass. I liked playing with Reeve if for no other reason than when he yelled, you heard him. He yelled like a father angry at a child.

"Elizabeth!"

"Dave!"

Elizabeth won the puck from a Chinese defenceman, who'd chased her into the corner. It was a memorable image: small Elizabeth with her curly blond hair hanging below her collar being checked by an elder in hockey socks wrinkled around his skate tops, poking at her feet with a stick stamped with Chinese characters along its shaft. But Elizabeth came out well in the battle. She flung the puck out into the middle of the ice and I was there to collect it. I spanked at it and my wood found rubber. The puck climbed up the goalie's shoulder and hopped into the net.

I felt good. Before the game, Harry O'Mealia told me that he'd scored a goal in every country the Foxes had visited, and it made me realize the importance of not coming away empty-handed from a country you might never visit again.

The ref blew his whistle to signal the end of the period. We took a five-minute intermission so that the Zamboni, an old grey beast with rust biting at its flanks, could clear the ice. I sat down. Our benches were a few feet from the boards, so you had to take two steps before jumping on. The inside of the boards were made of pine planks painted white, and there were old iron radiators behind us, none of them expelling heat. When the puck hit the boards, there was no *boam*, but a kind of muted thunk. Exposed pipes ran below the bench and you had to be careful not to scrape your skate blades against them. The ads along the boards were so old they were flaking; you could drag your stick and scale them. There were about fifty little flags with blue and red lettering suspended across the ceiling advertising car dealerships. A sign next to the pixelboard read IIHF 90th Anniversary, and above it, black scrim covered what appeared to be a window overlooking the city. I thought that I could see the night sky behind it and I asked Lu if it might be opened.

"No. The glare. The problem is sun."

"But it's evening. There's no sun. Maybe it's snowing."

"No, no," she laughed.

I had learned that the Chinese have a different laugh for every situation. This was Wang Lu's Don't-ask-me-to-move-the-black-scrim-again laugh.

"But it could be beautiful!" I said.

"No, no. Not beautiful," she said, shaking her head and laughing some more.

I went over to the Chinese bench and said hello to the players in Chinese. As you can see, I'd added a few words to my verbal reper-toire and could now form one complete sentence: "Hello! I play ice hockey!" Actually, the first hundred times, I said it wrong. The word for hello is *nihau*, but more often that not I said *mihau*, in a good impersonation of a cat. But the Chinese players cut me some slack. They huddled around eagerly and waited for me to torture more words in Chinese.

I called Janet over.

"Tell them that they play very well. For their age. No, wait. Don't tell them that last part."

Janet thumbed through her Mandarin phrase-book. We leaned in as she scanned the pages.

"Okay. Wait. No. Okay," she said. Then, as was the case every time she pieced together a sentence in Chinese, she held up one finger and moved the guide book in front of her face like a myopic granny. She said, "You are very excellent players. You skate ably and with pride!"

"Ahh. Ahh," they smiled, nodding appreciatively.

"Ask them if they've ever seen an NHL game."

"Gee. Okay," she said, flipping. "Okay. Do you know hockey in Canada?"

"Uh. Ungh?" they muttered, confused.

"Hmm. Try this one: 'Where can I find the Daur?'"

Janet glared.

The elders and I leaned over the boards and looked at each other and nodded silently. I started an accidental pantomime that seemed to get things rolling. I took out my blue mouthguard, bent it, snapped it back in my hand, and shook my head, scowling. The old men laughed. Then I showed them my Morningstars sticker on my helmet. The Morningstars are the team I play on in Toronto. I said: "*Bing xi*. Mine. *Bing xi*. Mine!"

"Ah! Ah!" they said, nodding their heads.

"Tell them the Morningstars are a very popular team throughout Canada," I told Janet.

"I will not."

I took out my mouthguard a second time and pointed at my fake tooth. I tapped the tooth with my finger and, with my other hand, I pantomimed the motion of a blade carving into my gums. I tapped it and scowled some more. Then a fellow who looked as old as math removed his red helmet, then showed me his teeth.

"Ha! Ha!" he said, his eyes alight.

I gave him the thumbs up.

"Ha! Ha!"

He stepped away as one of the younger players, Mr. Lui Wen Wu, moved in. Mr. Lui was in his early forties and he was the coach of the Harbin junior team. He could manage a little English, so we played a word game.

"What do you know of the NHL?" asked Janet.

"Ungh. One. Night. Television?"

"Yes."

"Ungh. Television. Hockey. NHL."

"Do you know the Leafs?" I piped in.

"The . . . what is?"

"T-O-R-O-N-T-O. Toronto Maple Leafs."

"Umm. In red? Team in red?"

"Montreal?"

"Yes! Yes! Montreal!"

As a Leafs fan, it galled me that the Canadiens evoked such enthusiasm. I'd travelled thousands of miles from home to a remote part
of northern China, only to discover that I was in Habs country.

"Hmmm. What about Detroit?"

"Yes. Detroit. Not so good."

"Well, not this year."

"No," said the coach, lowering his head as if Detroit had dis-
honoured their fans.

"Who are some of your favourite players?"

"Fave . . .?"

"Best players. Best."

"Um . . . Gretzky."

"Yes!"

"Jagr?" he asked

"Very good."

"Um . . ."

"What about Hasek?"

"Oh. Hasek. Yes. Yes. Hasek."

A few other members of the Chinese team gathered around the
bench and added to the chorus. They leaned in and listened as I
spun out the names.

"Selanne?"

"Um. No."

"Lindros?"

"Lind?"

"Kariya?"

"Korea?"

"Yzer . . . man?"

"Yzer . . . man?"

"What about the Russians?"

"Oh. Russians, yes. Makarov!"

"Ha!"

"Yes. Yes. Makarov good."

"Okay: Krutov?"

"Yes!"

"Larionov?"

"*Yes!*"

"Fetisov?"

"YES!"

"Kasatonov?"

"*Oh!*"

"Bykov?"

"*Bykov!*"

"Kamensky?"

"KAMENSKY!"

"For me, there's only one," said Janet. "Fellow by the name of Vladislav Tretiak."

The old men scrunched up their faces. I continued the count.

"Balderis!"

"Ah!"

"Vasilyev!"

"AHHH!"

"Mikhailov!"

"Kharlamov!"

And it ended there. We were speaking the language of hockey. In naming the Russians, the old men and I had shared the same vision: Kharlamov speeding over the blue line, skating down the ice like a leaf passing over a wave, slipping towards the net, and snapping the puck over the goalie's shoulder with all the ease of a boy throwing a chestnut. It was visual telepathy. We wouldn't have shared the intimacy of these visions had we been discussing art, literature or film. As much as I wanted to ask them about the Cultural Revolution, the Japanese occupation in the 1930s, the collapse of the Soviet Union, the Gang of Four, and the Siberian prison camps (which lay just north of Harbin) – I couldn't have raised these subjects with single words, for they were too complex. But the name of a hockey player was all it took to understand a small but significant piece of each other's hearts.

The ref blew his whistle, and we skated to our respective sides. On my first shift of the new period, I took a pass and streaked across centre. One of the old fellows put out his stick and caught me flush in the ribs. It felt like a tap, but when I returned to the bench at the end of my shift, I was having a bit of trouble breathing. When I bent over, it hurt. I lifted my shirt to discover a bloody welt running five inches across my chest.

The old fucker.

10

The next day we dined with the Foxes at a restaurant called the Swan, which Paul Theroux once dubbed the Frozen Swan for its lack of heating. I didn't find it so bad. We had traditional northern Chinese cuisine – an entire roast duck, a champion-sized steamed fish, flying-dragon soup, and the most delicious small ribs I have ever tasted – as well as three items that were not named for me until I tried them: grilled bear's paw, moose snout, and monkey brains.

One of the questions my friends most asked when I told them that I was going to China was "Don't they eat monkey brains there?" I admonished them for their ignorance. So I was startled when we were served grey goo spilling over glutinous, rubbery ears.

"Monkey!" I shrieked, pointing at the plate.

"Yes. You like it?" asked Wang Lu, smiling.

"It's monkey!"

"No. It's mushroom!"

"Monkey!"

"No. No. The monkey only looks like the mushroom. I mean, the mushroom only looks like the monkey!" she said, laughing into her small hand.

I was confused. Was Lu trying to cover up by saying that the monkey was actually mushroom? A man came out and cleared the air. He told us that the dish was a type of fungus that looked like the brains of a monkey. How he knew what the brains of a monkey looked like I never learned.

The moose snout and the bearpaw, however, were exactly that. The paw was served as flat, pale pink medallions and squares. They tasted gummy and were covered in a sweet slime that made the dish inedible (it was the first time I'd been in a restaurant where I was thankful that the food was terrible). The moose snout was stewed. It had a delicious, salty flavour. After the moose course we were presented with a shot of clear liquor. As I sat there in front of a plate of half-eaten moose snout, sipping pure alcohol while snow fell outside on the Manchurian plain, I'd never felt more Canadian in my life.

Reeve told us that the Foxes had already paid for the meal – it was part of the tour package – yet another example of their generosity. The Foxes were a paradox. They were unique not only in that they were globe-trotting hockey enthusiasts who hailed from a country that has never really fallen in love with the game, but in that they also came from an elevated socio-economic stratum, shared by politicians (the governor of New Jersey was Reeve's cousin) and bankers (Frank Nelson was the former vice president of the Marine Midland Bank, and Harry O'Mealia's business card read, "US Trust of New Jersey"). Their hometown was a patrician enclave where hockey alternated with fox hunts and horse jumping. They were the last group of people I expected to meet on the hockey road. But while their search for athletic adventure was commendable, they showed little desire to plumb the culture of northern China. They spent a lot of time in the hotel piano bar. Only Reeve Junior, after the third day, said, "I don't want to go out to dinner. I want to go and see some of this town."

While the Foxes played hockey for fun, they were highly competitive. Reeve Senior was the most annoyed whenever they lost. He went so far as to complain to Wang Lu that the competition was too stiff. The Foxes had forked out thousands of dollars for their trip – it would take them to Shanghai, as well – but complained that the fees for ice rental and refereeing and the goaltender in Harbin were too high. I watched Harry O'Mealia spend half an hour in the dressing room trying to wrench the cage off his helmut so that he could give just it and not the whole thing to a young Chinese player, but he also was in the habit of peeling off crisp one-dollar bills for children he met on the street. It was strange. Jim Cummins, the Manhattan book anti-quarian who looked like David Crosby, specialized in collecting old hockey books, yet I heard him complain about a pair of old skates that his wife had made him bring so that he could give them away. "I've been carrying these damned things around since the USA. I'm sick of 'em," he groused, stamping out of the dressing room in search of some kid whose skates were falling apart, of which there were many.

The Foxes were a complex study. To their credit, they calmly went about their business without letting a writer who was docu-menting their every travail get in the way. They never once suggested that I was ever out of bounds, and I felt very comfortable among them. They hid nothing. They were uninhibited even when their actions were suspect. After a game against the Harbin junior team (we played them twice after losing to the Oldtimers), the Foxes spent thirty minutes outside the arena haggling with our guests over the trading of hockey paraphernalia. At one point Dave Whiting ran up to me and said, "This player wants to trade me his old jersey for my stick, but my stick cost me forty bucks!" The tradition in international play is to swap jerseys and equipment after games. The Foxes had already travelled to a dozen different countries, so it's unlikely they didn't know this. And it was obvious through the windows of the tour bus that Harbin was a suffering town, but the Foxes appeared not to notice. That our decrepit gear was desirable to the juniors should have alerted them. They had enough personal wealth to equip themselves many times over, so it was strange to see them try to talk down the players. At one point, Jim said, "Hey, buddy. You want this?" and held up an old towel. Dave boasted, "If I pull this deal off, it'll be the steal of the century!" while trying to trade his sweat-logged Cooper elbow pads for a beautiful Russian jersey. But the player wasn't interested in Dave's equipment so he could wear it to parties and announce "Check out what I scored in China!" He was going to use it to play, to extend his career a year or two before he quit to work in the smelting plant. Dave zipped open his hockey bag and showed the kid his stuff. The kid put up his hand and walked away. We climbed into the tour bus and headed for the hotel.

At times, I was also troubled by the Foxes' behaviour on the ice. Mike Moran, the speedy defenceman, was hot-headed. He was young and freckle-faced and square-jawed, with a close crop of red hair. He looked like Opie on the verge. In the first few minutes of the game against the Old Boys, he banged his knee into the boards after getting tied up with a Chinese forward. He hobbled to the bench yelling and complaining that one of the Chinese seniors had taken him out, even though it had clearly been an accident. On his next shift, he skated towards whichever Chinese forward was carrying the puck and got a piece of him, slamming knee against knee. The septuagenarian he'd checked looked surprised, then skated away, disbelieving. It was hard to imagine any of the pandas responding in kind, and I think it goaded Mike. For the rest of the game, he glowered on the bench, at least when he wasn't banging his stick and yelling, "*Chippy shit!*"

Later in the game, Mike turned to Janet, who was standing behind the bench, and apologized for his language. Then he said, "But the guy took my legs out and I've already got a bruised ACL." Janet told him, "Hey, you're in China playing a game you love." Later that evening at the hotel bar, the two of the them discussed movies, and Mike confessed to her that he liked only violent films. He listed *Payback* and *Face/Off* as two of his favourites, then added, "But there's no better movie than *Reservoir Dogs*." Mike was a classic type – a tightly wound, aggressive, white male. As such, he was alone among the Foxes. I wondered who'd invited him.

I just have to bring up a subject that is obvious to anyone who has ever played hockey competitively: the game harbours assholes. I won't sugar-coat it. It gives them a place to flourish. They're in every league. Assholes who shoot pucks at refs. Assholes who chase you down the hallway after the game. Assholes who smash their sticks into splinters along the boards in full view of their wives and young children after a missed play or bad call. Assholes who attack the other team's smallest player. Assholes who refuse to serve their penalty. Assholes who play drunk. Assholes who berate league officials and phone them at home and threaten their families. Assholes who assault the timekeeper. Assholes who wreck dressing rooms and smash up Zambonis. Assholes who wait for you in the parking lot after the game with a tire iron.

But being an asshole is a relative thing. A lot of hockey players have assholish tendencies, the asshole gene. Some might call me an asshole while I'm on the ice. I admit to having tripped, slashed, speared, scraped, butt-ended, knifed, harpooned, hacked, carved, slew-footed, kicked, head-butted, twisted, punched, slugged, strangled, thumbed, elbowed, gored, gouged, jousted, jostled, cross-checked, nailed, knuckled, hooked, gutted, clawed, hoed, hammered, slapped, shanked, and bludgeoned opposing players in an effort to help my team win hockey games. Like many others, I have tasted hockey's bloody, salty intoxicant.

And I have loved it.

But there are those who step beyond the pale. I have a friend who is a perfectly reputable citizen by day but, once strapped into his gear, he affects the look of a murderous duck, behaving accordingly. Once we had to kick him off the Morningstars for spitting into an opponent's eye. A few years later, he landed a spot on another club, but was again relieved of his position, this time for spitting blood. He is actually a mild case. A few years ago, I was playing in a tournament when another friend, Steve Stanley, was attacked by a thug who tripped him to the ice, then rained blows upon his head. Steve lay there shouting, "My leg is broken! My leg is broken!" as he absorbed the blows. It was a horrible thing to see. When they wheeled Steve out of the rink (with a corkscrew ankle break, no less), the thug told him that he hadn't meant to hurt him. A few hours later at Don Cherry's, I spotted Steve's attacker sitting nearby. When I walked over to growl something at him, he raised his glass of beer to me and smiled.

On the ice, people change. It's what Hugh MacLennan said: "To spectator and fan alike, hockey gives the release that strong liquor gives a repressed man." Hockey is a game that shows people (okay, men) at their best as well as their worst, but usually it's the latter. I've never written an angry letter to a newspaper, called back a waiter to complain about my food, or fought with a fellow motorist, but many is the time that I've spent entire games stalking opponents on the ice, seeking revenge. I've cold-cocked strangers in the helmet, covertly speared and slashed them, and altogether behaved nastily in an attempt to even the score after being pushed around on the ice.

My most regrettable moment came during a recreational league game against the Black Stokes, the Morningstars' arch-rivals. Actually, it didn't happen during the game, but afterwards. The Black Stokes are the Habs to our Leafs, the Yankees to our Red Sox. Like us, they represent the part of the music community that's obsessed with hockey (similar outfits also exist in Winnipeg and Vancouver, with whom the Morningstars have no quarrel), each team resenting the existence of the other. The Stokes are a collection of men from groups familiar to pop fans – Cowboy Junkies, Blue Rodeo, Skydiggers, *NOW* magazine – while the Morningstars come from bands that would send the average listener thumbing through a local guide – Lowest of the Low, Rheostatics, Morganfields, Local Rabbits, Guh, Nothing in Particular, Cottage Industry. Both teams claim to have been around longer than the other and, in addition to league play, we hold public games that each considers better run and more vital than the other. Our league games are marathons of angst that verge on Pier Four brawls. Traditionally, they're the only contests on our respective schedules that friends and families come out to see.

In 1999, tension between the two teams reached a fever pitch, and I was the first to snap. During the season, we lost a close game, 6–5, which ended with a goalmouth scramble and their captain shouting, "Morningstars lose again!" During the post-game hand-shake, one of their players said to me, "Good game, asshole," and I lost it. My synapses melted. Once he'd skated away, I charged after him screaming. When he refused to turn around, I grooved my stick into him. From behind. He flew into the rest of his team, toppling them like dominoes. He scrambled back to his feet and came after me, so I put my hands up and tried to grab his head. But by this point, both teams had intervened and were yelling, and the last thing I remember was the hot breath of one of my teammates on my face, shouting at me to calm down.

When I realized what I'd done, I felt remorse, regret. I could have injured the player badly. I could have broken his neck. I was both frightened and awed that hockey had transformed me into someone I'd never been before. Whatever poise and good sense I'd learned had been dissolved by rage. The game had poisoned my heart, flooding it black like ink poured into an aquarium.

What worsened the situation was the fact that the Black Stokes were obliged to answer my hit, yet another barbaric principle of this fierce, competitive game. You may regard Jim Cuddy, the dignified and handsome singer for Blue Rodeo, as a calm and good-hearted person with a lovely voice and a fine set of friends with whom he makes music. And while I'm sure that's true, this time it was Jim Cuddy's turn to behave like a fist-swinging thug. I even have the scar to prove it.

We met the Stokes in that year's semi-final, and in game two Cuddy snapped. In the first game, he'd skated over to me and said, "Ah, Bidini, you're not so tough," meaning it good-naturedly. I laughed and repeated something my friend had told me to say: "What's the matter, Jim? You want a piece of me? All you've got to do is *try*," referring to a popular Blue Rodeo song.

Cuddy is no Bugsy Watson. But in the second period of the second game, he flipped. It all started with a check. I rode him out against the boards, firm. He was furious. He screamed over and over at the top of his lungs, "*Bidini! Fucking Bidini!! Fuck you!*" and started swinging wildly. I felt like I was being hit with a sack of yams.

I went down.

From behind his face-cage, I saw his eyes. They were like hot cinder points. Froth bubbled at the sides of his mouth and he bared his teeth. Seeing this sweet pop singer transform into a monster tickled part of me, and at one point the thought entered my head: "You are being attacked by Jim Cuddy of Blue Rodeo. Cool."

He hit me once, twice, a third time. He was almost hysterical, crying. I tried to put an arm under my face to prevent it from being mashed into the rink, but could not. He pressed the back of his hand against my helmet and ground my face into the ice like a man juicing a grapefruit. I felt the rink crush my nose and forehead.

Months later, Janet told me that she'd had a dream in which I attacked Jim Cuddy's car with a tire iron. After destroying it, I went looking for him. I dragged him out on the driveway like Ray Liotta in *GoodFellas* and I beat him to within an inch of his life. People on the street were pleading me to stop.

"It was terrible," she said, shaking her head.

The truth is, that was my dream. I'd pictured this scene many times. Anyone who has ever battled an on-ice enemy has had these fantasies. I imagined him being electrocuted on stage, impaled on a goalpost, falling to his death, getting run over by a streetcar, beat up by thugs, buried alive. Because of what happened on the rink, I will never look at Jim Cuddy the same way again. When I think of settling the score, my heart races, my hands sweat, and I get that salty taste in my mouth. It makes watching the country music channel very difficult.

I'm always astonished when one NHL player is interviewed after assaulting another. He never stares into the camera and says, "I did it because I hate that fucking guy's guts. I wanted to murder him out there." That's what I would have said had a camera been pushed at me after my escapade. I always expect hockey players to behave like pro wrestlers: blood caked on their faces, raving psychotically. Some would argue that the reason players don't comport themselves like this is so that they can teach kids sportsmanship and respect, but these are the same players who pour drinks over waitresses and wreck cars and get arrested for smoking crack. You often hear admissions of hatred from old-timers, but rarely from today's players. They have a kind of mundane respect for each other. Maurice Richard once said, "These days, rivals are going into business with each other. All of this fraternizing takes something off the competitive edge. I know that when I played, fraternizing with the enemy was out." Brad Park was of the same view: "Sometimes I dreaded getting picked for the all-star game. The last thing I wanted was to play with the enemy."

I think this modern, measured behaviour is another reason why fans feel so detached from the players. I was there the night Dino Ciccarelli nearly decapitated Luke Richardson at Maple Leaf Gardens (Ciccarelli was later charged with assault). It was one of the most violent things I've ever seen one man do to another. He brought his stick down across Richardson's neck like a man axing a stump. Despite the obvious passion of this incident, both men issued solemn notices of regret after the game – something that happens after every egregious act of violence on the ice. But these admissions sound untrue, like spin jobs. We never hear why a player has gone on the rampage. Bill Berg once told a writer that, in order to get under a rival's skin, he would find the worst possible thing to say to him – terrible, reprehensible things. Knowing this, what did Richardson do to make Ciccarelli so mad? Did he call Ciccarelli's wife a skank? Did he tell him his brother had had a sex change? This was the case with one player, who was dogged for years by taunts from opposing teams. For once, I'd like to hear what the player was feeling when he committed his heinous act. I want a measure of Eddie Shore hatred in my hockey, because it's what I feel when I'm playing. What would happen if players stopped cloaking their feelings and let it all hang out? Would it bring into the open all the furtive spearing and hitting from behind and stick-work and head clubbing?

A few seasons ago, much was made of Claude Lemieux's refusal to apologize to Kris Draper after tearing away half his face with a dirty hit. Lemieux was grilled in the press for not saying he was sorry, but his refusal struck me as frank and genuine. Players in the golden age used to wait to eat until their train came into a station so that they could walk around, instead of through, the other team's car to get to the dining room. Their dislike of each other was legendary. Today, there's a perception of brotherhood and commonality among the players but, frankly, I think it's all bullshit. Anyone who has ever played a competitive game knows that brotherhood can only go so far. While it's true that sport gives life to dreams of personal achievement, it also provides a place for demons. Hatred, as well as love, lives in my hockey heart, and I would never trade one for the other.

I I

A CERTAIN MR. LIU

The Harbin hockey program was influenced by men of three generations. Guo Hong was the eldest; in the middle was Jin Guang, whose nickname was Golden Sunshine, a fatherly ex-goaltender who coached the junior netminders; and the youngest of the three, Liu Wen Wu, was the junior coach and a former hockey hero from the 1980s. When I first met Jin, he was decked out in a Buffalo Bills jacket and hat. Lu asked him on my behalf, "Why do you like the Bills so much?"

"Who?" he replied.

We brunched with the players. Brunch in a Western-style restaurant in a Singaporean hotel in northern China is a meal all its own. I ordered eggs and toast, but after weeks of not eating Western food, they didn't taste right. I went for shrimp dumplings and a steamed bun, but that was about as satisfying as chomping on a salted bathtub plug. Finally, I settled for copious cups of Chinese coffee while Guo drowned his dumplings in Thousand Island dressing.

Wang Lu provided translation for our conversation; that is, she tried to. The players' answers were long and dramatic, but Lu distilled them into short sentences heavy with times and dates. Still, it was the closest I'd ever get to the living history of Chinese hockey. It was like being able to sit around with members of the Ottawa Silver Seven. Before we began our interview, I played the name game with Guo using Soviet players from the 1970s: "Maltsev! Bodunov! Petrov! Shadrin! Tretiak!" He repeated them back to me until I came to Bobrov. I said the name once, twice. Bobrov had been a linemate of Tarasov's in the '50s and was the Russian coach in 1972. Finally, Mr. Guo's expression broke.

"Ah, Bobrov!" he said, raising a finger.

"You remember Bobrov?"

"Yes. Bobrov, Bobrov, Bobrov," he said, nodding his head and reaching for more dressing.

The most significant statistic about hockey in China is that in a country of more than one billion, there are only 800 registered hockey players. It's never been more than that. Not counting the game played by the elusive Daurs, hockey has been played in China since 1915 in Shenyang (formerly Mukhden), a region in northeastern China (although none of the players I talked to were aware of such distant roots). The first organized games happened on January 26, 1935, in Beijing at the First Winter Spartakaide Games, a domestic version of the Olympics. In 1951, the Ice Hockey Association of the People's Republic of China was formed, and hockey started to gain in popularity. In February 1953, a tournament was held in Harbin with teams from the northeastern, northern, and northwestern regions. This led to a Chinese league, and the championship has been contested every year since 1955. In 1956, the Chinese national team had its international debut at the Universiade in Wroclaw, Poland, which resulted in a Czech team – VZKG Ostrava – touring China for five exhibition games against teams from Beijing, Changchung, and Harbin. The Chinese lost all five games, but they gathered invaluable experience. In 1957, the Japanese national team came over, and later that year, the Chinese junior team visited Poland and the Soviet Union and participated in hockey camps. In 1957, China became a member of the IIHF.

Mr. Guo, with glasses, and teammate

"In 1956, two coaches from Russia visited Harbin and picked out the best young players," said Guo, forking a tomato slice. "Since I'd played ice hockey as a child, I knew the game well. My father played volleyball, but switched to becoming a speed skater, so I too became a speed skater. I was chosen to train with the Russians. Each time, I stayed for one month away from home. We had no helmets and the goalies had no masks. The equipment was very poor, but it didn't matter. Our skates were made in Russia and they were very thin, very weak. You could hardly stand up in them, but we did our best. Tarasov, the coach, was very strict. He was skilled and serious and wanted our full participation, no matter what kind of equipment we wore."

"You were taught by Tarasov?"

"Yes. We had many exchanges with the Russians due to the relationship between our countries. But since their country has been broken up, things have changed. Tarasov last visited here in 1983. He was like a big bear. Sadly, he was very, very fat," said Guo, filling his cheeks with air.

"The Russians helped us learn the game, but hockey had already taken root here," said Jin. "It is hard to put an exact date to it, but ice hockey in China started around 1950. In 1952, there was a competition for the three provinces in the north but, since there was no formal ice-hockey team from Harbin, they chose students from the schools to learn the game. Mr. Guo was one of them. He was one of the first ice-hockey players in China."

"We did all our skating out of doors!" said Guo.

"We had to!" said Jin. "Ice hockey was not paid any attention by the government, so there were no proper facilities. I couldn't wait for it to get cold so I could play! When I was a child, many boys played outside on the river, and some of the schools would freeze their grounds in the winter. I remember the men doing this; they were heroes for making the ice. We used to have one stick and a small ball. We'd chase after it, not really knowing the rules. The trick was to be a good skater. We have long winters here, so we had plenty of time to learn how to skate and play the game."

"Around 1952, the government got involved and built arenas for the players," said Guo. "More people joined in as the game became popular. Then in 1960, the national team of East Germany came to the Harbin rink. They were a real team, with beautiful jerseys and fine equipment. This was a team that finished fifth in the A-Pool World Championship the following year, so they carried their heads high. It was an unforgettable game! The score was 3–1 for Germany, but it was a very close game. Much closer than the Germans expected. You could tell. The crowd was excited by it and you knew that Chinese hockey was going forward. To where, we didn't know, but it was a start."

"Did you score?" I asked.

Guo rubbed the table with his hand and tilted his head. "I passed the puck to the player who scored. It was as good as a goal. A feeling like never before . . ."

Jin chimed in, "That was an important step for the Chinese program. At one point, we dreamed that Chinese hockey would be the future game for our country. At first, the members of the government would rarely come to watch us play, so we never thought we'd be noticed on the level of other sports. We felt isolated, on an island: an island of hockey players. Then they started to watch the games on the television and they enjoyed it. One of the leaders who was the head of the Communist Party at the time saw a game on television. He said, 'People should have the spirit that the ice-hockey players show! It doesn't matter what job you have, but you should perform the same way!' He was using hockey as an example for how the entire country should conduct their lives. We were getting attention."

"We made great strides," said Guo. "I remember from 1960 to 1963, China had a very serious drought, so the government had no money to send the team abroad. We didn't know the level of our play. Then, in 1966, Poland – who were the world's champions – came to northern China and we beat them."

It was a significant achievement for the Nats. The Polish team featured a couple of players from the national team and other young stars, but China won six of the seven games, with the seventh game ending in a tie.

"But it could not last," said Guo, lowering his head. "All the momentum and advancements were lost due to the Cultural Revolution. In that period, we stopped everything. Training for our team stopped. For five years, our program was completely destroyed. Imagine having your sticks and skates taken away from you, being told you cannot play the game you love? When the Polish team returned to play us in '72, they won easily. We lost a lot of ground during that empty period. We had achieved so much in only ten years, but the government put a stop to it. Some of our better players from that time period – like Jin – they had those years taken away . . ."

"I started playing in '62. But in '66, hockey disappeared," said Jin, looking into his plate. "It didn't start again until 1972, and by that time I was a little too old. Still, I was one of the members of the team that played in the world competition in Romania. We finished third. I was the number-one goaltender, and it was the first time I'd played at such a level. I was very happy when I saw the Chinese flag being raised twice. I try to teach that to the kids: that love of the motherland, that feeling of winning for your country."

In the early 1970s, the first indoor arena with artificial ice was built in Beijing (capacity 18,000) and this gave hockey a bit of a boost. At the end of 1971, Romania's national team visited China where they both trained and played against Chinese teams, and then, at the start of 1972, the Chinese national team went to Romania and Sweden to sharpen their technical skills. China made its international debut that same year in the C-Pool World Championship in Miercurea Ciuc, Transylvania (a town which I would visit that fall), where they finished fifth after winning two of their games, beating Holland 11–4 and Denmark 6–1. They also won the Fairplay Cup in the tournament.

"It took a long time to get things back to where they were before hockey was banned," said Guo, forlorn. "Liu got the best period, I think."

Liu looked away, embarrassed. You could tell that he was saddened by the stories of Guo and Jin's hockey past. Liu was tall and handsome and he was often seen in a track suit: the mark of a serious athlete. When he spoke to his junior club, they looked up to him as if he were a god.

"I learned to play in 1973, at school," he said. "In 1975, I joined what we called the Physical Training School and in '78 I was chosen to be a member of the national youth team. I was sixteen. In '82, I joined the National Team. The 1980s were the best time for me because the team entered several international competitions. I was able to go abroad two or three times – to the United States and Canada. I once played at the University of Toronto."

The University of Toronto. He phrased those last few words as if passing the whole weight of them over the table. He took out a black-and-white photo of himself standing in the corridor of Varsity Arena with three medals hanging around his neck, his eyes dancing. It's the look of a man who has been swept into the world, skating from country to country, experiencing the adventure of being in exciting and strange places, playing the game he loves. I know the look well. It is the look of a hockey nomad.

In nations that are still closed – China is one of the last – being a top-rank athlete means being able to see the world beyond what your neighbours and countrymen can see. You are able to do things that the average citizen could not dream of doing. You are elevated, freed from the purgatory of ordinary life. Top athletes in every nation are privileged, whether it's Andrei Trefilov, the NHL goalie who grew up in a town without a television; Orlando Hernandez, the Yankees pitcher who found himself in the major leagues throwing a baseball to Joe Girardi after years on Castro's blacklist; Mats Sundin, skating in the glorious arenas of the world after learning his game on frozen lakes; or Diego Maradona, living in a house made of gold and marble after growing up among brothers who scrapped over fish bones. In Communist China, it was possible to achieve through sport, if not outright freedom, then a freedom of the mind.

But this liberty is not without a price. The next photo Liu showed us was of his wife in her home in San Francisco. She had emigrated to the United States two years previously in hopes of finding work and setting up a home. Until she was established, Liu would stay in China and take care of their three-year-old daughter, and then he'd follow her to America. But at his immigration hearing, Liu was denied entry to the United States because he had once been a member of the Communist Party. It was not his choice, he told us; in order to represent his country in sports, he had had to join. We suggested that he might try Canada, where political allegiance was not as important an issue. He said he would try, adding, "I would like to come to your country. What cities in Canada are close to the United States border?"

Liu put his photos away and continued telling the story of his life in hockey. "The shining moment for me was in 1986 at the Asian Games," he said. "It was there that we won our first gold medal in hockey, the first of four consecutive first-place finishes. The Japanese team was better, but there was too much pressure on them. The papers in Japan said, 'No other medal matters except the gold medal in hockey. They must defeat the Chinese.' But they could not respond and we won. They were too frightened to win."

Jin leaned forward: "Liu scored a very important goal in that series. It was a wondrous goal. He led China, he led our team. He became a hero in that instant."

Liu said, sheepishly, "It was important for us to win. For myself, my teammates, and my country. We were playing for those who'd played before us, too."

Guo said, "I remember the 1930s and '40s. I remember what Japan did to the people of northern China. When I played against them, I thought of these things. From 1950 to 1960, we played against the Japanese team many times and, in 1957, after they won a competition here, they played the national anthem of Japan. It angered me. It was not right to hear the Japanese anthem played in China. I didn't feel right hearing that song."

"Was there ever the same feeling towards the Russians?" I asked.

"No. The Russians helped us," said Jin.

"But not anymore," said Liu.

"The great exchange is finished," said Jin, knifing his hand through the air.

"Was there ever recognition of Canada's role in hockey. Were you aware of Bobby Orr?"

"Who?

"Orr. Gordie Howe?"

"I do not know these names. I only know Wayne Gretzky," said Guo. "I have a photo of myself with him taken in the 1980s. I was introduced to him after a game. They said to him, 'We would like you to meet one of the first Chinese hockey players!' He was very gracious and friendly."

Liu said, "We'd heard about Canadian ice hockey, but not much. We had more influence from the Russians. They would speak of the Canadian teams, but only about how to beat them. It has all changed, of course. Now, we get one game a week on television. We watch it to see the NHL teams and the Canadian players. But also to see the Russians, some of whom we know well."

"The reason I heard of Canadian hockey, I think, was from our equipment," said Guo. "We had shoulder pads and sticks that came from this place, this place called Canada. So we knew that there was a connection to hockey. My skates came from Canada, too. They were much too big. I put paper in the toes to make them fit. Once I did, they were beautiful. I skated well."

"Do you remember what they were called?"

"They had letters."

"Letters? CCM?"

"Yes! They were called CCM!"

Guo wore Tacks.

With that, we finished our interview. Liu asked if I could supply him with a list of NHL teams he could contact. My first thought was of Dave King; the former coach for the Flames had been to Harbin many years ago and had assisted the Japanese national team with their program. With his wife already in the United States, Liu was looking to continue his life in North America. But it would not be easy. Unless he had a job offer from a company in Canada with a work permit authenticated by the Canadian government, it would be very difficult for him to get into Canada or the United States.

Wang Lu had designs similar to Liu's. She, too, wanted to work abroad. "I will take the interview," she told Janet and me later, on the steps of the Hotel Singapore, "and I will come to Canada, possibly America, to study in my field."

"You seem pretty certain," I told her.

"I have the money, the experience. China is changing so that it is easier to do these things," she said.

She was right, but it was hard to tell just how much it was changing. Years ago, it might not have been possible for three former national-team players to sit down and tell their story to a writer from the West without being studied by a third party. They might not have been able to say "the Cultural Revolution destroyed hockey!" into a tape recorder and get away with it. But now they could. Sort of. Things were opening up, albeit with the slowness of a stone being winched off a sarcophagus.

That evening, Janet and I and a few of the Foxes went to a local tavern, which was decorated in a quasi-Western theme with checkered tablecloths and imported beers. I ordered a bottle of Guinness, while Reeve and a few of the others drank Johnny Walker Red. The bottle was brought to them on a large tray by three waiters, each more eager and excited than the last. They put on a Whitney

Houston tape that sounded like it had been chewed by a dog. To my ears, Ms. Houston never sounded better.

Above an unlit fireplace, cardboard photocopies of pictures of young Western models were propped up on the mantle. There was a yellow Yield sign next to them that read "Honk If You're Horny," a poster of the cast of *Friends*, and what looked like half a swan's wing stretched out and taped to the brick façade. The waiters checked in on us, oh, once every twelve seconds. They brought us nuts and candies, and kept relighting the candle at the table. My ear caught the faint sound of another type of music blending in with Ms. Houston's, and when I went looking for the washroom, I realized that the club had a room upstairs that was used for live music.

I dragged the Foxes to the second floor. There were two young men performing on a little stage. The room was dark and it had the feel of a small cottage. There were three tables; we took one. There was no one else in the room.

The duo started playing. One of them strummed a slightly out-of-tune Yamaha acoustic guitar, reading sheet music propped up on a stand. The other teenager – who had the impressive northern cranium and a fabulous mop of black hair – sat on a stool and sang into a microphone with all the heat of Joe Cocker. He gave it his all, and I think he scared the Foxes. This endeared him to me. His hair was flying and he clenched his fist when he sang. The stool rocked as he unleashed a deep, booming tenor, singing what I took to be Harbinian folk-rock songs; they were mostly in waltz-time in minor keys. Each song blended breathlessly into the next. At our applause, the singer's face turned red and the guitarist buried his chin. After they'd been playing non-stop for about half an hour, two things struck me. One: it was quite possible that this was the first time either of them had ever performed in front of an audience, let alone an audience of Westerners; and, two: it was one of the most impassioned, nerve-fuelled performances I'd ever seen.

I invited them over. The singer came and sat down and laughed nervously at everything we said. The guitarist remained on stage and tuned his guitar. We spoke bad Chinese to the singer, and he spoke good Chinese to us. None of us could understand a word the other was saying. He sat for five minutes. I picked up my bottle, and said, "Cheers! Good set!" tipping it towards him before I drank. After I put my bottle down, he grabbed it, said, "Ha!" and drained it. Then he slammed it back down on the table, laughing some more. He bolted to the stage and huddled with the guitarist. Then he grabbed the mic and gave us another half hour, full-on.

When we left the club, the streets were empty except for the snow, which fell in great spinning medallions from the sky. It covered the road in a fine, white foam and brightened the streets leading up to our hotel, which shimmered in the distance like a drive-in movie screen. We could have been in Canada for the beery wobble of our bodies and the way our feet squeaked in the snow. We were reviewing the events of the day when Janet said, "In China, behind every smile there is a story to smash your heart to pieces." She was right. The young folk singer's howl had been the musical equivalent of Liu's tale of longing. Their voices had the same desperate tone, the same hopeful resignation. It had been a day of heart-grabbing stories and I was affected hard. At first, travel gives you the feeling of having seized control of your life, but encountering people who are simply trying to survive every hour of the day drowns that self-assuredness and sense of achievement in the sad blue of life. Liu's tale reminded me of the precarious nature of my own happiness, and made me ambivalent about having fulfilled my own life quest while he was struggling to take hold of his. The sense of self-determination that I'd felt on my journey was non-transferable. I would leave Harbin the next day, and the lives of those whom I'd met would continue independent of mine. Though we had shared the same ice, played a game we both loved, and crossed lives briefly, in the end, we were all adrift. That the game had provided a few hours when we were just men playing together was precious. But it was also terribly sad. In the end, hockey was a poem, but not an answer.

12

EIGHT BALL FOR THE WORLD

The snow was still falling when we left Harbin. We said goodbye to Wang Lu and the Foxes in the lobby of the Hotel Singapore. I thanked Reeve for letting me play and he said, "No, thank you. You were the guy who said we could beat the juniors. And you know what? We beat them!" So now Reeve could go back to Pea Pack and tell his friends, "We showed the Chinese what for." I told Reeve that I might come down to New Jersey and play with him some time. He slapped me on the shoulder and told me to do so.

We hailed a taxi. Lu leaned into the car and gave the driver terse instructions. It was harder saying goodbye to her. We hugged and said that we'd meet somewhere down the road, even though we knew we probably would not. It was the kind of goodbye that makes you sick when it's happening and makes you sick again when you think about it years later. At that moment, I felt very far from home, imagining myself years from now remembering the trip, and feeling that Harbin was on the other side of the universe. Coming here would seem as if it had happened in another lifetime, and perhaps never at all.

The cabbie watched television while he drove. He had a little red box screwed to his dashboard that showed a black-and-white Chinese soap opera. He dropped us at the train station and we took our seats in the passengers' lounge, a cold white room where I bought an instant coffee that tasted like hot-and-sour soup. Janet ate chocolate and looked sad. After spending five days in the company of the Foxes and Wang Lu, we were suddenly alone, vaulted into China. But the feeling didn't last long. The train out of Harbin was packed with bodies. We shared a hard sleeper with four other passengers, one of whom was a very drunk man. I watched him fall out of bed in an attempt to pull my running shoes over his large, stockinged feet. He grunted and moaned, finally wedging one foot half inside my Converse. He started to skid-shoe away from the berth, but I grabbed him and pointed to his own shoes, which he had kicked underneath his bunk. Later on, I was in the dining car drinking tea (every car had an old, coal-burning samovar that spouted hot water, and you could fill up your glass thermos at any hour of the day) when he walked in, his eyes half-closed, looking for the toilet. The train rocked and he swerved along the car, taking each table in the gut like a linebacker running a contact drill, bouncing off one, then another, until he crashed through the doors at the end of the car.

Ah, toilets. For both the drunk and me, the toilets on Chinese trains were a terrible ordeal. I refused to use them, even at the risk of intestinal cramps. As soon as I lay down, the cramps started, which did nothing to ease the discomfort of trying to sleep on a plank squashed against the berth's dirty linoleum walls, my head buried in a filthy pillow, my cold body swaddled in century-old wool blankets. I lay there half-frozen, my insides twisted. By now I'd gathered that it was a national sport in China to see how long one could go without being warm. It was certainly more popular than hockey. I'd doze off and awake to see clouds of breath puffing up from under the blankets. I resisted leaving the relative warmth of my bed until the cramps got so bad that I had no choice but to use the toilet. I looked over at Janet and said, "Now is my worst nightmare." She touched my hand. "Just come back, okay?"

And with that, I took the walk of shame. I moved through the corridor past innumerable dour people, many of them sitting on fold-down chairs against the window and chain smoking. Everyone in China smokes. And when they're not smoking, they're horking great clods of phlegm. Even those who don't smoke seem to have smoker's hack. After a while, it was all I could do to suppress the tingle of nausea, even though I am a hockey player and actually enjoy a good hork. In China the spitting and the smoking goes on twenty-four hours a day. On the train, this creates a sea-green murk through which light is filtered, so as I marched towards the toilet at the end of the car, I felt as if I were passing through the kind of subterranean mist you might find in a catacomb. Those who stared at me as I went by had all the robust panache of the undead. They gave no sign of wanting to reach out to warn me: "No, mister! Don't go down there! *Not there!*"

The toilet reeked. Not the billowing cloud of stale flatulence you find in a hockey dressing room, but a sharp stench of shit and piss, a stink that came at me like a board with a nail in it. I had to adjust my trousers to keep them out of the glinting urine pools beside the hole, and then squat. Janet told me: "It's actually better for your bowels. South Asian women have easier pregnancies after years of going to the bathroom this way." Not being a South Asian woman, this was hardly comforting. My ass was goosed from the cold breeze that sneaked under the door, and I stopped breathing so as not to swallow the stench. All I could think was, "If only there was an airbrushed photo of a pony running along a beach for me to look at." Then it was over. I walked back along the corridor past those same faces, their look unchanged. I told Janet, "That was horrible, but it's done. It's over." She gave me a look of pride, as if to say, "Darling, you have finally arrived." An hour later, she was forced to do the same. I told her, "Actually it's not so bad," knowing that, of course, it was. She went through with it, only to report, "Man, there was a mound of shit piled up beside the hole. It was like someone didn't even try to sit over the toilet. They just shat right there." I took her hand. It was a very touching moment.

This was not as bad as it got. A few weeks later, we were in Yangshuo, a picturesque city nestled in the mountains where backpackers bivouac before heading off to less accommodating points on the map. A woman named Peng took us on a bicycle tour of the countryside and then on to her ancestral home outside of town, where she prepared lunch over an open fire. Peng was a remarkable woman. She had learned English by listening to and speaking with the tourists who came to Yangshuo, many of whom had taken her tour. The first time we met her, she came at us waving a book of letters and photographs from other tourists who'd enjoyed the trip. At first, I was annoyed by her, then became smitten with her entrepreneurial spirit and ability to communicate with people from all walks of life. She had a young child and a husband in the army. When we asked her what her one dream in life was, she said, "To one day visit Beijing."

When we arrived at her stone and thatch home, I asked if I could use the toilet. She led me down a country lane until we reached a small cement hut with a door made from pieces of old fencing. She pointed inside and laughed: "I hope you're not afraid of pigs!"

Now, when you ask someone to use their washroom, the kind of reply you expect is, "Sure, just down to the left," or "Up the stairs, second door on your right." You're almost never told, "I hope you're not afraid of pigs!" When I opened the door, I looked in to find two pink hogs snuffling across the cement floor. Just opposite them was a sluice with a couple of wooden planks balanced over it. The sluice was a whitish-brown colour and I realized that this was Peng's toilet. The one thing it had going for it was an absence of fecal smell, although there was the pungent scent of eau de livestock, which might upset some, but not me. I positioned myself on the planks, took down my trousers, and did the deed. The pigs came up to me like dogs and sniffed my feet. I petted them, then looked between my feet to see clumps of maggots wriggling in the sluice. Flies buzzed around and the pigs snorted. Then I heard voices outside the hut. It was a tour group.

I could hear the tour guide chattering on, her voice getting louder. I looked through the slats in the door and saw about ten

German tourists gathered outside. One of them tried to look in, but she was too short. "What's in here?" she asked the girl. "No, Christ, no," I muttered. The pigs honked. The tourists walked away, and that's as bad as it got.

After Harbin, our destination was the biggest tourist trap in the world, The Great Wall. After four hours on a bus, we arrived, and several hundred vertical feet later, I found myself sitting atop a fifth-century BC stone ledge looking over a hillside, its terraces spotted with new snow, golden tufts of trees, and the bones of a long dead cable car. The Great Wall ran like vertebrae over the mountainside. The sight of it took me back to being ten years old and sitting at my desk in history class, running my thumb along the page titled "The Seven Wonders of the World: Great Wall of China." But as I sat on the wall in my toque, spitting sunflower seeds over the edge, taking in the beauty of the only man-made object visible from space, my thoughts turned from the monumental achievements of mankind to, well, to Johnny Bower.

I thought of him for two reasons. One, Johnny's nickname was the Great China Wall (a *nom de guerre* since bequeathed to Hong Guo, goalie for the Chinese women's team); and two, we were joined en route by a group of small, kerchiefed women from a nearby village who sold us Coke and water and packets of cookies and who, quite frankly, looked like the old Leafs netminder. Their faces were folded and pinched with age, as if they too might have been clubbed with the odd puck, and their teeth reminded me of broken toothpicks, slanting above wind-blistered lips and gums.

When they first showed up, Janet turned to me and said, "Oh-oh. We're about to be Walled." Along certain parts of the Wall the locals live off the tourists, and we figured we'd stumbled into one. But as is her way with total strangers, Janet was soon deep in conversation with them. This allowed me the opportunity to meditate on the ledge. I'm not talking the incense-candle-and-tinkling-synthesizer kind of meditation, but rather the kind where you're swept into your own thoughts by the sheer calm and beauty of the scene. The breeze made a gentle sound and there was a cold snap to it that reminded me of late autumn, that time when sticks are ferreted out of basements, skates are shorn of rust, gloves patched, sweaters pulled out of drawers, and cups and mouthguards washed, maybe. I wondered what was happening back home with my team. It was still winter in Toronto. I imagined the Morningstars climbing into their rusted cars, pulling toques over their heads, blasting their heaters, and rolling through the crunchy streets of the city to get to the rink. If the game was at St. Michael's Arena, they might thaw themselves while walking beside the back wall of the rink, which is lined with photographs of players who have competed there – everyone from Red Kelly to Gerry Cheevers, from Eric Lindros to Tim Horton. Before entering one of the dressing rooms – perhaps the Frank Mahovlich or Dave Keon room – they might think to themselves, "Shit. Syl Apps played there. Right there!" pointing at the blue line. In the dressing room they would hang up their coats, have a piss, tape their sticks, stone their skates, and fill the air with the kind of babble and wise-cracking you would have heard ninety years ago in the same place, until, one by one, the team walked out the door dressed in red and white.

I missed them. This trip meant having to give up my team for the season, and now I felt the pull of wanting to return. I went over to Janet to see if she was ready to leave, thinking that the sooner we left the Wall, the sooner I might return to skate with the guys. But she was busy talking to one of the women, and I resisted interrupting them. Janet was pointing and saying something and the woman was laughing.

"*Feng shuo*," said Janet, touching her ear.

"*Feng shou?*" repeated the woman.

"*Feng shuo.*"

"Ah! Ya!" said the woman, smiling.

"What's going on?" I asked Janet.

Her eyes were bright.

"I just told her, 'The wind is talking.'"

Janet was determined to find Ping Yao. I was reluctant, because no one could prove to me that it existed. My wife didn't say it, but I knew what she was thinking: "I've travelled half-way around the world with you so you can play hockey; you could at least let me try to find Ping Yao." It took three visits to the travel service office in Beijing before the travel agent located the town on a map; or rather found the space between two towns that the agent claimed was Ping Yao. I was wary of looking for a place that may not have existed, but Janet was convinced that it boded well if fewer people had heard of it.

We bought our train tickets and left Beijing.

We told our steward that we wanted off in Ping Yao. She nodded agreeably, but being a nervous traveller, I wasn't sure she'd understood the import of the question. So at each stop, I poked my head out of the berth.

"Ping Yao?"

She shook her head until finally, at around eight o'clock the following morning, she rapped on our berth. "Ping Yao! Ping Yao!" she exclaimed, pointing out the window. We had about twelve seconds to disembark.

The day was breaking as we leaped from the train and made our way to the city's stone walls. The four square walls were 1.5 kilometres long and 12 metres high and had been erected during the Ming dynasty (the town itself had been built in 770 BC in the Zhuo dynasty). The city built them equidistant from the centre of town to resemble the markings on a tortoise shell.

There were two sections of the wall over the city's main archways, and from there, you could take in all the activities of the town. Janet and I stood and watched as two dozen school children were led merrily out into the schoolyard by their teacher. "Look at the little peanuts!" exclaimed Janet. We expected to see a little hopscotch, maybe some four square, but instead the teacher lined them up, barked an instruction or two, and the kids pulled down their pants and peed sparkling streams of wet sunshine.

On the other side of the wall, cars, bicycles, horses and buggies, auto-rickshaws, rickshaws, mules, and mopeds passed through the narrow, unpaved streets. Almost always, the scooters were driven by fashionable young women whose look seemed drawn from Swingin' London of the early 1960s: teased-hair, pantsuits, and high heels. At one point, an old man in rags climbed off his horse to talk to a woman with crimped black hair who was dressed head-to-toe in a long purple coat with fur collar and cuffs. She wore striking red lipstick and looked like a moll. The old man chewed on his cigarette and patted his shaggy horse, which had been hauling pots of fresh manure. Chickens clucked at their feet. An auto-rickshaw sputtered past and children played in the road. The woman drew a long cigarette from her purse, smoked it languorously, and then climbed on her moped. She sped away in a cloud of purple dust like a Bond fatale exiting the scene.

After navigating the rest of the wall, Janet checked her watch, and realized that we'd missed our train. Since the next train left in twenty hours, we had no choice but to scope out digs for the night.

The first hotel we found was the Ju Guang Ju. We ended up staying there for three days. From the outside, it looked like a grey office building from the 1950s, but behind its tall glass doors were three storeys of velvet chairs, glass chandeliers, and friendly young hostesses in burgundy and taupe suits, their matching hats angled like airline stewardesses' from the 1970s. The proprietors of the hotel wore pinstriped jackets and had waves of slick black hair. One of them was short and fat and looked like the Buddy Hackett of the Far East. There was a kitchen at the rear of the hotel and, during lunch and dinner, the lobby turned into a restaurant where you could watch everyone's comings and goings, and they could observe you. At times, the sight of us stopped patrons in their tracks. They'd stand a few feet away and stare at us. There were more people at any given hour in the Ju Guang than there appeared to be in the town. It was a hive of activity where all classes of Chinese rubbed elbows. Yokels passing on bicycles stopped in to sup at the lobby's bar, and old men in slippers, who looked like they'd just walked off a Workers Party poster, sat in deep chairs sipping green tea. There was a small military base in town, so platoons of soldiers would arrive after nightfall and head to large rooms upstairs. We could see them through the windows pouring each other shots of pure grain alcohol from mysterious bottles bearing a gold seal.

One evening, about twenty children filed into a dining room upstairs. A few minutes later, a hostess brought them a platter of fried chicken, trailing salty vapours. We spooled in our tongues long enough to call her over and point to two words in our phrase book: "fried" and "chicken." She nodded, and five minutes later brought us a fried chicken, complete with head, neck, and feet. We ate it with chopsticks. It was delicious.

Another time, I saw a plate of french fries being carried across the room. I ordered them immediately. It was ten in the morning but it didn't matter. We'd eaten so much good food – Peking duck, spicy mutton and eggplant, dumpling soup, hot pork buns made with fresh coriander, and stewed ham-hocks – that I craved some-thing fast and wrong and greasy from the West. The french fries arrived. They were slathered in maraschino cherries.

I spent one afternoon at the hotel reading the sports page, an activ-ity of which I'll never tire. I'd culled it from the *International Herald Tribune*, which I'd bought for seven dollars (US) at the Beijing Inter-Continental. I had resisted reading it until I could no longer go without sporting news and, in the isolation of Ping Yao, I was desperate. I'd brought along a taped broadcast of Prime-Time Sports – a twice-a-week sports talk show out of Toronto – which I listened to on my Walkman while lying in bed. When it was done, I flicked over to the radio, and searched the dial. In Ireland in 1985, I'd come across an orphan Armed Forces broadcast of the Cardinals versus the Mets, and it had been a feast for my ears. But now, from the top to the bottom of the dial, nothing but silence. There was no radio in Ping Yao.

The only report of hockey in the *Trib* sports was a column of numbers no thicker than a blade of grass: game summaries of

mid-week matches played ten days earlier. But it was enough to get
me through. Summaries are to hockey fans what hieroglyphs are to
archaeologists. To the untrained eye, they are just names and
numbers, but once you know what to look for, they evoke the images,
sounds, and feelings that bring the games to life. Summaries tell
stories. They have, as poet Mark Cochrane says, their own arithmetic.

The paper was dated March 22, 1999. It began: "BUFFALO 3,
RANGERS 2." I filled in the blanks and provided my own commen-
tary. *No Gretzky. Must still be injured.* "Satan for Buffalo." *Were Satan
running for mayor, that might be his bumper sticker: SATAN FOR
BUFFALO. Miro Satan looks Manchurian, but he comes from
Czechoslovakia.* "Mathieu Schneider for the Rangers": *the Jewish-
American defenceman with the French-Canadian first-name. Was a Leaf.
Hated by teammates. Saw him once in Toronto at Alice Fazooli's, eating
dinner with his agent. Hockey players live lonely lives, too.* "From Graves
and Leetch": *Leetch, sweet Leetch; Dave Shaw once said that Brian Leetch
was the greatest player he'd ever played with. Likable on the ice. The kind
of guy who'd stop to help you change a tire. Not a scratch on him, either.
Elusive. Norris winner. To the Hall of Fame?* "Nedved for Rangers.
Grosek." *And* "In overtime: Satan carries the day." *Satan Carries the
Day.* "From Barnes and Shannon," *one of the brothers, not sure which
one.* "Shots on goal in overtime for New York: none. In goal for Buffalo:
Hasek." *The Dominator. His parents took him to the doctor when he was
young because his legs were so flexible he couldn't walk right. So goes the
tale. After being caught driving under the influence, he met the press in
Buffalo to explain his new resolve:* "Next time I drink that much, I take
cab!", *missing the point my friend, Kyle, got, that you're not supposed to
drink that much.* "In goal for Rangers: Richter." *Hung with the loss. I
once saw him with a bag of ice like a beaverpelt taped to his shoulder.
Peewee. An accent like a Bowery Boy.*

"OTTAWA 2, DALLAS 1." *I forget that Ottawa has a hockey team. I
forget how good they are.* "Sydor for Dallas. From Modano, Zubov." *
Zubov: a great drummer's name.* "Ottawa: Dackell, from Van Allen and
Martins." *Who are these guys? There are so many players in the NHL, it's
impossible to know half of them. Dackell. Is he good? Twelfth goal. He's
okay. Satan has 32.* "Hossa, Ottawa. Third period scoring: none." *Check*

the shots on goal total. "I shot for Ottawa, 13 for Dallas." The Sens rolled up like a rug bug and took what the Stars threw at them. Typical '90s Trap hockey. "Damian Rhodes in goal." Goalie with a lisp. Was a Leaf. Backed up Potvin, but we gave him up to get Muller, or was it Clark? "For Dallas: Belfour." Tough. Some wise guy once said, "All the Manitoba goalies were the toughest guys on their team." Terry Sawchuk, Ron Hextall. Belfour looks like he shits nails.

And so it went. As I sat there musing my way across the NHL, a hostess brought me coffee, beer, and tea, feeding the connection. Even though I was a great distance from these games, I could see the players and hear the crowds and feel the flow of the action. I could imagine what every goal looked like from the patterns and references I'd memorized over the years, the same way musicians can hear a song after it is described to them in detail. It was quite a breakthrough for someone who'd grown so tired of pro hockey. Even though I was sitting in a hotel on the middle of the Chinese plain, I didn't feel very far from the league at all. For now, it had survived the stretch.

Later that day, Janet and I left the hotel and walked down the main street towards town. Shopkeepers stood in their windows and pointed. Little children cried "Hello!" and, when we answered in Chinese, they laughed and ran away. On our way, we came upon ten pool tables lined up on the sidewalk. The tables were old and weather-beaten, in varying states of disrepair. No one was using them, so I gestured to a young fellow nearby who was wok-cooking outside a noodle house. I pointed to one of the cues and he handed it to me. He racked the balls with his arms, then picked up a cue. He waved me to the end of the table. I broke.

The game was on.

The balls were scuffed and cracked and speckled with mud. There were crosses of silver tape on the table where the balls were supposed to be spotted, and the bunkers were sloped and weathered and dead. My cue was bowed worse than an underwater weed,

Pool in Ping Yao

with no sign that it had ever once been kissed by chalk. The table lurched right, left, then right again, so you almost had to miscalculate the angles in order to make a decent shot.

We played two games and the young fellow was clearly the more clever player. A crowd gathered – kids, young women on their way home from work, greybeards, a couple of local hoods, rounders, a very dirty smiling fellow in rags (possibly deranged), some men in military jackets with gold, star-shaped epaulets – locking their eyes on the ball whenever I was about to strike it, or not strike it, as was often the case. A mule brayed. A rickshaw driver rang his bell. After a while, my opponent's mother stuck her head out of the noodle shop and barked his name, so he handed his cue to a friend, a young fellow with windblown hair who proceeded to kick my ass worse than the cook had. I lost two more games, badly. Everyone could tell who the mook was.

In the next game, he let me off the hook, but I blew it. He played all the angles right (that is to say, wrong) and ran away with the game until he missed his last two shots. A little bit of light shone under the door. I sunk one ball, another, then another, but missed an easy shot in the end pocket. Once I closed the door on my own

foot, he wrapped up the game and I placed my cue on the table. But he handed it back to me and we played on.

By now, there were fifty or sixty people watching us. I nodded to my first opponent, who had returned from preparing a dish for one of his patrons, a hunched mandarin with a moustache as long as my arm who dined at a small wooden table in front of the shop. He took the cue from his friend and broke. It was a bad shot, and he slapped his head with the flat of his hand, a bit of comic relief. I held up my arms and stuck out my tongue. Why I did this, I don't know. The gallery laughed. I was headed for better things.

I banked a shot, then a second, a third, missed, and after a little push and pull, I was left with one shot before the eight ball. I leaned across the table and struck the cue ball hard. It popped off the stick and pinballed around the green baize, hitting four bunkers before landing against the target. The ball dived into the pocket and the crowd ohhhhhed. The shot had been played perfectly, if by accident. I counted my blessings, then walked around the table stalking the eight ball, which lay at the end of the stretch.

My opponent sighed, then laughed. It was the so-here-is-a-visitor-from-the-West-with-a-chance-to-vanquish-his-Chinese-opponent laugh. Enough to add a little pressure; to twist me, just so. His friend leaned against a wall and picked his teeth. He gave me a quick smile, then looked away.

It was an eight ball for the world. The crowd represented China and I represented everywhere else. There was Canada, the United States, the Faroe Islands, Tonga, right there on my back. The circle of onlookers tightened against the table. Children pressed their fingers to their mouths. An old fellow sipped tea from a glass jar. The sun glinted off someone's gold teeth. The deranged man giggled and clasped his hands. I drew the stick back, looked up, down, up again, then measured the shot and breathed.

Thrack!

I sank the bastard.

I thanked my opponents and headed back to the hotel. The crowd melted. The sun dipped below the wall, and night fell upon us.

"How'd I do?" I asked Janet, walking beside me.

"You didn't need a phrase book," she said.

"I mean my playing."

"I know, but you didn't need a phrase book. There was a common language. You both knew the rules and you reacted to each other," she said.

"I beat them one game. They beat me five," I conceded.

"Ya, but there was constant dialogue, even though none of you spoke."

"Did you hear the crowd go 'Ohhhhh!' when I sank that ball?"

"You mean the shot that you didn't really mean to make?"

"Ya. That one."

"I heard it. Very nice, dear."

PART TWO

The United Arab Emirates

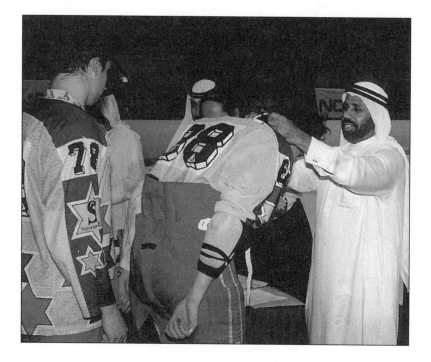

13

MERLIN SNOWS THE DESERT

My Koho shot down the baggage chute at Dubai International Airport dressed like a prop in a Christmas parade. When we left Hong Kong the baggage handler at the airport had decorated it in the colours of a candy cane, so you couldn't miss it. What was once just glossy blond wood, black lettering, and fibreglass ripple had been made over into a showy staff. The attendant had plastered red *Fragile* stickers over the curve of the blade – creating a snug, paper sockette for those 40,000-foot chills – and had stapled a cardboard *Fragile* flag to the shaft. Elton John might choose such a stick were he equipping himself for a pickup hockey game. It was beautiful, but I feared that two thugs in jumpsuits would grab the stick at the other end of the baggage chute and bash it to pieces.

But it was fine, so we collected the rest of our luggage and headed towards the taxi stand, where we were stopped by a cop who wanted to know what we were doing in Dubai. By cop, I mean a teenager in a red beret and blue uniform waving a handgun.

"I'm here to play hockey," I told him.

"There is no ice hockey here!" he said.

"Yes, there is. The Mighty Camels."

"Field hockey, yes, but I have never heard of ice hockey."

"You're sure?"

"In the UAE? Impossible!"

"But the tournament starts tomorrow."

The soldier scrunched his face.

"Really: hockey," I implored

"You are crazy," he said, waving his gun towards the door.

It was nightfall. Outside the entrance to the airport, a hundred men were standing around. I thought I'd stumbled upon a Sheik look-alike contest. I hope I'm not tempting the fatwa here, but back home whenever I encountered a man in robes, I assumed he was an oil baron with many wives. The sight of so many berobed men in one place confused me, until I realized that you don't have to be worth $70 million to dress this way. All of them were tall and dark-skinned, with thick torsos and moustaches. They were draped in flowing robes coloured light blue, cinnamon, pearl, and lavender, and walked around with placards held over their heads with the names of hotels and their guests scrawled in pen. I looked for the Al Khaleej sign, but when I found it, it was the wrong Al Khaleej. "No, you want the other Al Khaleej," the fellow told me. When I asked him how he knew it was the wrong hotel, his reply was "Is your last name Sanji? Are you Mr. Sanji? Do you know Mr. Sanji?" He was the size of a garage and upset that I'd asked.

When planning my trip, I thought it only fitting that, while living the life of a hockey nomad, I visit a country where nomadic life had been a given for thousands of years. The UAE was Bedouin country. Bedouin tribes had dominated Emirate lands for centuries, in par-ticular the Bani Yas tribal confederation, whose descendants were now the ruling families of Abu Dhabi and Dubai. Theirs had been a culture of camel herding, small-scale farming, and falconry. For hundreds of years they'd co-existed with the Portuguese and the British, not to mention migrant caravans from whom the Bani used to extract money. They were a wandering people who moved from place to place in search of pasture. One of their folk heroes was one Ahmed Bin Majed, a fifteenth-century adventurer who sailed around the world looking for peace and writing poetry. He lived by the creed: Love goodness and hate evil. Here was a people who might understand my quest.

When I first decided to come to the desert in search of Canada's game, I cast myself in the role of a treasure-seeker in pursuit of a rare and magnificent bounty. I dreamed of meeting dry-land swash-bucklers with silver teeth and, when I read that the British had once dubbed the UAE area the Pirate Coast, I was struck with visions from *The Thousand and One Nights*: gold-laced tents, torchlit marches, sandstorms, beautiful veiled girls playing finger cymbals, fried lizard, tea-drinking sultans travelling by carriage, machetes slung low through their belts. The Temple of Doom, Sinbad versus the Cyclops, Johnny Quest. Peter O'Toole. A flaming heaven of sun and sand.

So when I first walked out of the Dubai airport, I hoped against hope that I'd be greeted upon arrival by a gathering of wrinkle-faced migrants riding camels and looking at my stick quizzically, then retreating in awe as I stickhandled a deck of smokes. But, except for their robes, the men outside the airport couldn't have been more different. They all drove minivans, and their job was to shepherd guests to their hotels. There was not a falcon or a cutlass in sight. And when we finally located our man from the proper Al Khaleej, our drive into the city deflated my dream of finding a shimmering desert town. We passed retail promenades, car dealerships, hotels, office towers, bars, discos, restaurants, and a proliferation of bowling alleys. Dubai looked more like a North American city than Lawrence's Arabia. They'd built Regina on the red sand.

But this impression did not last. In our hotel room, I opened the drapes and saw a winding street, bustling with men and women in robes and sandals and lined with shops the colour of chalk and sand: Al Jabar Optical Centre, the New Avon, the Crystal Cup Trading Company, the Victoria Hotel, Tunlees Watches, Khaleed Jewelry, Mariana Hotel, the Hatam Restaurant. All the signs were in English and Arabic. Even at this late hour, the street buzzed with life. The Al Khaleej was in the heart of Dubai, not, thank goodness, its new outskirts. Downtown Dubai, in fact, wasn't even called Dubai, but

Deira. The city's two regions, Bur Dubai and Deira, were separated
by a river that flowed to the Persian Gulf, plied by dhows and abras
(motorized water taxis) carrying tourists to the other side, and ships
transporting goods to and from ports as far away as Bombay. We
stood on the balcony and felt a hint of cool coming from the water,
a breeze pushed along by the Arabian Sea.

Dubai came alive when the sun disappeared, for it was too hot to
do anything during the day. The evening was soft and steamy, the
sky was the colour of grape juice, and it hung low, spilling out to
the horizon. I was reminded of the richness of the midsummer
prairie sky, and this wasn't the last time the UAE would evoke the
Canadian prairie. Both places were old, flat, dry, and built upon
buried rivers of fossil fuel. And both were hotbeds of hockey.

Among the first things I did when I got to Dubai was to telephone Chris Reynolds, one of the fathers of Arabian hockey. Chris
was a Calgarian whose architectural firm had won the commission
to build the Jumiera Beach Hotel, Sheik Maktoum's waterfront
monument to himself, complete with heliport and rooms at $2,000
a night. During his relocation in 1992, Chris had organized the
Mighty Camels Hockey Tournament, in which I'd be playing.
Together with Abdullah, the chairman of the UAE Ice Hockey
Committee, whom I'd met in Hong Kong, Chris had put Arabian
hockey on the map. He made Dubai the focus of the desert game
by bringing together teams from Bahrain, Dhahran, Riyadh, and
Kuwait. Even though Arabian hockey was still so small it had yet
to be acknowledged by either the North American or European
hockey communities (there was no Arab membership in the IIHF,
nor an entry in *Total Hockey*), Chris had done the near impossible:
he'd conjured hockey on the scorched plain like some kind of
sporting Merlin.

On our first morning in Dubai, we attended a press conference
where Chris announced the start of the Mighty Camels tournament, officially known as the '99 Nokia International Ice Hockey

Tournament. In China, I was usually troubled whenever hockey was referred to as "ice" hockey, but over here, it seemed a sensible thing to do seeing that a more likely use for ice would be to rub it across your neck and forehead. I'd tried convincing both Wang Lu and Tom Barnes not to call the sport ice hockey if they hoped to gain credibility in Canada, but I didn't press the issue with Chris. Besides, having the word "ice" in it probably helped sell the game in Arabia, where a rink was the perfect place to escape the awesome heat of the desert.

Standing on a street corner trying to hail a taxi to take us to the press conference at Al Nasr Leisureland, we nearly melted in the sun. For those first few minutes I felt I was being assaulted.

"I feel like there's an oven on my head," said Janet, shading herself with the flat of her hand.

"Taxi!" I yowled.

"Shade. I need shade," she choked.

"Taxi!"

"It's like there's a giant foot pressing down. A giant wool foot!"

"*Taxi!*"

"My eyebrows are on fire!"

And so on. The sun attacked without mercy, as if it carried a grudge ("*Turn away, foolish visitors, or suffer the wrath of the Sun King!*"). I thought the bill of my baseball cap would burst into flames. I finally waved down a cab, and we scrambled inside, sucking the air-conditioned air as if we'd just run a marathon.

"Are you here for shopping week?" asked the driver.

"No," I said, debating whether to tell him the reason for our visit.

"Shopping week is very popular!" he said.

"What goes on?" I asked him.

"It is very popular. Buying. People buying. The souk. The gold souk. You are going?"

The gold souk was one of Dubai's most popular tourist attractions. Souks are canvas-covered markets where spices, fabric, and all varieties of goods are sold. The souks were the centrepieces of the Dubai Shopping Festival '99, an event made necessary by the fact that, since Dubai City has only been around since 1971, there are few anniversaries of revolutions or military conquests to cause public holidaying. The Shopping Fest drew visitors from around the world. For one month, every clock radio, T-shirt, handbag, and solid-gold miniature Corvette was discounted, turning the town into an endless bargain table. Street posters asked "HAVE YOU EVER SEEN A CITY ON SALE?" and commanded "SHOP UNTIL YOU DROP!" You can imagine what this did to my dream of finding tents made from animal hair, men with cracked brown teeth, and flatbread cooking over a open pit.

The Mighty Camels tournament was part of the festival, which included a ton of other events. Draws were held daily at which cars, furs, and money were given away. There was the Iron Man of Oman competition (whose winner would have the satisfaction of walking into any bar on earth and proclaiming: "I am the Iron Man of Oman! Beer me!"), the dhow sailing race, the Dubai arm-wrestling competition, beach soccer for seniors, and bowling for the disabled. The city put up water slides and staged concerts by James Brown and the Temptations. Thousands of ex-pats working in the Middle East came for the festival and to take in some of the city's hundreds of clubs, the only venues in Dubai licensed to serve liquor, banned in most Muslim countries.

Most of these clubs were located in hotels, and during Shopping Week they operated at full tilt. When I arrived at the Al Khaleej, I pored over my complimentary copy of *What's On* and discovered that Dubai was some kind of lounge-band purgatory. The names of the groups were like those you'd find on the marquees of Holiday Inns: the Real Deal, Nightshift (playing at 49er's), Denise Fuller ("a pleasant change from her previous stint at Disney World, Orlando. In addition to tinkling the ivories, Denise will be offering ballet instruction to the fleet of foot"), D'Friends, Touch (performing at Bugsy's), Joker, the Surprise Trio ("Guitarist Nick's Carlos Santana, Jimi Hendrix, and Jimmy Page impersonations – and his tendency to jump disconcertingly close to the low ceiling – does the trick"), Two's Company ("Veterans of the South African music scene"), Roger Goldfinger Yarwood, Billy International, Side Effects, the Rage

Duo (at Biggles), Slip of the Tongue, Prime Jive, Ozone, the Rubettes (appearing at the Inter-Continental in Muscat), the Johnny Duo, Express ("Live and direct from Poland!"), Finnegan's Blind Date, Grafite, and Atco West, after which was written, "Diners tempted to strut their stuff are also invited to have a go at line dancing with instructor Mohammed Sherif."

The taxi pulled up in front of Al Nasr Leisureland, a long, flat building with an unlit neon portrait of a penguin holding a parasol. We made our way inside to a second-floor restaurant above the rink, where pictures of Indian film stars lined the hallways, the influence of the UAE's large South Asian population, nine per cent of whom were Pakistani. There was a head table set up in the restaurant with a couple of microphones and some tournament programs. I picked up one and read "Dave Bidini, Canadian" under the heading "Beijing." Chris had arranged that I would play with a team from the Chinese capital, a collection of ex-pats working in Beijing with whom Steve Chiu played weeknight hockey at the Chinese National Sports Centre. The tournament's other teams were listed as well: the Abu Dhabi Blades, Riyadh Rangers, Bahrain Buds, Dubai Mighty Camels, Dhahran Saad Falcons, Kuwait Mooseheads, Ticino Tigers, and EHC Meinisberg (the last two hailing from Switzerland), as well the Al Ain Falcons, who were, more or less, the UAE national team. Nasser. Mohammed. Ahmed. Juma. Kareem. Omar. The young heroes of Arabian hockey.

Chris Reynolds walked into the room, followed by Abdullah. Chris asked if I'd say a few words to the press about why I was here and what I'd seen of Arabian hockey in Hong Kong. Abdullah said, "You'll mention our victory, I hope."

"Of course. Do you want me to mention you?"

"These people know who I am," he said.

Three reporters came into the room and settled at a table opposite the dais. Waiters poured water and passed around plates of ginger cookies. We were joined by a Swiss forward named Marzio Brambillo. He used to play in the UAE's domestic league, which was made up of the Abu Dhabi Blades, Al Ain Falcons, Dubai Red

Chris and Abdullah

Wings, and Dubai Nokia. Their scoring leaders were printed in the program and, although dominated by North Americans, Juma Al Dhaheri and Omar Al Shamsi stood fifth and sixth.

When Chris called the conference to order, there were ten, maybe twelve people in the room, including three reporters, a print photographer, a handful of waiters, and one television cameraman. We each said a little something. Chris mentioned the tourney's sponsors, Nokia, many times, and stressed that the tourney was in its seventh year and was a sanctioned part of the Dubai Shopping Festival, to which the fifth estate nodded its heads approvingly. He said that there would be 144 players participating in this year's tournament, a new record, and that skaters from as far away as Canada, China, and Finland would be competing. Then he passed the microphone to me. "We have a Canadian right here with us," he said, at which the fifth estate finally opened its notepads.

I did my best imitation of a diplomat. *Unity through sport. Shared culture. Meeting of minds.* Having been on the other end of these speeches, I stole a glance at the reporters to see if they were writing anything down, but I was doing little to move them. I finished, then Chris wrapped things up, but not before Abdullah reached in for the mic after my speech and said, "Dave was at the tournament in Hong Kong. He will tell you, if you'd like, about seeing the UAE team play." Abdullah passed the mic back to Chris and shot me a look. I'd forgotten to mention the Nats. Janet sat in a corner chewing a nail, wondering whether I'd pissed off the big man. Maybe there would be a story in that.

Chris asked if there were any questions, but the press had none. They closed their notepads and, like all good reporters, reached for the ginger cookies. It wasn't until I read both the *Gulf News* and the *Khaleej Times* that I realized that these writers weren't being rude or lazy. Judging by the size of their sports sections, the poor fellows were chronically over-worked. The April 6 edition of the *Times* was a killer. It ran stories on the Pakistani cricket team in town for the Coca-Cola Cup, the Australia versus West Indies cricket match in St. John's, Antigua, the Adidas Soccer Cup in Abu Dhabi, the Inter-Continental Aquatics championships, local power-boating politics ("The marine sports community has hailed the decree of his Highness Sheik Hamad bin Mohammed Al Sharqi, Member of the Supreme Council and Ruler of Fujairah, regarding the incorpora-tion of Fujairah International Marine Sports Club"), the Jebel Ali race course, UAE rally driver Khalifa Al Mutaywi (winner of the Golden Sword), the International Bowling championships ("the UAE women bowlers were exempt from participation fees to give maxi-mum opportunity to gain experience"), the Crown Prince of Abu Dhabi's support of bowling ("the Federation has decided to engrave his picture on the trophy"), the Golden Flake tennis cham-pionships, UAE mini-motorcross, National Football League (the Arabian one), Bell South Classic golf tourney, Davis Cup tennis, the Grand National, English League soccer, the NHL ("WINGS BLAST STARS"), and, of course, the NBA, complete with black-and-white and colour photos.

After the press conference ended, the manager of the restaurant came over and introduced himself. He had a Sergei Berezin mullet that hung down his back. He was from India and told me that he had relatives in Toronto. One day he hoped to move to Canada and work there.

"I am an enterprising type, like a Canadian."

"Canadians are enterprising?" I said, raising my eyebrows.

"Well, you are the enterprising type, coming to the UAE to play hockey!"

"Ya, I guess so."

"Truly."

"Thank you."

"It is no problem. Only my enterprise did not turn out quite the way yours has."

"How so?"

"Well, it is a humorous story. Humorous for you, but not me. You see, last year I decided that what Dubai really needed at Christmas time were Christmas trees. So I went around to a few stores and they said it would be a great thing to have a tree in their shop during the holidays. In Dubai, there are many Americans, British, and Germans – people who celebrate Christmas.

"So I ordered hundreds of trees. Beautiful, tall, trees, straight from Canada. But when I went around to rent them out, most of the hotels and stores said, 'No. We can only use these trees for a few days, because of Ramadan. How do you think our other customers will feel if we put this tree up, but not something for them as well?' I am Indian, yet I did not see this. I wanted to bring Christmas to the UAE – it was my goal – but no one wanted my trees. I was left with hundreds of them, not to mention a very substantial bill."

"Well, I guess it's a one-step-at-a-time deal," I said. "First, they get hockey. And then, Christmas. The next thing you know, you'll be walking around in a white beard and red suit."

"Yes. Perhaps if the people like the hockey, they'll demand Christmas."

"Do you notice more people getting into hockey?"

"A small number, yes."

"When did people start to get interested?"

"Oh, it was back in 1979, when the British built the Al Nasr rink. Many people think it was the sheiks who built it, perhaps the

Canadians. But no, it was the British Petroleum Company. They wanted to give their employees some pleasurable activity."

"Hockey? The British?"

"Well, not hockey. Ice skating."

"When did they start to play hockey?"

"You'd have to ask one of the players," he said. "Perhaps the Colonel could tell you."

I asked Abdullah, who referred me to Ala Ghanem, an occasional member of the Arab Nats who'd taken it upon himself to document the history of hockey in the UAE. Ghanem told me: "It wasn't the British at all. No, at first there was the Al Nasr sports club, which was chaired by Sheik Manaa Al Maktoum, who decided to open a leisure club adjacent to the main football grounds to serve the growing ex-pat population. The club opened its doors to exclusive members in 1979. It contained a swimming pool with a wave maker and an out-standing, larger-than-life fibreglass fruit garden, which was very popular with families and children. Al Nasr had more bars than any other sports club, as well as an eight-lane bowling centre. The club included a North-American-sized ice-skating rink, but the ice-hockey lines were not laid down until a Canadian fellow – I can't remember his name – suggested that they introduce the game in Dubai. His suggestion was accepted; the Sheik is an educated man and he was conscious of being the first proponent of hockey in the UAE.

"This was the start of the Dubai hockey league. The first teams were the Dubai Penguins, made up of Arab players; the Vikings (Swedish and other Scandinavians); the Dugas Oilers (Canadians, mostly from Alberta); and the Tigers, who comprised all nationalities, but mostly British. It was dynamic, full-contact hockey, and we pulled great crowds. As far as I can remember, we've never had the kind of crowds we had in the beginning.

"Soon, we developed three divisions of hockey: peewees, juniors, and seniors. The coaching was done by expatriates who volunteered. Several of the kids went on to play college hockey. Over the years, many teams from Europe came to play in Dubai, among them a team from Finland, as well as the German Red Devils from

Frankfurt. But by the end of 1985, hockey started a spiral descent due to ex-pats leaving the country, a result of the drop in oil prices and the economy. Those who stayed lost interest, or switched to golf when the first world-class course was opened here.

"Then, in the early '90s, a new breed of hockey enthusiasts arrived on UAE soil, and the game was reborn. We competed in Hong Kong and won our division. The popularity of ice hockey is growing in the Middle East, with three more rinks planned here, as well as one in Jordan and one in Egypt."

It was a longer story than I'd imagined. Already, the UAE had a hockey history, and soon they could start planning their Hall of Fame. "No one ever thought we would see hockey here in the UAE," the restaurant manager told me. "Even skating was strange to us at first. We'd never seen it before."

"Did you ever think the UAE would have a national hockey team?"

"Of course not. I remember the first few days the ice was in, there were people – Bedouins – still living in the desert. They came in from the sand just to see if it was true. They wanted to see for themselves that ice could be made on the desert. I remember their faces, their eyes. One day, a whole family came in. They were astonished. They walked out near the benches and reached down and they touched the ice. They couldn't believe it was real."

14

JOURNEY TO THE TEMPLE OF THE DOG

My first day at the Mighty Camels tournament started with a cab ride to the tournament's other rink: Hili Fun City in Al Ain, a town one hour west of Dubai. My journey began at a hotel on the other side of town, where I hooked up with Team Beijing. It was an inauspicious introduction. The first skaters I met were Lyle Hartley from Saskatchewan, and John Davy, a soft-spoken British Columbian who had come from Riyadh, where his wife worked as a doctor, to referee the games. They were both middle-aged, so I assumed that Team Beijing (the tournament would pass without us ever having a moniker) would be close to the Foxes in age and ability, but when the rest of the team arrived, most were in their mid-twenties. They looked in good shape, if a little tired or hungover, their hockey bags slung over their shoulders like small children rescued from a fire.

They were more like real hockey players than any of the Foxes. This troubled me slightly. Even though I may comport myself like a typical player, I do not mix well with just any group. Forced into an atmosphere of bubbling testosterone and machismo, I'm reminded of the worst of my youth: denim stoner jocks throwing me to the ground in front of their feather-haired girlfriends, who leaned against the portable and laughed in hiccups. Jocks who won Best Athlete awards, flaunting their abilities in Sunday morning house-league ice games, yelling at me for not keeping up, their bodies muscling into shape, emerging confidently, lords of the hallways, calling the weak faggots and queers.

I extended my hand to one of the players, an American named Andrew.

"Hey."

"Hey. I thought you guys would be a lot older," I said.

"Why?"

"I played up in Harbin with this American team, the Foxes. Most of them were in their sixties, some might have even been older. They were grey-haired, well-off. They were nice enough to let me play, but I couldn't really relate to them. Half of them had Roman numerals after their names."

"Oh ya? I've got one after mine," he said.

"Ya, but . . ." I said, backing up.

"And I know the Foxes, too. Some of them played with us in Beijing. Helen's father's team, right?"

"Ya. Reeve Schley."

"Ya. Reeve," he said, looking away.

Most of the team rode in a bus that Chris had rented. It was too small to carry everyone, so Lyle, John, Janet, and I hired a taxi to take us to Al Ain. It was the first time I'd been in the desert and I was thrilled. As we left the city, the ivory buildings of downtown Deira grew smaller, and soon all the concrete and asphalt turned to rippled red sand. Unlike Saskatchewan's unbroken gold and green, the Arabian prairie changed every few klicks, from barren flatland to writhing dunes to rusty mounds spiked with afros of green. We drove past two young, male hitchhikers standing along the shoulder of the highway. They were dressed in celadon and pale-blue robes that swooshed like summer laundry as we passed. Behind them, camels stood still as boxcars on the rough plain. The sun blazed in the milky sky. Burkas. Wooden teeth. Falcons hunting their prey. I was getting closer.

Having lived in the Middle East, Lyle and John had seen it all before, but Janet and I pressed our faces to the window.

"What do you guys do for a living?" asked John.

"I'm a musician," I said. "A writer, too. Sort of."

"Me, I'm at my leisure," said Janet.

"What kind of music do you play?" asked John.

"Oh, a little bit of everything . . ."

"I'm in music, too. At least I was, before I started my career as a referee."

"Where did you ref?"

"The NHL."

"The NHL?"

"Ten years, 1986 to 1996. You might not know me because they gave me a lot of games in the United States, in the south. I did a lot of mid-week and secondary market games."

"Where?"

"Dallas, St. Louis, Florida. Los Angeles."

"What was your most memorable game?" I asked.

"That would have to be the time I gave Wayne Gretzky a ten-minute misconduct."

"You gave Gretzky a misconduct?"

"I had to."

"What happened?"

"He skated over to me and said, 'Do you know what the fuck you're doing?'"

"And you gave him a misconduct?"

"Yup."

"The league must have been pissed!"

"They weren't too happy. Neither was Wayne."

We all laughed, including the cab driver, who wouldn't have known Wayne Gretzky from Wayne Newton. Just as John finished his story, the radio in the taxi locked onto the signal of a Dubai pop station, and the opening bell chimes and descending notes of Blur's "Country House" filled the speakers. To appreciate how amazing this sounded, it doesn't matter whether you like Blur or whether you've even heard of them. But understand: this was the first bit of rock and roll I'd heard in weeks, not counting the thirty-second sound clips at SkyRink and Festival Walk. I was elated. The song exploded out of the radio as we cut loose on the highway. My head swam. I air-drummed and mouthed the words.

"You like this song?" asked John.

"This fucking song rules!"

The taxi driver laughed and showed us his brown teeth.

"We haven't heard any rock and roll since we left Canada," said Janet, staring out the window. "All they listen to in China is the Carpenters."

"Oh no," said John, shaking his head.

It was true. The only Western band we'd heard on the Chinese mainland were the Carpenters. On one particularly torturous taxi ride to the airport in Guilin, I was held captive by a young woman who drove the whole way thirty miles an hour in first gear and forced us to sit through *The Carpenters Greatest Hits* album. It made me feel like I was being dipped into a cauldron of boiling lead.

"Well, I hear there's lots of good music in Dubai," said John.

"Most of the bands here look pretty schmaltzy," I confessed.

"It depends on what you like, I guess."

"What do you like?" I asked.

"Oh, lots. I produced lots of different bands."

"You were a producer?"

"Yes. And an engineer."

"As well as being a ref?"

"The refereeing came after."

John Davy had worked at BJ Sound and LaBrea Studios – two of America's best studios – in the 1970s before refereeing for the National Hockey League. When I asked him which groups he'd produced, the first name he mentioned was the Allman Brothers, the pioneering Southern rock band of the '60s and '70s. I looked at him disbelievingly.

"You worked with the Allmans?"

"Yup. Dickey Betts solo, too."

"Did you know Skydog?"

"Yes. I knew Skydog."

Skydog is the name that Wilson Pickett gave Duane Allman. The name is shorthand among music fans. You drop "Skydog" and the right people know who you're talking about. They can read your musical tastes. Skydog made me think of Gord Cumming, the person who introduced me to the Allman Brothers. The first time I heard Skydog's name, Gord said it. He was a reservoir of musical knowledge, and I spent the greater part of the 1980s at his place listening to music I'd never heard before, discovering books I didn't know existed. One night, he reached under the coffee table in his living room and pulled out a copy of Paul Quarrington's *Home Game*, a novel about a baseball game between a team of circus freaks and a team of monks playing for possession of a town. It was life-altering stuff. Gord also got me into W.P. Kinsella, Thomas Boswell, Ed Linn, and David Carkeet, writers who wrote about the spirituality of sports, sports as life. If I hadn't been shown these books, I probably never would have come to the desert.

It was Gord who gave me the idea of exploring hockey beyond the television screen. Together, we hatched the idea of experiencing the NHL from a place other than our seats on the couch. We decided to take our fandom into the realm of the absurd. We were inspired to do this by Pat Riggin, the small ex-Bruin goaltender who, during the 1984 world championships, said that he was "sick and tired of Americans taking away jobs from Canadians in the NHL" (five years before Tiger Williams claimed, "Americans are taking over the game. When I broke in there were two Americans, now there are sixty of the bastards"). Riggin also gained a degree of notoriety at those championships when he became the only goaltender to carry the puck over the red line in international competition, which he did against Poland on a dare from his teammates. He stood out from an NHL fraternity that was becoming ever more dumb, colourless, and predictable. It became our mission to meet him.

But we couldn't just call Pat on the telephone or hang around the rink whenever the Bruins came to town (there's a term for that: stalking). So because we had no credibility, we created some. Along with my friend Ozzie, we doctored press clippings using a friend's newspaper production office. I took columns from American dailies and pasted my byline above them. We lied about our identities, invented a bogus portfolio, and tricked public-relations employees of pro hockey teams into believing that we worked for *Nerve Sports*, a fictional university paper.

We contacted the Bruins rep, who said that an interview with Pat could be arranged the next time the Bruins were in Toronto. It would be my second time meeting a pro hockey player. The first was when I was a kid and I lined up at Shopper's Drug Mart at the Westway Plaza to get Paul Henderson's autograph. "What should I say to him?" I asked my mother. "Why don't you ask him about his watch?" she offered, referring to the Timex that Henderson had been given by the Leafs for his goal in '72. As I moved up in the line, I became progressively nervous, sweating a terrible sweat. When it was finally my turn to meet him, I think I said haltingly, "Nice watch, Mr. Henderson," to which he replied "Thanks!" and signed my Esso Power Player folder. He had an impressive looping signature, with circular hooks that connected like a magician's secret rings.

We were told to meet Riggin at the Westin Hotel on the afternoon of the Bruins' game against the Leafs. We waited on pins and needles in the lobby. Ozzie had the worried look of a man about to be hit by a car. He wore a bulky winter jacket his parents had bought for him and jeans that were a size-and-a-half too small. Gord arrived in his leather jacket and Kodiaks. He had long hair and looked like a hoser drug dealer. I wore a blazer and carried a tape recorder and notepad, pretending I was a junior-league Dick Beddoes.

When Riggin walked out of the elevator, we called him over. He was probably expecting one of the new breed of beat writers, all Hugo Boss and hair gel, but he sat down and we talked for an hour. He pulled out a Mars Bar and started gnawing away. When we brought up the American controversy, he asked us to turn off the tape recorder. This thrilled us. He was cool, and we thanked him for the interview. We left the hotel giddy that we'd crossed paths with a real-life NHLer.

From there, our adventures broadened. Our next escapade took us to Buffalo. The Sabres were always complaining that they were getting overshadowed in the media by the Leafs, so I contacted them and said that I was working on a story about that very subject. The

Sabres' media rep told me that he'd leave us passes for the next game. I told him that I'd be bringing along another writer as well as a photographer – Ozzie – who, while he might not have ever taken a photograph, certainly had appeared in a few of them, most often alongside strippers who charged two bucks a polaroid.

On game day, we went to the rink's offices to pick up our press passes. Ozzie patted down his bedhead with the flat of his hand. Gord looked around the office and lit a smoke. I was dressed like a 1950s muckraker in an old coat, my spiral notepad flipped up as if to shorthand the media rep's greeting. But there was none. He came into the office and looked startled to find us there. A few seconds of silence passed and then he spoke:

"What organization did you say you were with?"

"*Nerve Sports*," I said.

"That's out of Toronto, right?"

"Right."

"I'll be right back," he said.

"I have some clippings right here," I added, pulling out a binder of papers.

He stopped and you could tell what he was thinking: "Perhaps I should just give these freaks what they want."

"No, no. That's fine," he said, turning back. "Your passes will be ready in a second."

And that was how it worked. We sat in the press box and drank Budweiser. We watched the game and talked hockey with Buffalo's press row. Ozzie got a photo pass and I could look down and see him with his camera crouching in the penalty box like a nervous animal trapped inside a pen. Before the game, we dined at the buffet along with the other beat writers, among them Ed Kilgore, Buffalo's broadcasting legend, who took an interest in what we were doing. He was a good guy, but I can't say the same for Jerry "King Kong" Korab, the six-foot-five ex-Sabre defenceman who was employed by the local broadcast crew. While Korab ate, he glared at Gord, forking his roast beef and sneering at our table. It was as if he knew what we were up to. He spoke to the others at his table, all the while staring straight at poor Gord, who whispered into his plate, "Shit,

Korab's looking. He's looking right at me." We ate our food and got the fuck out. We could feel Korab's eyes burn through us as we scurried out of the room.

In 1987, we took our charade a step further: we sneaked into Rendez-Vous '87, the two-game, mid-season hockey summit in Quebec City. Matching the Soviet Nats against the NHL All-Stars in a run-up to the Canada Cup tournament, the contest replaced the league's traditional all-star game. I'd read somewhere that Marcel Aubut, president of the Nordiques, wanted this event to be the biggest gathering of players, management, media, and fans in the history of the game (this was back in the days, of course, when Quebec City had its own team, before the Nordiques moved to Denver and the league went all screwy). He said that press would be coming from as far away as China and Africa. I figured that three more press passes wouldn't make a difference, so I faxed bogus press clippings and media requests to the number provided by league officials.

I sat and waited, and three days before the tournament, the phone rang early in the morning. On the other end a woman named Chantal told me that our accreditation was in order. We hopped on a train and headed for Quebec. We arrived at eight-thirty at night, five hours later than expected because of frozen railway tracks. We'd neglected to arrange a place to stay, but Gord remembered that a friend of his, hockey archivist James Duplacey, was travelling with the Hall of Fame's touring exhibit. So we headed there. We nearly froze as we made our way to the building. Once inside, we looked for James, but he was nowhere to be found. We took the time to browse the trophies and memorabilia that had been transported for the event. There was an autograph booth with Eddie Shack sitting in it so, while I phoned the Hilton to see if Duplacey had checked in, Gord lined up to get Eddie's signature. Duplacey wasn't registered there, but Gord got what he wanted. Sort of.

"I told him to sign it 'To Bev,'" he said. "Then he asked me to spell it, so I did. Here, check this out," he said, holding out the autograph book. It read: "To Beb, Love, Eddie."

We were stranded in Quebec City. While we stood shivering outside the building a car drove by with a Rendez-Vous logo on the door. My hand went up like a flare. The car stopped. We piled into the back seat and asked the driver to take us to the Hilton. I told him that we were visiting media. "*Nerve Sports*," said Gord, lighting a smoke.

The driver passed a wineskin filled with homemade whiskey to us as the car weaved through the cobbled streets and narrow alleyways of old Quebec. He pulled up in front of the Hilton, where ice sculptures of all twenty-one NHL logos circled the entranceway. We gathered our luggage and thanked him, and he gave us his number in case we needed to be taxied, free of charge, anywhere in Quebec City. As we stepped through the doorway into the hotel, a camera crew backed out in front of us holding television lights, followed by a sartorial procession of the biggest names in hockey: John Zeigler, Alan Eagleson, Sam Pollock, Harry Sinden. If you had tuned in to TSN at that very moment, you would have seen us standing before them, holding our suitcases and looking bewildered. You would have thought, "Who the fuck are those guys?"

We checked in at the hotel's media centre, where they treated us with all the respect and attention we didn't deserve. We were each given a complimentary carrying bag, Rendez-Vous notepads, pens, coupons, and press passes. We were told to register at the hotel's front desk, and when we did, they said that because we were late, the only room available for us was the executive suite on the twenty-fifth floor with windows overlooking the Plains of Abraham and a ten-foot marble committee table.

We said that would be fine.

The next day, we attended practice at Le Colisé, where I met Gordie Howe, Wayne Gretzky, Mario Lemieux, Ulf Samuelsson, and Mark Messier. The lights were up and the rink was full of reporters from around the world, hockey agents, GMs, celebrities like Alan Thicke and Gordon Lightfoot, and contest-winning fans. Ozzie took photographs; Gord and I drank beer. No one ever asked who we were or what we were doing. I made my way into the NHL dressing room, where Mark Messier walked around naked talking to reporters both male and female. I asked Kirk Muller if he remembered where he was when Paul Henderson scored to beat the Russians. "Woodstock," answered Kevin Dineen, sitting beside him.

Later in the day, Gord and Ozzie got stuck in an elevator with Scotty Bowman. The three of them stood there in silence until Gord said, "Uh. Maybe we should do something." Scotty, who was starting to sweat by this point, reached for the phone, started to speak into it, and then threw it back against its saddle in anger when no one answered. The elevator hiccupped and then started again. A while later, in that same elevator, I met Gordon Lightfoot coming back from a gig.

"How'd the gig go?" I asked him, nervously.

"Well, 'Early Morning Rain' was a little fast," he said, scratching his hand.

We attended practice and watched the Russians in their colour-coded practice jerseys: green, red, and yellow. Their drills were based on rhythm and timing and the execution of geometric figures on the ice: an odd ice ballet. One player would streak through the middle of the rink while a defenceman would break from the boards and skate cross-ice – yet another would skate backwards behind from the net – moving continuously in a seemingly blind pattern that resulted in both goaltenders being peppered at either end of the rink. Pucks and players were constantly in motion. I'd never seen anything like it.

We watched the first game of the series in our room. Canada won on a goal by Dave Poulin. Afterwards, we spent the night in the hotel bar, where Trent Frayne and others were holding court. I got shit-faced trying to go toe-to-toe with Gord, and later that night I puked on him.

It was a fantastic weekend.

I was thinking of Quebec as we dashed across the desert. It made me wish that I could summon my friends – Gord, Ozzie, the

Morningstars – so that they could see what I was seeing: a rink rising over the horizon like a giant blue beret, a temple of ice standing alone in the golden vista, a monument not to time, God, or the universe, but to Canada, to hockey, right there in the middle of the desert.

The rink glowed. Two spires on its roof speared the great nothingness of the sky and across the roofline, triangles were painted lavender and teal in the pattern of a Persian head-dress. At the front of the grounds stood tall orange gates, over which "Al Ain Ice Rink" was painted in English and Arabic. Behind the gates, a fountain set in red rock shot streams of water into the sky, and beyond was a manicured garden rich with pink and white blossoms and bushes with yellow flowers. There were date and coconut palms with tapered fronds on either side of the grounds, and in them parakeets and doves and parrots flitted. It was more like the setting for a thoroughbred race track than a hockey arena. The front of the arena had a tall, glassy proscenium with large round windows, Al Ain Ice Rink hanging in gold letters above the entrance, glinting in the light. It was a building of substance, a hockey parliament or a courthouse or hall of letters. It looked as if its architect had carefully drawn up plans and then, after an evening of food and drink, simply decided to fill the sky. It made McCormick Arena seem as noble as a cardboard box. While our rink back home had a little marquee out front that announced things like "GOOD LUCK TAMMY IN NATS" and "SUNDAY SHINNY: FIVE DOLLARS," here white columns raised the building to the sky where it boldly kissed the sun, knowing that it was protected by an icy heart. Our heart.

As the taxi pulled up, I saw three women in black robes approach the building. They looked like moving triangles, their bodies stooped under the hammer of the heat. The rink dwarfed them, and that's when I realized what the Al Ain hockey rink was supposed to look like: a mosque. A place of worship. Sanctuary from the outside world.

The Arabs had got it right.

15

THE SUDANESE CYCLONE

The rink was as beautiful inside as it was out. Like the rink at Harbin, the ice surface was Olympic-sized but, while the arena in Dong Bei had been dark and sombre, Al Ain was swimming in gold light. It smelled like lemons. Its capacity was two thousand, including a carpeted VIP area that was decorated with ferns, rubber plants, and red velvet curtains draped over the back wall. (Abdullah would tell me later: "They usually bring out sofas for the sheiks and sports minister. You know, people with soft asses.") A window behind the south end gazed out on the Al Ain desert landscape, and if you looked hard enough, you could see camels treading across the horizon. The rink was only a few miles from the site of the world's oldest archaeological find, dated 4000 BC. The first time I took to the ice, I was aware I was skating across civilization's cradle, of carving ice with metal the way the first men might have chipped a pick into a wall-face in the same kinds of shapes and patterns I was making with my feet. I swirled, celebrating the genesis of life in an impromptu Canadian folk dance, a dance cast by the sun. The sky poured into the arena and painted the ice blue-gold, the same quality

Al Ain Ice Rink

of light that would have spilled down on the world's first sports: a date pit tossed into a basket, a cane tapping a rock along the ground, mumbletypeg with a dead bird's bones.

There was a snack bar at the front of the rink that sold samosas, falafels, and stuffed vine leaves. You could sip Turkish coffee mixed with sweet condensed milk while your skates were being sharpened for twenty-five durhams a pop. If you gazed up at the mirrored ceiling during a game, you could see the play backwards. Up there, all giveaways were goals, all missed passes breakaway darts. It was a game of perfection played in the sky, and it combined with the forgiving hue of the afternoon to make me conclude that it was impossible to look bad playing hockey at Al Ain.

I walked my gear to our dressing area behind a curtain next to an arcade (Al Ain being their home arena, the Arab Nats occupied both proper change rooms). My entire team was there – a mixed bag of Swiss, Finnish, British, Russian, Italian, Canadian, and American players – a ragtag UN of hockey. When Steve Chiu first told me about the team, he said, "There's a Russian guy, Roman Lebedev. He used to play in Moscow with a few guys who made it to the NHL. He's really good. You'll do well if he makes the trip."

The first person I looked for was Roman, but no one in the room fit my image of a Russian hockey player. I imagined Starshinov, the USSR's pre-1972 star: coldly handsome with high cheekbones, thin lips, darting eyes, and the build of an athlete who trained on dry land as well as ice. But when Roman was pointed out to me by Andrew, I saw that the same fate had befallen him as Vladimir Krutov, the left winger of the KLM line and one of the world's best players in the 1980s. Krutov was signed by the Vancouver Canucks, then cut after confessing to an addiction to hot dogs. Like Krutov, Roman had become a victim of food. His face was as round as a volleyball and his midriff could have plugged a rain barrel. Before the tournament, I'd relished the opportunity to play on the same team as an athlete who represented Canada's greatest (and most symbiotic) hockey rival, but Roman looked more like a parody of a Soviet athlete. He seemed better suited for the Pro Bowlers Tour than the Izvestia Cup. When I asked him what he remembered most about his time with Moscow Spartak, where he played alongside NHL stars Valeri Bure and Alexander Selivanov, he told me, "I remember too much running." Roman had left the grind of the Spartak club and moved to Beijing as a sixteen-year-old, where he'd traded in years of cabbage and borscht for life in the world's gastronomic hub. He seemed proud of his new shape, too. When prompted, he would lift up his shirt and fondle his enormous belly, saying "My baby is hungry."

I slapped my hockey bag down in the change room and sat at an old table next to Tomi, a young Finnish defenceman. Tomi was short and slight, but he skated with great strength; it turned out that his dad was a hockey coach. I'd spoken with Tomi on the phone when I was in China, and expected to meet a fellow with the proportions of a Viking because his voice made him sound like Krull the Conqueror. It was a deep, throaty baritone that belied his small frame, and when he shouted on the bench, it was a terrifying howl: "*Fawwwking shooot the puck!*"

Tomi sat next to Marcus Benz, the team's captain. Marcus had the unfortunate look of a pained stork. He was Swiss-German and he reminded me of a Hanna-Barbera parody of German royalty: a natural arrogance belied by a propensity for bumbling. When he wasn't trying to figure out where the team should party, he was talking sex. He would say things like, "Tell me: what does a pussy look like?" It was bait for Roman or Andrew or Dave Roberts, a Canadian living in Abu Dhabi who, like myself, had caught on with the team. While Marcus changed into his gear, he threw out phrases like "Oh, I wish I could touch a pussy!" The fellows joined in and it was pretty funny, in a juvenile, jock-scratching way. I wrote down a few of these exchanges, and while I did, Tom Burridge, an eighteen-year-old Brit who was in the Middle East visiting his dad, leaned over and said, "Like, what are you doing? Writing down jokes?"

"No, it's a book."

"A book? For what?"

"For Canada. About hockey."

"I guess you'll be writing about me, then."

"It depends," I said, not revealing to him my distaste for the British hockey accent.

"I play in Blackburn. Semi-pro. I'm a hockey player."

Tom Burridge was young and usually aloof. He had long blond hair and wore cool clothes. He looked like he could have been in Blur. Tom earned 125 pounds a week playing for Blackburn and had played briefly in the low-ranking Pioneer League for the Colorado Cougars. He'd also competed in the 1997 C-Pool World Junior Championships for Britain. He'd faced off against Lithuanians who stuffed newspapers in their legs to keep warm, and against Team Estonia, whose star player used a stick that was chopped in half. When Tom asked him why he did this, he said, "Because I only had broken sticks when I was a child."

Tom's dad was John Burridge, who'd made the trip from Oman, where he was the coach of the national soccer team. I never saw Mr. Burridge out of his track sweats, so I assumed he was one of those disciplinarian fathers who'd insisted his son take up sports. I was dead wrong. John was a nice man who held the English Soccer League record for most decades played by a goalkeeper, from the 1950s into the 1990s, more than 800 games. He'd also won the 1965 FA Cup with Aston Villa, and when I asked where I could learn about his career, he produced thirty years' worth of press clippings from the British tabloids. He always carried them with him.

But both father and son had issues. Whenever his father came to our games, Tom would get thrown out. His on-ice tantrums were hard to watch. The one game Mr. Burridge didn't come to, Tom scored twice. I asked Tom about it later and he said, "My dad is famous at home and he's right in with the English soccer people, Kevin Keegan and all that [Keegan was the coach of England's national side]. Alan Shearer used to babysit me in Newcastle; my dad coached him, too. But whenever my games are reported in the newspaper, they always say, like, 'Tom Burridge was the star of the game. Tom is the son of former Aston Villa goalkeeper John Burridge.' There are only so many times in life you want to hear that, right?"

Sitting at the table next to Tom was Jan-Erik Messell, our Norwegian goalie. When you think of great goaltending pedigrees, you don't usually think of Norway, at least not yet. Both on and off the ice, Jan was as quick as a wall hanging. He had a pencil-thin moustache like Inspector Clouseau's and looked unlike any goalie I've ever seen. When I met him, he was strapping on his pads while kneeling on the ground – like an eleven-year-old – with a lit smoke clasped between his lips. He grunted with each tug and huffed when he got up. He finished the smoke, then lit another. "Hello, Canada," he said to me, then grimaced and wiggled his hand back and forth as if it were injured. Jan always looked in pain.

Massimo Diem and Steve Conniff rounded out our line-up. Massimo was a smooth-skating Swiss-Italian who moved with all the swiftness of a young Serge Savard; Steve Conniff, by contrast, moved like Serge Gainsbourg. Steve was the oldest member of the team and one of the tourney's co-organizers. He had a George Hamilton tan and spoke with the rasp of a bingo caller after years smoking Kools. He liked to greet people good-naturedly with, "How ya doing? Ya big faggot." Steve's reputation was of hard-drinking and inveterate womanizing despite the fact that he was about as suave as Norman Fell. He was a failed desert rogue whom I took to instantly.

We were a goofy team without a name, bound for failure. Our first game was against the Ticino Tigers from Switzerland. During the warm-up, I saw that Tomi, Massimo, and Andrew were skilled – Roman had one of the sweetest wrist shots I've seen – but I also saw that we couldn't really get together. The Swiss team, on the other hand, were a fourth-division club who'd already played two seasons together. They were the products of a new policy that limited the number of foreigners allowed in domestic leagues: three in the first division, two in the second, and none below that. It had produced a rising national junior team and explained in part why the Swiss had overtaken Germany on the world's stage (the Germans had no import limits). This promised more high draft picks like Luca Cereda, the Maple Leafs' first choice, and youngest player in the 1999 draft, as well as high-calibre rec teams who would travel the world drubbing no-star ex-pat ensembles like us.

Our game was fast, but the Swiss were faster. I knew from the start that if we had any chance of challenging them, we'd have to play tough; that is to say, dirty. But I had difficulty welling up any kind of distaste for Switzerland. They played clean and were well-mannered, and about three-quarters of them boasted Italian heritage, which made it hard for me to play them as if they were the 1974 Flyers. Although they wore the gaudiest yellow and blue Euro jerseys, an affront to the style code of traditional hockey, it wasn't enough. Unlike the Harbin juniors, they hadn't been ordered by their coach to go easy on us, either, so whenever I ran them in the corner, they ran back. Their coach, name of Pepino, would not shut the fuck up. He had the look of an Italian Bronson Pinchot and talked trash from the bench. He wore designer sweats and a baseball cap, and he timed shifts with a stopwatch, as if the Tigers were competing in the NHL, not some scrub tourney in the desert. He took the game far too seriously (which probably explained why the Tigers were the among best teams in the tournament), and it was easy to get him riled.

It was late in the final period (we played twenty-minute halves), when Tom Burridge got kicked out. There was little sympathy for him on our bench because he hadn't done much to try to fit in with the team, at least not in the beginning. Andrew was troubled by it; he came up to me at one point and said, "Hey, what's the deal with Tom?" I told him what I knew. Tom was a fast skater and an assured puckhandler, but he didn't pass very often. He was the kind of fellow for whom dash and flair came naturally, and who had probably been the best player on his team at all levels. But because the calibre of English hockey was that much poorer, it had made Tom twice as insufferable as any young Canadian puck hog. Before the game, Marcus asked him what position he played, and he told him "anywhere," not as in "Put me anywhere coach, I'm just happy to be playing," but as in "It doesn't matter where I play; I can score from anywhere." This would have been fine if he'd come through, but the hockey was better than Tom had bargained for. You could tell it was important to him that he prove how good he was, and when he couldn't do it, it got to him. It wasn't pretty.

He clubbed one of the Swiss defencemen in the back of the head, and when John Davy called a penalty, he flipped. He chased the ref around the ice before turning his attention to his assailant. Tom was shouting "That was shit! *Shit!*" to the ref, to the Swiss, to everyone. His voice boomed throughout the rink – certainly loud enough for his dad to hear – and at one point, he skated over to the Swiss bench, took off his glove and pointed at the offending player, saying "I'm gonna git you pal! *Git! You! Pal!*" For me, his accent defanged his anger. There just wasn't enough snarl in that English short-pants, cricket-bat, strawberry-trifle, Upstairs-Downstairs voice, even though Tom's eyes bugged out and he spat when he shouted. Not one person in the rink was afraid.

Pepino wasn't, and being a consummate good sport, he leaned over the boards and swore at Tom in Italian. The Swiss coach employed the kind of European dramatics better suited to loamy soccer pitches than battlefields of ice. He looked as if he'd never been hit with a puck, let alone shot or stopped one. So when he started taunting Tom, the young Brit went for him, which was John's cue to skate in and tie up his arms. So, to recap: the guy who could have been in Blur was restrained by the producer of the Allmans. On a rink in the desert.

Typical hockey.

Tom skated off: "*I'll show you, pal! You're gonna get it!*" I made a note to tell Tom that, in order to piss off one's opponent, there are more effective words than "pal." "Fag ass fucker," for instance. It was the least I could do. After the game ended, 8–2, we found him sitting in the room with his head down, his equipment half-off.

"That's all right, Tommy," said Dave Roberts. "What'd he give ya?"

"A two-hander is wot. Right in front of the bloody net. Did you see it?"

"No, no," Dave said.

"Well, I did. And I felt it too! That ref is bloody blind. Bloody fucking blind!"

"It wasn't the ref," I said.

"Who the hell was it then?" he asked, throwing his shoulder pads to the ground.

"You flipped out. I mean, it's okay, but don't blame the ref. He reffed in the NHL, you know."

"That joke? In the NHL?"

"Ya, man. '86 to '96."

"Really?" asked Tomi.

"Ya, he gave Gretzky a misconduct once."

"That means you're in good company, buddy," said Dave.

But Tom wasn't laughing.

After the game we laid out our gear on the grass behind the rink and it dried in about ten seconds. One of the benefits of hockey in the Middle East is that the sun's natural disinfectant neutralizes the stench of hockey, and that's why Fun City smelled so much better than any other rink. Out here in the desert, there was no excuse for rank equipment, and while I tried to figure out whether this was a good thing, I made my way back inside, where the Al Ain Falcons were taking to the ice.

The Falcons roster was identical to the UAE Nats with the exception of three ex-pats: Dr. Tim Watson and his son, Dave, and goalie Don Bourguignon, whom they'd left off their Hong Kong roster. Don had reclaimed his position from Darwish, who had wisely quit the game after his triumphant return home. Abdullah was counting on these additions to continue the Arabs' tournament success, but the competition here was quite a bit stronger than in China. In their first game against the second Swiss team, Meinisberg, the Falcons were badly out-played. The Swiss were no Flying Frenchmen, yet they skated holes through the Arab defence. At both SkyRink and Festival Walk, Mohammed, Obaid, Nasser, Turqi, and the rest could get away with a certain lack of mobility, but on Olympic-sized ice, they were simply out-skated by the Swiss. The Falcons' elite scorers – Juma, Omar, and Ahmed – played as if back-checking was an affront, and they had difficulty getting the puck past the Swiss goalie, which aggravated their frustration. But that wasn't the worst of it. Near the end of the game, Nasser got tangled up and he went down in the corner. The Al Ain coaches – Bear and Bill Upton, the same pair who'd guided the Nats in China – jumped out onto the ice to see how badly their best defenceman had been hurt. Nasser climbed to his feet and glided to the bench hunched-over with pain. Up in the VIP area, Abdullah buried his face in his hands.

Team Beijing's second game was against Meinisberg and we fared a little better, losing 2–1. Roman scored the finest goal of the game. No one could figure out how he'd done it. He moved down the wing with all the urgency of a floating bathtub toy – out-skating no one – yet whenever someone tried to take the puck from him, he deked around them using what can only be described as sleight of hand. He bounced the puck off the inside of his skate, hid it behind his heel, all the while grimacing in concentration. Once he was within range of the goal, he snapped a wrist shot and the puck rang off the inside of the cross bar and banked into the net. The Swiss defence had been deceived by Roman's girth, and I knew exactly how they felt. Many times, I have defended against players with tub-bellies and pie-eating jowls in Toronto's rec leagues, only to have them slip the puck through me as if passing a letter under a door. Though Roman skated without any velocity, the way he cradled the puck and moved it around in his feet was the result of the countless drills he'd been put through by coaches in his youth.

After the game, the rest of the team headed to the restaurant. Instead, I skated over to where Kareem and a few of the other Falcons were standing by the boards.

"Hello," I said.

"Hello," he replied.

"Who do you guys play next?"

"Oh! Some other very good team," he said, shaking his head.

"Ya. The Swiss are good. Too good," I said.

Kareem laughed: "At least we are playing! That is the main thing!"

"Are you from Al Ain?"

He thumbed his bony chest: "No! I am from Sudan. *I am the first Sudanese hockey player!*" he proclaimed, throwing his arms apart.

"The first?"

"*Yes!*"

I remembered that Chris Reynolds had mentioned at the press conference that he'd had a few Sudanese players in the tournament before. I told this to Kareem, who shook his head and put his arm around my shoulder.

"Let me tell you a story," he said. "I talked to my grandfather in the Sudan the other day. I told him that I was playing hockey. He asked me what hockey was and I explained to him: 'It is a fast game played on ice.' 'Ice?' he said. 'Crazy boy! In the Sudan we are praying every day and every night for water, yet you are taking the water that you have and turning it into ice! This hockey; this is a stupid game!' But I told him, 'No, grandfather. All my life I have been looking for a smart game. And finally, I have found it. Skate. Shoot. Muscles. Think. It is a simple game, but I love it because it is a fast game. You have to think fast or you're dead. Grandfather, for me there is no other sport.' Then he said, 'That is my grandson, the first Sudanese hockey player. And such a stupid boy to be doing this!'"

Kareem's face beamed warmth. And as he leaned against the boards, closed his small hand into a fist, shook it gently, and said, "They call soccer the beautiful game, but what could be more beautiful than hockey?" I knew why I'd made the trip.

Before I could tell Kareem this, the Falcons' coach walked out of the dressing room to round up the team. "All right, guys. Get dressed," said Bear, clapping his hands.

"Good luck," I told Kareem.

"We'll need it, man!"

"How's your buddy who got hurt?" I asked.

"His elbow," said Kareem, touching his arm. "Nasser."

"Is it broken?"

"I don't know. But we are short a few men."

"Do you need another player?" I asked impulsively.

Kareem smiled the smile of a thousand candles.

"*Come! See!*" he said, wheeling his arm.

16

THE UNITED COLOURS OF LOSING

Now, I don't mean to boast, but I look like Charles Bronson. Sort of. Like Mr. Death Wish himself, I could be mistaken for many different ethnic backgrounds: Italian, Serbian, Greek, Russian, Portuguese, Spanish, French, Turkish, Arab. Just slap a few days' growth on my face and I'm the frigging united colours of Benetton. I've actually been mistaken for an Arab before, in Ireland, where a group of touring American nuns were convinced that I was the fellow who'd taken a pot-shot at the Pope. They thought I was Libyan. One of them even kissed my forehead and said she'd pray for God to show me mercy. So when Ahmed, the Falcons' captain, polled his team on whether they would let me play, I hoped that my swarthy looks and ability to incite fear in women of the cloth would tip the scales my way.

After about five minutes, the door opened and Ahmed emerged from the room in his pants and shin pads: "Okay," he said, grim-faced. "Okay: you play."

Though I'd represented Canada at the HK Fives, this was differ-ent. In the Hong Kong competition, there were Canadians playing for other teams, and besides, I didn't get to know any of my team-mates well enough to develop a kinship with them. But since the Falcons were more or less the UAE Nats, I considered this my official debut as an international rep, albeit for a country I'd been in only two days. At the least, I was representing the desert city of Al Ain, and when Ahmed handed me my sweater – it was purple and black with NASSER on the back – I felt like I'd become part of a team, not just a bunch of guys playing hockey.

The Falcons changed in a real dressing room. I took a place on the bench with the rest of the team. Once out of their equipment, I saw that they were younger than I'd realized. Some of them were just kids. Khalifa was only fifteen, and Ahmed, at twenty-three, was the senior member. Their beards made them appear older and more mature, but players like Omar and Juma were small-armed and scrawny-chested and had yet to develop the muscles of an athlete. They behaved like teenagers, too, snapping wet towels, crowding the bench space, and getting in each other's hair with taunts that made me wish I knew Arabic.

Bear came over and introduced himself. His hair was close-cropped and he looked like someone who'd served in the forces. He had a moustache and was solidly built for a man of forty-one. He also had a soft voice and gentle disposition, and when he told me, "It'll be good to have you on the team," I believed him.

"I'll run you through the pairs," he said. "You don't mind playing defence?"

"No, it's where I play at home."

"Good. It'll steady the guys a little."

"Ya. I saw you guys in Hong Kong."

"So you know a little bit about how we play?"

"I should. I've seen you more times this year than the Leafs."

After the team dressed, they came over one by one and tapped me on top of the helmet. The players had Easton sticks and wore CCM helmets, Cooper pads, Nikes and Tacks, which they'd ordered through the hockey shop at the rink. The UAE Hockey Federation had recently received first-time funding from the Emirate sports ministry, so they'd had a chance to upgrade. Kareem had a towel with the logos of all the NHL teams, and when I asked him where he'd got it, he told me, "I ordered it on the Internet!"

Mohammed, the tall shot-stopping defencemen who'd made an impression on me in China, sat down beside me. He introduced himself and asked, "David, you were in Hong Kong?"

"Ya. I saw all of your games."

"Yes. Yes, I think I saw you. Up in the rink."

"I was at the final."

"Yes. Now you will play. Together?"

Bear came over.

"Dave, you'll pair up with Mohammed here."

"Cool."

"David, this is good," Mohammed said, slapping my shin pad.

"I'll call you 'Mo' out there," I told him.

Mo thought about it.

"And I will call you 'Dave.'"

Janet sat up in the stands with the Beijingers and watched as the Falcons took to the ice. It was my first time playing on a team whose principal language was something other than English so, as we spun around the ice and warmed up, I asked Mohammed how to call for a pass in Arabic.

"Pass!" he said.

"What about 'shoot'?"

"Shoot!"

"And 'Heads up!'?"

"Head is what?"

Kareem wore a purple Jofa helmet and skated like he was on roller skates. It was an awkward style, but he managed to get moving when he had to. Of all the Al Ain players, Kareem had the hardest slap-shot, due in part to the fact that his wind-up started from behind his head. The only problem with Kareem's shot was that he had no idea where it was going. When he wound-up in the offensive zone, the Falcons ducked and covered, as if he were flinging dinner plates at them. Bear had to remind him: "Shoot at the goalie, Kareem, at the goalie." I also noticed that when Kareem shot, the brightness in his face faded. His eyes dimmed, his jaw clenched, and his brow furrowed into a hockey face. Ahmed also had the look, and so did Juma. Khalifa, too. The only person who didn't have it was Mo, whose eyes were continuously alight, his tongue wagging when he skated. He looked like he was having as much fun as a kid toboganing down a hill. I thought of the Bedouins who'd come in from the desert to touch the ice at Al Nasr, and wondered what Mo's ancestors would have thought if they could see him play hockey. Slippery ice. Snug pants and sweater. A tool made from Quebec timber. Cold face and ears. Mohammed was enjoying a child's Canadian winter right there in the desert.

When Skydog blew his whistle to start the game, Bear called us to the bench for some advice. Ahmed translated into Arabic. Bear said the usual stuff – "Don't take stupid penalties; play as a team; work together; stay focussed" – while Ahmed's voice murmured under his. After Bear finished his instructions, Ahmed spoke. His speech sounded more grave than Bear's, and he punched certain words and phrases with a sudden nod of the head. I looked at Kareem, Juma and Omar; none of them were smiling. After Ahmed finished his pep talk (though, truthfully, there was nothing peppy about it), we put our gloves together in a scrum of chaffed leather. Kareem closed his eyes, and each player bowed his head. There was a pause, and then Kareem sucked air through his nose. He held it for a second, and then exhaled, growling a prayer from the Koran.

Our opponent was the Ticino Tigers, the team I'd lost to massively in my first game. While it was their third game of the day, none of them looked the worse for wear. By the way they moved, you could tell that they weren't going full tilt; it was obvious that they possessed more speed and talent than the Nats. We ended up losing the game 8–1, but I was thrilled to be skating with the Falcons. The players spoke Arabic on the bench and, every now and then, Bear – who hailed from Montebello, just outside Ottawa – would unleash a torrent of French-Canadian invective: "*Maudite Tabernac!*" I loved it. Dave Watson, who skated on a line with his

The Falcons, featuring the author as Nasser

father, threw in his two cents: "*You little shit fuck!*" We only scored once, but we were good at profanity. I finally did my part when Marizio Brambillo, the Swiss captain, tripped Ahmed and was called for a penalty. I leaned over the boards: "*Take a seat, you fucking clock-making slob!*" I looked at Mo. He covered his mouth and laughed.

I think my swearing was an ice-breaker, because we communicated better from that point. At one point, Khalifa leaned over and shouted at Obaid. I think I knew what he'd said, so I asked him, "Body?"

"Yes, body."

"Use the body?"

"Yes. Using the body," he said, pointing at my chest.

After my best shift of the game, Ahmed told me, "Good play, Dave," and it gave me a boost. The captain didn't suffer floaters. He was the hardest-working player on the team and had a glare that could crumble stone. He used his Arab *gravitas* to full advantage – dark sunken brow, eyes hard and severe, chin and jaw gripped – but because I was the new guy, I wasn't targeted for the worst of it. I was thankful for that. When he yelled at Juma and Omar and Khalifa after bad shifts, they would stage long glowering contests that lasted until their next turn, and which Ahmed always won.

"You're doing good, Dave," said Kareem, nodding his head.

"You too, man."

"I must score!"

"Keep your head up. Go hard."

"I must . . ."

"You ever faked a slapshot?"

"How do you mean?"

"Well, every time you come over the blue line, you shoot. That's cool, but the defenceman expects you to do it, you know? Next time, pretend like you're going to shoot, but don't. Then you can fake him and you'll be in closer."

"Fake," he said.

"Yes, fake."

"I will try!"

But Kareem never got his chance. The Tigers allowed us very little room on the ice. Don had an awful time in goal. Ahmed did a lot of staring while Juma and Omar sulked. Mo got frustrated at not being able to stop the Swiss, who kept swishing around him. I tried to help Bear keep it positive: *"Keep fuckin' at 'er, boys!"* and *"One fuckin' play at a time!"* But pretty soon, not even Mo was laughing. Apparently, a loss is a loss no matter where the game is played.

Near the end of the game – the result already determined – I tried a rush from behind our own goal. It was a typical defenceman's folly, straying so far from my station behind the play that I had no choice but to keep moving into the Swiss zone. But with the momentum of my body went my thoughts, and as two Swiss defencemen met me at centre ice, I looked over their heads through the window at the far end of the rink to where a handful of Arab men were standing under a date tree, smoking. They reminded me of the clay men who show up in my neighbourhood around Christmas time – bearded, robed figures looming over the manger, eyes cast down at the child. With this vision came memories of winter: street hockey, jean cuffs frozen with snow, the salty warmth of Campbell's soup, my dad skidding towards the car from the gas pump with one hand clamping his hat to his head, the other holding a deck of Esso Power Player stamps, which I would pass across my fingers in the back seat like ancient tokens; and later, lying on the carpet in front of the Magnavox in our basement, "Hockey Night in Canada," Bob Goldham, Peter Puck; Santa Bower at Christmas, pickled on egg nog and shouting, "A Stanley Cup for all the kids!" I remembered running down the driveway on Christmas day with my new glove or stick or goalie net or pads and meeting my friends half-way up the street, where the Magi stood on front lawns, looking solemn on the happiest day of the year.

I had dragged these images of the Canadian cold half-way around the world to the sizzling heat of the desert. Knowing the Magi were here, I stepped across the blue line feeling free and relaxed and fanciful. I could see out the window to where, a few miles up the road, archaeologists on their hands and knees were digging into the sand, looking for artifacts from a lost time. They wore broad hats and shorts and drank from canteens while listening to Arabic music on the radio. As I flung the puck at the goaltender, I watched it sail over the heads of the Magi until it was picked up by the wind and thrown against the earth at the feet of those archaeologists, who would spoon the puck into a plastic bag, tag it, carry it into a big room with a high ceiling, and place it in a sliding wooden drawer, where it would sit next to dead bugs and arrowheads and bits of pottery as another symbol of the restless earth. Someday, a middle-aged woman in a lab coat eating a sandwich would stare at the puck and wonder how it related to Arabia, what its connection was to the land. As the goalie caught it and held it against his chest, I realized this was a question that I could answer.

"Fuckin' fuck," I said, skating back to the bench.

"David. Good," said Mo, who never called me Dave.

"No. It was a weak shot. Should have waited," I said.

"No. You have to shoot! In soccer, you never get a chance, but here, you shoot, shoot," he said, moving his hand as if brushing crumbs off a table. "It's why we play. It's what I like: to shoot and score and win the game," he said, smiling.

I leaned over and told Kareem what Mo had said.

Kareem thrust a finger into the air.

"Hockey is like a disease!"

17

A BUSLOAD OF ESPO

Espo-sito.

We caught a ride home from Al Ain with the Swiss team. The day had been tough on my nationhood. Since I'd already played for two totally different teams, being surrounded by Swiss-Italian kids with whom I shared an ancestry only further muddled my sense of identity. It's how I imagine a lot of pros must feel these days. During a recent World Junior Championship, I read about a Buffalo Sabres draft pick who was representing the Czech Republic for the second time while playing for the Tri-City Americans of the Western Canadian Hockey League. At that same tournament, the American team included the sons of Canadians Bob Sauve and Blake Dunlop, both ex-NHLers, while the National Hockey League's front-runner for Rookie of the Year was Hispanic – Scott Gomez, a New Jersey forward who'd learned the game in Alaska and British Columbia. It's not unusual for today's pros to have multiple home-lands. Brett Hull – reared in Belleville, Ontario – was the Americans' hero in the '96 World Cup; Washington's Brobingnagian goalie, Olaf Kolzig, was born in South Africa, yet competes internationally for

Germany; Tony Esposito, Mike Keenan, and Bryan Trottier all
traded south for passports; Igor Larionov and Peter Stastny became
hosers; and a few years ago, the once indomitable Soviet Red Army
struck a deal with the Pittsburgh Penguins, who stamped their
yellow and blue bird over the army's famous utilitarian logo. Not so
long ago, one didn't have to suffer the dilemma of cheering for or
against Mats Sundin when Team Sweden played Team Canada in
the Olympics, or whether to simply hope that he didn't get hurt and
imperil his season as captain of the Toronto Maple Leafs.

Once, there were only bad guys, and us.

Espo-sito.

I told the Swiss-Italians the story of Phil Esposito. I did this for
two reasons. One, I refused to let these eighteen-year-old hockey
players sleep while I still had the energy to talk hockey. It hardly
seemed right, considering they'd whipped both of the teams I'd
played on. Second, the confusing issue of my Canadianness made
me think about him. If I could go back and emulate any Canadian
Nat, it would be Esposito. He was the most complex of all Canadian
hockey heroes, and the most culturally significant, too. His contri-
butions to the game were broad and dramatic. He was part of the
most lopsided trade in hockey history – Espo, Ken Hodge, and Fred
Stanfield going from Chicago to Boston for Gilles Marotte and Pit
Martin – as well as the biggest – Espo and Carol Vadnais to New
York for Jean Ratelle and Brad Park. He had the league's first one-
hundred-point season, set records for goals scored (76) and points
(152), and was the possessor of the era's most fetching sideburns,
thick as rainforest growth. Espo was hockey writ large, all bombast
and braggadocio.

"Espo was the first," I told them.

"?"

"Italian. He was the first Italian. Before him, you never saw
Italians on television in Canada. It was all British and Irish. Tommy
Hunter. Juliette. "Front Page Challenge." The closest you got was
Stan Mikita. Stan was a man of colour. He was Czech, but he looked
Asian. But that was it. Until Espo became the de facto captain of
Team Canada, hockey was all Conachers and Smythes and Clancys.

Espo in Russia
(Brian Pickell)

But Espo was no cake Loyalist. No: he looked and sounded different and, by seeing him every day on television and in the newspapers,
you could tell that Canada's face was changing. He looked like the
men on my grandmother's street in Little Italy in Toronto. You
couldn't miss him because he was the biggest star on the team. Orr,
Hull, and Cheevers weren't on the team and Gordie Howe was
retired. You've heard of Howe?"

"?"

"Doesn't matter. Espo, right?"

"Espo-sito."

"King Wop. He was *it*. IT. Greaseball lid and sideburns like fat
Buffalo wings. Pasta fazoo. Garrulous. Emotional. Always sweating.
Wild-eyed, operatic. He did things big. He played big. He *was* big.
Espo went hard, you could tell. There's a photo at Shakey's Bar in
Toronto of Espo, Bill Watters, Frosty Forristal, leaning against a
bar in somebody's basement, cheering on Wayne Cashman in his

checkered blazer and tight brown slacks, who is up on the bar dancing. Booze and broads. He lived high and fast. The man. *The* man.

"But Espo paid for it. In 1972, Canada took on the Russians in an eight-game series: four in Canada, four in Moscow. Espo brought measured arrogance to the event. He'd just won the Stanley Cup with the Bruins. Everyone in Canada thought we were going to win. It would be easy. Automatic. A joke. The Russians had shitty equipment. Their sweaters looked like somebody'd found them at the back of a closet. Moth-gobbled. Old scrubby wool. Their sticks were cheap, knotted. The players looked small and seemed awestruck by the whole scene, the pageantry. Next to the rich NHLers, they looked like rubes, bumpkins, country bushwackers. But what did they do? They humiliated us. They marched in and killed us, seven to three. We mourned. Like in soccer. Like your Inter Milan, right? You know Inter Milan?"

"Eh!" they said. They called to a friend across the bus, who passed over his Inter Milan membership card. It had been a terrible year for the fans of Inter. The team had fallen apart and would not be competing for the Italian title.

"Yes, see? It hurts," I said, punching my chest.

"Eh, it does. Yes."

"Well, imagine that pain and multiply it by a hundred. A thousand. A knife in the heart. Canada is known for hockey, yes? It's all we have, really. We are not a country of wars, disasters, revolutions. We don't have thousands of years of art and poetry. We have Pamela Anderson. You know 'Baywatch'?"

"Yes. Yes, 'Baywatch'!"

"Well, we didn't have it back then. We only had hockey. Gretzky, right?"

"Yes, Gretzky. He played?"

"No. Not back then, later. That was the first time. *The first.* You understand? Our country did not talk to the USSR. The United States didn't. Italy didn't. No one did. They were just these huge shadows on the earth. Not until we faced-off did we see them. We never saw pictures or television from Russia, nothing until their team showed up to play, and humiliated us. We gave them no respect because we knew nothing of them. We hated the Russians. I hated the Russians. Do I still? I don't know."

"This man. Espo-sito. He was angry?"

"Yes and no. Probably shocked, like the rest of us. Anyway, listen: the Canadian team was dying at home. Dying. We got hammered by the Russians in Vancouver. Hammered. The fans booed. They booed again as the team left to play in Moscow, the first time a pro team had ever travelled behind the Iron Curtain. Only fifty fans showed up at the airport to see them off, whereas one week earlier, the whole country had boasted that we'd win the series easily. Now, we were sickened by the hockey – frightened, too. After the game in Vancouver, Esposito was interviewed by a reporter on television, Johnny Esaw, a very famous Canadian broadcaster. It was live. Live and sudden. We watched the interview through our hands as if it were a horror film. Yet there was Espo, his big *scungilli* face filling the screen, eyes dark and heavy, shoulders hunched, panting. Fucking Dago. That's what they said on the Prairies. You could hear it. Fucking Wop. Espo, Cournoyer, Henderson, Savard, Park, Dryden: they'd let us down. I was just a kid, but I knew. We turned up the volume on the set to hear what the big fuck had to say for himself. How he was gonna apologize. How he was gonna try and get out of this one, defend his team.

"But he didn't. He didn't defend anything. Instead, he gave us shit. He gave Canada shit. He called us quitters. He looked the country straight in the eyes, and he pointed his finger at us, and he said, 'I'm really disappointed. I mean, we're trying. We might make our money in the United States, but we're doing this because we love Canada.' He threw down the gauntlet. Remember: this wasn't some polite, erudite CBC type in a suit and a bow tie. This was no Massey College lecturer. No, it was Espo, the greasy lummox, staring at us through the eye of the camera, asking, 'You. Are you afraid? Good. I'm dying and you're afraid.' He was half-way between screaming and crying. It was impossible to look away. He invaded our homes, our consciousness. He was the first. The first Italian. Afterwards, no one in Canada could deny that we Italians existed. And when he brought the team back from the brink of elimination and we beat the Russians in their own house: oh boy."

"Numero uno."

"Yes. Number one. About a week later, three thousand Canadians flew to Moscow – the biggest airlift since the relief of blockaded Berlin in 1948. Espo carried the team on his back. Him and Henderson, the God-fearing Leaf who was born in a sleigh. After a faceoff, the camera locked onto Espo bending down to argue with one of the refs. Espo with his nose pressed against Ragulin's face, blood against blood, Espo saying *Fuck me up. I want it. Fuck me up and watch me love it. Then watch me give it back.* Espo with his arms raised to the crowd like Caesar. Many years later, I saw a film by Nikita Mikhalkov, the great Russian director. It was a documentary about his daughter, but it was also a poem to Russia, an ode to its turbulent history. The narrator said, 'In order for Russia to be a great nation, we needed great enemies.' Then he showed a clip. Not of the United States' nuclear arsenal. Not of Hitler. But there in the penalty box, sneering at the world: Espo. A great enemy. Italo-Canadian. Like me."

"He still plays?"

"No. Retired. After the team returned home, they held a parade in Sault Ste. Marie for Phil and his brother. They hung banners across the main street. They built a great wooden podium where the mayor and the community leaders sat. They polished the key to the town and boxed it in royal-blue velvet, hooked up a television feed around the province, called in cheerleaders, marching bands, honoured guests from cities around the Nickel Belt, paved the pot-holes, prepared big slopping pots of osso buco on the sidewalks, and readied the firework cannons to greet the car that carried the guests – Phil and Tony in their shades and mohair coats and leather boots – so they could sweep down the street, catch confetti, blow kisses."

"A special day."

"Special, ya. They never showed up."

18

CHICKEN NIGHT IN DUBAI

"*Do the Finnish Chicken dance! Do it!*"

"Do it, ya faggot!"

Steve was shouting at Marcus.

Janet and I found ourselves drinking at a party for the visiting teams and players held at Crocodiles, an Australian-themed sports bar in the heart of Dubai. The bar itself was a little bit of Mississauga in the heart of Arabia. It was also the place where the Beijing team got on a three-day carousel of booze, hockey, and the pursuit of loose girls, who prowled the night clubs and discos in search of Western men.

As soon as I walked in the door, I knew what I was in for. The Beijingers were messengers of hockey's jock culture, for better or worse. When I told Dave Roberts what Kareem had said about hockey being like a disease, he added, "Ya, it's like some kind of testosterone ritual. Guys from different parts of the world get together, play some games, get drunk, and then leave feeling like they know one another. There aren't many ways that you can do that." He said it with pride. Like the rest of the guys, Dave believed that hockey teams produced the kind of male dynamic found in hunting camps, frat houses, cub scouts, and other bastions of male-dom. For the few hours I spent at Crocodiles, women were ogled, balls were jockeyed, dicks were grabbed, hats were stolen and flung away, asses were protruded suggestively, and more than once, Steve Conniff mimed a rutting goat to demonstrate Marcus's corrupt sexual proclivities. It was a typical hockey bar scene, which Dave and the others believed possessed a kind of magic.

"Fuckin' Chicken dance! Do it, faggot!"

For a group of straight guys, the team, like most men in sports, played at being gay a lot of the time. It is an extension of that weird inverted macho stance which, by pretending you're queer, shows how comfortable and assured of your heterosexuality you are. I've actually played against all-gay teams before (do they stand around their dressing room pretending to be straight?). One of them was entered in our summer league. When I first skated against them, I thought of all of those kids in school who were bullied by jocks and toughs, whose feyness didn't give them a fighting chance. I antici-pated a team of players who had persevered through the bullshit despite the fact that hockey (and most of pro sport) refused to acknowledge their existence. It was Tiger Williams who once told *MVP* magazine, "This ain't a game for fags."

What I hadn't anticipated was that the All-Gays would be stocked with hard-muscled men with an axe to grind. They were in better shape than most teams. They were a tough and vengeful group, and the experience was an eye opener. Foolishly, I'd expected a team of swishy "whipper-wills," but they hit hard and used their sticks like carving knives. They were the most intense bunch I've ever played.

Steve and Marcus weren't half as tough on the ice as they were on the dance floor, where they ground each other ass-to-ass. Marcus moaned, "That's right. I love it baby," in a long German drawl and the fellows laughed and cheered and drank more. At one point, Steve was rebuffed by a woman, and as she turned away, he said, "That's because *we're all faggots!*" so loud that everyone in the bar could hear. Then he pointed: "Especially Marcus!" at which the Swiss-German did his chicken dance.

Finally.

I was grateful for being included in these escapades. While I was ambivalent about the nickname I'd finally been given – Andrew decided on the Espositoesque the Big Dago – I enjoyed the chicken dance. Very much. The whole scene, however, reminded me of why I'd turned away from sports in the first place: all of that dumb macho heat, the pressure to fall in with a crowd or be cast out, to drink, fight, and fuck, or else. At times like these hockey culture is at its most dubious. When the team gathered around the bar, wrapped their arms around each other, sank a trayload of lemon vodka shooters, and yowled *"Beijing! Beijing!"* I was reminded that I am in love with a game that possesses the worst qualities of maledom.

Booze is often the source of such eyebrow-raising behaviour. Under the influence, the Beijingers acted the way they did because they believed it was how hockey players were supposed to behave. I couldn't blame them, because the NHL has always been as obsessed with beer as sport. The league is as much about Molson (owners of the Habs), and Labatt (proprietors of "Hockey Night in Canada"), and Carling O'Keefe (former owners of the Nordiques), as Jones–Butler–Boutette. On "Hockey in Night in Canada" broadcasts, we're bombarded with hockey-themed beer ads. Wayne Gretzky recently signed on as the spokesman for Bud Lite, the official beer of the National Hockey League, while other minor Canadian breweries are always scrabbling after hockey to help sell their product. As well, the reputation of hockey players goes a long way towards the promotion of booze culture in hockey. Stories of a player's prodigious drinking bouts are often as compelling as stories of his athletic achievements: Jim McKenny and BJ Salming driving on the wrong side up Toronto's Yonge Street in the middle of the night, then spilling out of their car after being stopped by the cops, and being escorted home by Toronto's finest; Don Cherry and Bobby Orr driving a Mini into the lobby of a hotel, trying to stuff it into the elevator; Gump Worsley getting the trainer to spike his post-game water jug with vodka; the taverns and brasseries owned by Henri Richard, the Courtnalls, Sergio Momesso; and, of course, Derek Sanderson's famed escapades, like the time he impulsively

flew fourteen patrons of his bar – Bachelors III, which he co-owned
with Joe Namath – to Hawaii for two weeks, which he confesses he
can't remember.

On King Street in Toronto there used to be a bar called Peter's
Hall of Fame, which was a popular hang-out for athletes. My friend
worked there and he says, "Guys like Semenko would come in and
order bottles of Grand Marnier and threaten me if I didn't put on
their Pantera tapes." For a while, there was a series of photos outside
the bar (they've since disappeared) which depicted Wayne Gretzky,
Mark Messier, and other Oilers in the full bloom of youth. I used to
take my out-of-town friends there because it was the only true rep-
resentation of what life must be like for rich, young hockey players.
The photos showed the Oilers surrounded by a gaggle of young Teri
Garr–like blondes – fingers slipped through shirt buttons, hands on
asses – their tables spilling over with beer and shot glasses. Here
was the portrait of young hockey players living in the pulp of fantasy,
smiles melting their faces, eyes bright and bloodshot, looking
delirious with their romp through the garden of earthly delights.

It was this orgiastic nirvana to which Team Beijing aspired, and
while you had to hand it to them for aiming high, their behaviour
was as much rooted in Turk Sanderson's reptilian strut as the
cocaine cool of the '84 Oilers. Turk's story is a cautionary tale of
the excesses of hockey's booze culture. Sanderson was the former
star and small-town hero of the Niagara Falls Flyers, whose father
boasted of collecting the surgical thread from the first hundred
stitches of his son's career and storing them in a cigar box. After
being drafted by the Bruins, Turk ascended in the ranks as a penalty
killer and defensive forward during the Bobby Orr era. He was
named Rookie of the Year in 1968 and was considered the best
faceoff man of his time.

He told broadcaster Mike Anscombe that, during his first Bruins
training camp, he joined the team for a post-practice party at a bar
without the intention of drinking. Phil Esposito warned him, "If you
start drinking now, you won't be able to stop," while goaltender Gerry
Cheevers taunted the rookie, "You're not a hockey player if you don't
drink." Turk drank. He drank and smoked and snorted and dabbled

in every stimulant known to man. He came to embody the emerging sexual and cultural posturing of youth in his on- and off-ice habits: long hair and sideburns, Nehru jackets, wavy bell bottoms, tie-dyed scarves, turtlenecks, and beads in a league still full of neckties and crew cuts. His phone number was published in the New England directory. A local radio station, WBZ, invited female listeners to describe, in 103 words or less, why they wanted a date with Turk, and more than 13,000 women wrote in from thirty states. The woman who'd given the most evocative answer turned out to be a seventy-three-year-old grandmother of twelve: Mabel Hocking.

Turk's home in Boston was like Hef's Rumpus Room. It had bearskin rugs and sunken play areas. He installed a mirror on the ceiling of his bedroom so he could observe the services of his women, and later wired a video camera so that guests at lavish, Caligulan parties could watch Turk get down on closed-circuit televisions around the house. He bought an eight-foot circular bed and coated his home in ankle-deep, wall-to-wall white shag carpeting. He boasted of trading girlfriends with Rod Gilbert and Bob Nevin, and published a list of cities with the best and worst groupies (Montreal at the top, Pittsburgh at the bottom). He had the habit of entering motel rooms through the window, which he did during one training camp, only to crash into a room where three strangers were having a card game. Turk was wild. He hosted a TV talk show and called the first draft of his autobiography "I'll Smash You in the Face." He appeared on Merv Griffin and Johnny Carson. He was one of the last star players who openly questioned the direction of the league, often antagonizing president Clarence Campbell to the point of near-suspension.

But Turk's fall was hard. After signing a ten-year contract with the WHA's ill-fated Philadelphia Blazers for $2.35 million (he played only eight games before begging the Bruins to take him back), Turk couldn't parlay his superb defensive skills into the scoring that his best years with the Bruins had promised. He was let out of the contract and bounced around with a few other teams, getting deeper into booze, blow, and debt. His lifestyle, combined with ill-prescribed steroids for a stomach ailment, ruined both his hips. He quit hockey, or hockey quit him, which led him to a series of menial jobs, among them bagging groceries at a supermarket. He lived the immediate years after his retirement in Central Park, sleeping under bridges. He once told Dick Beddoes about the time he took another vagrant's newspaper to use as a blanket. Sanderson told Beddoes, "I sneered at the bum: 'Do you know who I am?' 'Yeah,' he said. 'You're a boozed-up hockey player. Now give me back my fucking newspaper.'

Turk's isn't the only story of a pro leaguer taken by booze or drugs (see Busher Jackson, Doug Harvey, Dutch Gainor, Bill Durnan, Bruce Gamble, Howie Young, Spinner Spencer, Steve Durbano, Borje Salming, John Kordic, Bryan Fogarty, and Bob Probert). This is to say nothing of the players who never had enough of a profile for us to ever know their sorrow. There are thousands of former athletes hanging out in rinks, at donut shops, or on skid rows who were raised in a culture that encouraged the behaviour of the Harveys and Proberts. The hockey world is littered with once-promising skaters for whom having a few beers meant acceptance into the hockey fraternity, but who weren't important enough to be protected by league or management once it was discovered that their wrist shot had no heat.

I know the story of a junior player who decided to drop acid with his friends the night before a nationally televised prospects game in Vancouver. He had a typical evening planned: get a little high, watch TV, chase some tail. But the acid turned out to be bad, laced with strychnine, rat poison. It hit others worse than it hit him. His best friend freaked out and tried to kill himself, so the prospect stayed up with him and made sure he did not. Ten o'clock became midnight, which became morning, which passed into day. Finally, the friend settled down and fell asleep. The prospect went to the arena and suited up, telling no one what had happened. You can only imagine how he played the most important game of his life. Parents and coaches attended the game, confused by his poor performance. You'll never know his name.

The prospect went on to have a life, but there are many others who did not. For a lot of ex-players, hockey opens onto a sewer that swallows their lives, and as the Beijingers got progressively more wasted, waving shot glasses and hounding babes, I realized that their behaviour was not so much a celebration of camaraderie as a mocking dance of the hockey dead.

At one point during the party, a rock 'em, sock 'em video came over one of the bar's many television sets. The video showed boda-cious women intercut with fast edits of guys beating the shit out of each other. The crowd in the bar whooped and hollered at the sight of these nubiles, who flashed their tits and midriffs and asses swathed in leather and spandex. Janet covered her face with her hand and the other women in the room turned away. Blood splattered off noses and nipples poked through sweaters. Heads slammed against the glass as vixens lifted their shirts and wagged booty at the camera. The Grim Reaper. The Little Ball of Hate. Tits and Fists. A snuff film for sports.

"Now that's Canadian!" yelled Steve.

"Check out her rack!"

I told Marcus that I had to go and that I'd see him at the rink the next day.

We left the club and stepped into the sensuousness of Dubai at night.

It was all starlight and neon and mysterious, robed women and the shuffling of sandals. Al Marraqat street was a swirl of global voices, what writer Jonathan Raban once called "a muted Babel." There were Palestinians, Iranians, Jordanians, Qataris, Yemenis, Indians, Arabs, Pakistanis, and Europeans, people speaking Urdu, Hindustani, English, and Arabic, filling the streets with a river of voices. We were swallowed up by the crowd: soldiers in blue detail; Sikhs in yellow turbans and white robes; Indian women in tangerine saris; hawk-nosed men with caramel skin and thick beards; groups of men strolling, their fingers entwined, arms wrapped around each other; a young Arabian woman, only her eyes showing above a gold burka; and a moon-faced girl wearing a black hood and a string of pearls draped over her head. The Arabian women slew me. Some of them exposed only a wrist, the palm of a hand, the quivering of an eyelash. The less I could see of their bodies, the more attracted I was. One woman was draped entirely in black cloth, but her eyes, lined with deep kohl, peered through the window of her *chaodor*. She looked at me and smiled. I could not see her mouth, but I was enraptured. The women were every shade of ash, milk, burnished brown, chocolate, tar. Their lips, when visible, were painted deep red and their bodies were robed in every colour of nature, showing womanhood in all her foliage, smelling of cinnamon, rose, licorice, and lemon. I thought of the fellows back at the bar. Here was beauty, waiting for them.

Janet broke my trance.

"What the fuck's a rack?"

19

KUWAITI KICK-ASS BREAKDOWN

The tournament continued at the Al Nasr rink in Dubai, the site of the pre-tournament press conference. Al Nasr was more a typical rink than Al Ain, if you can call an arena in an industrial park on the red desert typical.

The Falcons' first game of the day was against the Kuwait Mooseheads. When I saw Kuwait on the tournament schedule, I'd hoped it would be the Kuwait national team, whose performance in the 1999 Asian games, their international debut, had made waves over in Canada. This was, in part, thanks to the recruitment as head coach of Maritimer Brian Smith, who returned home with stories of players who kept lions and tigers and drove Porsches and Lamborghinis to the rink. The Kuwait team was formed at the behest of five brothers – or cousins, it depends on who you ask – and while they'd scored only a single goal in the tournament, the experience was, according to the Kuwait Sports Ministry, a significant achievement in the development of hockey in the desert. I wouldn't have argued with that, but to hear Abdullah tell the story, it meant very little to Arabian hockey: "Anybody can hire a coach and start a program. But to lose like that in front of the whole world? No. We will not go that way. We will build until we are ready. Kuwait is arrogant. They think they can just strap on skates and play. But they are an embarrassment. They show little respect for the game."

Chris Reynolds agreed, sort of: "The Kuwaitis are frowned upon over here. They have a reputation for being a little difficult. You know, when Saddam invaded them, a lot of people over here were going, "Go get' em, big guy!" because people in the Emirates and all over the Middle East have a problem with the Kuwaitis. We've invited the national team down here before, only to regret it. They turned down our initial invitation, then hopped in their Chevy Caprices the day of the tournament and whipped across the desert – the distance is comparable to Vancouver to Calgary – expecting to play. They brought bags of money and paid entirely in cash. We sat down and reworked the schedule to accommodate them, but after they lost their first game, they started an all-out brawl with one of the other teams. The next day, they were gone again. A year or so later, someone approached us with the idea of arranging a friendly match between the Mighty Camels and Kuwait. We were aware of their temper and behaviour, but we reluctantly said yes. As it turned out, we beat them convincingly, but after the game this time, the five brothers started whaling on each other, right there in front of everyone."

Kuwait forward Patti Rempell, one of the organizers of the Moosehead program, remembers the time her team of local ex-pats played against the Kuwait Nationals: "It was a fun game and a big event. They even charged people to get in and we had a good crowd. I remember being in the hallway getting dressed – the Nats changed in the dressing room – with all of these young kids gawking around the corner at me, watching me put on my gear alongside the men, staring at me as if I were a shameless Western hussy. The stands were filled with Westerners and Arabs, even the Canadian ambassador, Terry Colfer, his wife Lynne, and son Derek were there. The ambassador dropped the ceremonial puck and things were fine until the insane, full-out bench-clearing brawl. I was on the ice at the time. The Kuwati team jumped our guys and threw them to the ice. There was total pandemonium. Paul, our goalie, skated from his end down to where the action was and squared off against the other goalie. The fight seemed to last for days. Needless to say, we haven't played them since."

The rink in Kuwait was one-third regulation size and had a glitter ball hanging over the ice. Patti told me, "The arena has a room for prayer in it. There's a proper dressing room, too, but the ex-pats aren't allowed to use it. It's reserved for the national team, who don't play regularly, but we dress in the hallway anyway. I'm the only woman on the team, so sometimes I find myself asking no one, 'Did you see the ass on that player? Get a load of those undies? And he calls himself a man?' It's hard enough being a woman on a guys' team – let alone a woman on a guys' team in a Muslim country."

At Al Nasr, all twelve teams dressed in a gymnasium underneath the stands. There was a small stage at the far end of the room which the Falcons claimed as their own personal change area. I spent the day moving back and forth between Team Beijing's and the Falcons' quarters, stepping over hockey bags splayed open and spilling balls of socks, gloves, sweaters, jocks, and water bottles. The players dressed while sitting on wooden chairs with their gear at their feet, and several times over the course of the day, I saw a naked man with a towel over his lap sitting back-to-back with a gladiator from another team armed head to toe in gear. It was like being backstage at a Broadway production of *I, Claudius*. All the mouldy hockey detritus – not to mention a dense musk that roiled over the room; the chatter of players walking to and from the ice; the squelching of water bottles; tearing of tape; stoning of skates; and wheezing of men and women – gave me the sense of being at the heart of hockey, desert or no desert.

Eventually, I took my place on a chair and started taping my stick. The quality of hockey tape has declined in recent years. It's feathery and gets waterlogged, but it's something that we've all learned to live with. Taping a stick is the closest most men ever get to home decorating (besides choosing between green and black garbage bags), mostly because of the care put into the routine. Some players scrub their tape with a bar of wax to guard against blade slush, while others crown the top of the stick with tape to provide an ideal grip for a gloved hand. A tape job must be perfect before a stick can be used in a game. If it's not, it just doesn't feel right in your hands when you bring it down on somebody's pumpkin.

Before the match against Kuwait, I handed out little Toronto Maple Leafs stickers to the Falcons in the hope that it would give us a touch of luck in our game. I unfolded the sheet and asked each player to take one. Mo said, "Ah, I wondered where you were keeping these!" He stuck his on the back of his helmet while Ahmed and Omar slipped theirs into tournament programs. Years from now, I imagined them looking through a book of clippings, old notices, tickets, and pennants, and coming across the blue and white patch, picking it up between thumb and forefinger and wondering what it meant and how it had once fit into their lives. This is to say nothing of the feeling I got when we took to the ice and I saw Mo's tiny blue leaf. For the first time, I was struck with the weight of being a representative not only of my country, but of my city, and when I handed one to Nasser, who was with us in his street clothes on the bench, I said, "Toronto. This is my team," my throat choking.

We defeated the Mooseheads 4–0. It was a game high with emotion, because we needed the win to stay alive in the tournament. Since the Al Nasr ice surface was smaller than Al Ain's, our forwards were more effective. This meant that their perilous end-to-end rushes resulted in quality scoring chances and, for the first time all tournament, Juma and Omar played with the kind of flair I'd seen in Hong Kong. Bear marched up and down the bench and double-shifted them. They responded by back-checking in earnest, the first time I'd seen them do this. Don the goalie responded to their hustle with cries of "That's right, *boys!*" and "*Way to clear! Way to clear!*" Kuwait never stood a chance.

Kareem played as well as anybody. Near the end of the first half, Turqi passed him the puck from behind our zone, and he sped across the red line like a man chasing a runaway stroller. His eyes were tiny lanterns, his eyebrows arrowed. He eluded one check, then skated towards Kuwait's right defenceman, who immediately came at him. Kareem wound up as he had countless times before, but this time, he brought his stick down half-way to the puck. The defence-man braced himself for the shot, but Kareem feinted and slipped the puck around him. With that one deke, Kareem elevated his game. It was a moment of invention in the tradition of all the great, quick-thinking hockey players he'd never seen: Orr flying through the air to win the Stanley Cup in overtime; Paul Henderson beating three Russians to win game seven in '72; Gretzky's shot over Lump Vernon's shoulder in '88; Mario Lemieux undressing Ray Bourque from centre ice. Watching Kareem's move was like seeing a game burst open. *Skate, shoot, muscles, think.* The Al Ain players leaned over the boards, their mouths wide with excitement, their hands pounding the wood. Bear put one knee on the top of the door as Kareem, pro-pelled by his move, skated in on the goalie. He took one stride, then another, and in all his excitement, he shot the puck with great force, sending it ten feet over the net.

With the win, the Falcons moved into the division final against the Dhahran Saad Falcons, one of two hockey clubs in Saudi Arabia. Before the game, we took our warm-up, then formed a shell of black and purple around Bear, who gave us his pre-game talk while Ahmed translated. Once again, after Bear had finished, Ahmed said a few things to his team, and then we stood for a moment in silence. Ahmed and Kareem murmured prayers under their breath, their lips quivering and eyes half-closed. Ahmed held out his glove and we stacked ours on top. I dipped my head and leaned in. Kareem shouted a prayer from the Koran, ending his incantation with two words that we hollered as one: "*Al Ain!*"

The puck dropped and we charged out of the gate. We swarmed and pressed and took away everything the Saudis threw up the boards and the middle of the ice. Each time they tried escaping from their end, we pinned down a corner and held them in. We passed the puck with authority and skated with desperation. Since both teams were coming off miserable tournaments, we went at each other a little harder. Ahmed gritted his teeth and played like a tough-assed, Western League centre – Brian Skrudland, Bucky Buchberger – flying into his checks with his head and elbows first. Because it was the deciding game, both teams played the body, gently enough to stay within the rules, but always leaving something extra behind the play: a face-wash here, a rib tickle there, a forearm shiver, a zipper of wood down the calf. Dhahran gave it back, too, which was fine with me. Late in the first period, I pushed one of their players into the boards, and he reached around and locked his arm around my head, pulling me to the ice. We wriggled around a little like two pups fighting over a bone. He wanted the puck as badly as I did, the way it should be.

We continued to attack, getting chance after chance to shoot on goal. Juma hit the crossbar and Ahmed slid the puck wide of an open net. Somehow we could not score. The Saudis' goaltender was a short, balding fellow who moved with all the swiftness of a potted plant, but he stopped everything we threw at him. Sometimes goaltenders get in a groove despite their lack of skill or athleticism – a trait that only compounds forwards' suspicion of them – and every time we broke over the blue line, he was squared and ready for the shot. Pucks curved around legs and skates like small fish darting through the reeds, but he saw everything. Soon, we became a team racked with frustration. After every missed shot we buried our faces in our gloves, our heads thrown back, our voices crowing in pain. Bear yelled, *"Keep pressing!"* and *"Dig hard in there.* HARD! DEEP!" but after a while, he resorted to spitting French invective.

With about ten minutes left in the game, I had a chance to put us in front. Omar had the puck at centre ice, but was tangled up with a Kuwait forward. I stood behind him at the right point and noticed that Juma and Ahmed were both on the other side of the rink, so I took off from my point and skated beside him, shouting *"Heyyy!"* the way I would have were I warning him of an onrushing car. Omar looked up and slung me the puck. I collected it in full stride and whipped up the ice. I travelled around one player, eluded the poke check of another, then curled past the last Saudi defenceman. I was home free. I came in from the left side, the goalie's right. The Saudi goaltender darted out of the crease, then slithered back into his net as I charged up. I skated unthinkingly. I lowered my head, imagined the two top corners of the net peeking out from over the goalie's shoulders, and launched the puck into the air – a low, sagging arc, heavy and determined – lifting my head just in time to see it hit the middle of the goaltender's chest and drop to his feet.

I stopped in front of the goalie, who looked up at me and showed me his eyes, which were cold and red. I skated with my stick across my knees to the bench.

I stood beside Mo.

"David. Very close."

"Shit," I said, saddened, my head hung.

When I looked up, the Saudis scored. It was a stupid goal, a deflection that hopped on the stick of a player standing at the open side of the net. The tide turned against us. With thirty seconds on the clock, the game ended with a faceoff in their end. Bear pulled Don the goalie and sent out Tim Watson, Dave, Ahmed, Juma, Omar, and me to try and net the equalizer. I stood on the right point, but cheated to the top of the circle. I told Juma and Omar, "Thirty seconds is a lot of time. You're always thinking faster than the play is moving. So don't panic. Take your time. Don't kill time, but don't panic, either." Then Ahmed added something in Arabic. They answered him with fierce words and lined up in a wedge facing the net.

Tim Watson took the faceoff. He tried drawing it back, but the puck hardly moved. We dove in and scrambled for it like ants over crumbs, but someone ended up falling on it, killing ten seconds in the process. We set up again. I told Tim, "Just try to punch the thing forward. Get it to the net and we'll just bail out and go for it." But instead, he drew the puck back, and it landed on the stick of Dave Watson – his son. Dave corralled it and fired, but the goaltender kicked out a pad and then fell on the puck like a cat pouncing on a mouse, covering the disc with his glove. My heart was pounding. I repeated my suggestion to Tim, "Try pushing it." John Davy made sure every player was where they were supposed to be. He arranged the skaters like figures on a chess board, held the puck at his waist, then slapped it down. Tim pushed it and it sprang free. Ahmed swiped at it, nearly pushing it past the goalie into an open side. But the puck squirted behind the net to a Saudi defenceman's stick, who wristed it along the boards. It disappeared up the ice and the score-clock honked. Dave Watson broke his stick over his knee and swore. Ahmed bit his lip. I looked down at the ice, refusing to raise my head and acknowledge the numbers:

1–0, Saudi Arabia.

It was a hard loss, and my heart couldn't take it. In 1952, after scoring a semi-final winning goal against the Boston Bruins, Rocket Richard walked to his dressing room, sat in front of his cubicle and broke down. He sobbed and sobbed and could not stop; this great, fearsome man, his head in his hands, crying. Nothing could stop his tears, so a doctor was called in and he was sedated. The Rocket fell asleep weeping.

This is how I felt when I returned to my hotel room. Jet lag, the multitude of games, the strange environs, the foreign tongue – all of these things finally caught up with me. I stepped into the shower and, standing there in the cascading water, I felt my soul split open. Raw emotion poured out of me, my hands pressed to my eyes, tears squeezing through my fingers. Janet heard me through the door: "Dave? Are you okay?"

I was a wreck. One of the beautiful things about sports is that, even when you feel terrible, at least you feel. Sports taps into emotions we guard for the rest of our waking hours. Those who play sports, or who pledge love for their favourite teams, often find it impossible to express these feelings to wives, husbands, or children. We use games to vent our spirit, behaving in ways we can't at work or home. Because we spend so much time in offices talking to people we don't know or pretending to be someone we aren't, sports is an outlet where we can suddenly be ourselves, where it's okay to tour the extremities of passion and despair.

During my seven days in Dubai, I'd grown as close to the Falcons as any team I've played on. It's what Dave Roberts had tried to express earlier, but couldn't. Hockey had allowed me a rapport with these strangers, my Arab brothers of the ice. Playing on the Falcons gave me the same feeling I've had countless nights while skating with the Morningstars: love and acceptance and brotherhood. But with one difference – I would never see the Falcons again.

As I crouched in the shower, these emotions were shaken from me like fruit too heavy for the vine. The intense physicality of the game, the mental anguish, the heart-arresting highs and lows had opened parts of me that had been closed for a long time, and I fought to dam the sadness and pain.

"Are you okay?"

The puck. It hit him in the chest. The chest.

Let it go.

20

THE MOTHERLAND OF HOCKEY

Team Beijing's last day at Al Nasr was not the best. We were due to meet the Abu Dhabi Blades in a game that would crown the winner of the Shopping Festival Trophy (effectively, the silver medal), and I thought we had a pretty good chance to finish in the money. But when the team showed up at the rink, they were in a terrible mess. The first person to arrive was Steve, whose eyes were barely visible.

"Oh my god. Are you drunk?" I asked him.

"Ungh. Maybe."

"What happened?"

"Twenty bottles of vodka. Last night," he said, rubbing the flat of his hands over his eyes.

The team had spent the night at Cyclone's, another one of those Dubai-by-way-of-Mississauga party joints, where Tomi, it turned out, was the evening's star. He'd gotten shit-faced and had passed out in a toilet stall. He was found at four in the morning by a member of the cleaning staff, who thought he was dead.

When Tomi showed up at the rink, his face was puffed and pale, and he moved in a painfully slow shuffle, trying to muffle the sounds of his steps, which were resonating like cannon fire inside the booze-soaked cavity of his skull.

Once we settled into our dressing room (being division finalists, we were given a separate area to prepare for deciding games) all our eyes turned to Tomi, who sat on the bench and stared through the floor like a catatonic, his arms hanging limp at his sides, his fly splayed open on his jeans.

"So, did you have your pants down?" asked Andrew, pulling on a skate.

Tomi gripped his head with both hands.

"I threw out," he said, groaning.

"Threw out?"

"Yes. Out," he repeated, squeezing his eyes shut.

"No. You threw up," said Andrew.

"Yes. I threw up," said Tomi. "Up. Out," he repeated, holding his arm up, then letting it flop against his body.

It took Tomi about forty minutes to put on his gear. His hair was like a giant thistle, spiking in every direction but down, and there were thundery shadows under his eyes. Every now and then, he'd lower his head and groan. When I asked if he was sure he felt good enough to play the game, he said, "I am shit. But I will play."

"Tomi. You're not going to throw out on the ice, are you?" asked Andrew.

Tomi turned his head slowly, side to side.

Team Beijing had nothing. We played as if our skates were made of stone. Steve Conniff covered about as much ice as a stone column. He smoked on the bench and swore whenever Abu Dhabi came over the red line. At one point, he was sweating so profusely and his face was so flooded with red that he looked like a tomato bathed in oil. Roman had gone to Cyclone's, too, and he was moving slower than Lent. Andrew and Massimo tried leading the attack, but they had little to work with, and after twenty minutes, we were down 4–0. Tom Burridge took a ten-minute misconduct for ref baiting and was eventually ousted from the game. Tom's dad had given us a pep talk before the match, guaranteeing yet another undisciplined performance from the junior Burridge. The old man, dressed in his Omani national team sweats and trainers, stood in front of the team and said wise things like "Be relaxed" and "Don't worry about the other team; just worry about yourself" while keeping one eye on Tomi in case he vomited on his skates.

The best players for Abu Dhabi were two Finns: a defenceman and a winger. The winger reminded me of Mats Naslund, the Little Viking. He moved so quickly down the boards that my body pretzeled trying to catch him. At one point, he executed perhaps the most astonishing play I have ever witnessed. He was coming down the wing with the puck when he tried, as he'd done all game, to slip past me along the boards. This time, I measured my turn perfectly and got my stick between his legs, up-ending him as he moved past. But still he kept the puck in front of him, controlled it as he started to fall, and slapped it while he was going down. His blade caught the rubber and it shot towards the top corner of the net, which our goalie – Jan-Erik had been replaced by the backup netminder from one of the Swiss teams – barely defended with his catching glove. The Finn landed hard on the ice, not for a second taking his eye off the puck's flight. He slid hard into the corner and the whistle blew. I went over to help him to his feet, amazed at the focus and intensity of his play.

It was the first time I'd seen a great European hockey player do his thing first-hand. I'm among those who find it hard to concede that Forsberg or Jagr or Bure play any better than the finest of Canadian athletes. But in Dubai, I finally saw my attitude for what it was: bullshit rooted in pride and vanity. While the majority of players in the tournament were Canadian, they certainly weren't the best players. It was the same at the Hong Kong Fives. Had I selected this tournament's MVP, I would have chosen either of the Finns (the award went to Ticino's captain, Brambillo). On my own team, Andrew the American and Massimo the Swiss-Italian were the best players. The tournament mirrored the trend in international hockey. Part of me had wanted to show up to these world tournaments as a Canadian hockey wizard, skating unchecked around rink rats grateful for a lesson. It would be my chance to be a hockey hero like those players I'd worshipped as a kid. I'd wanted to prove to the Europeans that there was something about my play that they simply could not approach. I'd wanted them to lean against the boards, point at my moves, and admit, "Ah, so that is why Canadians have been so good for so long."

But I discovered that the strength of my Canadian game was also its weakness. Though I played with great will and enthusiasm – straightening up attacking wingers, diving across the ice to break up plays, kneeling on one leg to block shots, tying up players in front of the net – it didn't amount to much in the way of goals or scoring chances, at least not compared to the Finns, who were better shooters, or the Yanks and Swiss, who were more accomplished skaters. I made very few players or fans wish they were me. In other words, I shared the characteristics of the modern Canadian hockey player – toughness, guile, and hustle – the same qualities that Canadian stars in the NHL have come to represent at home and abroad. Owen Nolan, Mark Recchi, Eric Lindros, Brendan Shanahan, Steve Yzerman, Rob Blake, Chris Pronger, and Theoren Fleury are all tough, big-hearted natural leaders. Occasionally we produce a Kariya, a Turgeon, a Lecavalier. But then the world answers: Jagr, Hasek, Bure, Selanne, Sundin, Demitra, Stefan, Elias, Ozolinsh, Hejduk, Teverdovsky.

The nerve.

We only have ourselves to blame. We gave the world our game, taught it to them. It was the writings of Lloyd Percival – the erudite athletic scholar who was scorned in Canada, whose work Dick Irvin Sr. once called "the product of a three-year-old mind" – on which the great Tarasov based his teachings in the USSR. The rest of Europe followed the Soviets' lead, and now there are generations of Canadian kids who can't, and will never, know how it feels to dominate the world of hockey.

At the end of the day, no matter how much Don Cherry or anyone else tries to work the numbers, our current influence on the game comes not from placing a percentage of guys born in South Porcupine or Kirkland Lake among the league's elite scorers, but from having made it possible for the rest of the world to play this beautiful game.

After Team Beijing's 5–0 loss to Abu Dhabi, I was interviewed by a Swiss television crew who'd flown in from Zurich to cover the progress of their two teams. (The two eventually met in the Nokia Cup finals.) The reporter asked, "What do you think, sitting here watching a game in the desert, having come all the way from the motherland of hockey?"

His words sent a shiver down my spine. *The motherland of hockey.* The Swiss reporter had singled me out of the crowd simply because I came from a place that, in his mind, defined the sport that he'd travelled thousands of miles to film. In Canada, it's hard to know how other countries view our influence on the game. Without that feedback, we tend to moan about imported athletes perfecting the game we invented. But the truth is, abroad we're worshipped for our game. Canada is *the motherland.* Hearing the Swiss broadcaster describe my country in those words made me proud, thrilled. It was a compliment I treasured for the rest of my stay. As I sat there in the stands and watched the Dubai minister of sport sling medals around the necks of the winning team from Ticino, I felt I was being rewarded, too, for it was my people who'd made this scene possible, and without us, it was just dust and sunshine.

Before we left the UAE, I wanted to make one last visit to the Al Ain rink, to make certain that it was real by taking one final whip around the oval.

Our last day in the desert was about closure in more ways than one. While packing our luggage, I saw a broadcast of ESPN World on the television in our hotel. Included in their short highlights package was footage of Maple Leaf Yanic Perreault scoring four goals. Naturally, I was drawn to the screen, but when the action ended, my thoughts turned back to skating in Al Ain, and I realized that I was no longer absorbed by the NHL, but by hockey of a different kind.

I was glad. I'd been unhappy with NHL hockey even before that summer's day in 1998, and I was looking forward to getting weaned off the pro game. A few months before I'd gone to China, the Leafs moved from the old Maple Leaf Gardens to the shiny new Air Canada Centre. To many, this signalled a new beginning for the franchise, but to me it meant the passing of the last shred of the team's dignity and distinction. Leafs management defended the new building on two principles – more leg room and better parking – and, while many fans reported that it was indeed more comfortable to sit there than in the Gardens, one of the charms of the old rink was that you had no choice but to make contact with the person sitting next to you. The Gardens brought people together, but the ACC, like many of hockey's new arenas, suffered from ear-rattling between-faceoff music, crude lighting, enormous Jumbotrons belching ads and movie trailers, and HOME DEPOT and IBM beacons flashing above the exits.

To me, the decline of the NHL is embodied in these arenas, which are more about wedging people apart than binding communities. Rinks were once meditative places sheltered from the swirl of the outside world. You used to buy a ticket in hope of escaping the travails of real life, not to be boiled in hype. But NHL hockey games have become cheap electronic carnivals, orgies of sound and light and music. They've helped turn the league into a trend-conscious, style-driven operation fumbling for a piece of the youth market. The game itself has changed, too, its pace slowed by TV time-outs, which were inserted by NHL Commissioner Gary Bettman to sell more advertising time. These time-outs corrupt the inherent rhythm of the game, but then, after haphazard expansion, the neutral zone Trap, and superstars wrecked by their mid-twenties, it had already lost much of its zest.

What's a shame about the state of the NHL is that its slide has come at the same time that other kinds of hockey – minor leagues, women's hockey, the international game, roller and rec hockey – are humming with life. According to the Canadian Amateur Hockey Association, more adults are playing the game in Canada than ever before, proof that people are reaching for something they can no longer find in the National Hockey League. Now that I had been away from pro hockey for six weeks, I realized that players in the NHL don't play what I call hockey. Rather, they play NHL hockey. There's a huge difference and, as I turned off the television, collected our bags, and hailed a taxi to take us to Al Ain, I knew that I was cured.

I was NHL-free.

Nasser met us at the gates of the rink. He pulled up in a gold Mercedes with Will Smith pumping from the speakers. The first thing he did was apologize: "Sorry," he said, haltingly, "I have a better car, but it is being fixed."

Even though Nasser's English was spare and my Arabic was, well, whatever is less than that, we managed to talk hockey. I asked him how it had felt to compete in the Hong Kong Fives, and he told me that the worst possible thing to have happened to the UAE Nationals was winning the tournament in China. He said it was too much, too soon.

"Some of the players became different people. They went on television, talking about themselves, not the team. They changed and it was not good for us. Before we went to Hong Kong, we were like one hand, but coming home, we were many fingers. We used to practise together every Friday, but now we don't practise at all. We celebrated as a team in Hong Kong, but when we got back, everyone went away on their own. That's why I want to make a junior team. If you don't work, there's someone behind you."

I suggested that it was all part of growing as a team, but I'm not sure I convinced the young Arab skater. I asked Nasser what future he saw for himself, for the team. He told me that his dream was to one day visit a hockey camp in Ontario. I imparted two words: "Harris–Keon."

"Who are these men?" he asked.

"They used to run a famous hockey camp, the Harris–Keon Hockey Camp. Bobby Orr had one, too, I think. I don't know if they're running it anymore, but when I was growing up, I wanted to go there, too. Dave Keon was the captain of the Leafs, number 14, a great faceoff man. The pamphlet on the camp showed kids playing hockey with him and Harris by day, swimming in a lake in the late afternoon, and sitting around long tables playing games after dinner. It looked like a paradise in the woods. I wanted to go."

"You didn't?"

"No, I'd stopped being interested in hockey by the time I was old enough to go."

"That's a sad story," he laughed.

"No, no, it's not. I love hockey more than ever now."

I ran down my hockey schedule for him: Monday and Thursday night, Fridays in the afternoon, a league game Saturday or Sunday, and then my regular Sunday night skate. I told him that, in the winter, there are so many outdoor rinks in Toronto that I'd yet to skate on half of them. I told him, "Some of them are open twenty-four hours a day. If we were at home, we could just stop the car, put on our skates and go."

Nasser looked to the ground and shook his head.

"I can't believe it!"

"It's true," said Janet. "He's always going out the door with his hockey bag. It's fine until he comes home and tries to sit next to me smelling like that."

"Hey, it's a beautiful smell."

"Beautiful, no," said Nasser, holding up his hand.

At the rink, we strapped on our skates. Nasser had arranged the ice time so that he could watch the beginners he'd recruited to form a UAE junior team. Bill Upton told me that Nasser went into high schools in Dubai and talked about the game. He tried to convince kids to sign up for lessons, telling them, "If you play hockey, you'll never play soccer again! Soccer is such a slow game compared to hockey." The last time he did this, he recruited ninety-two kids, enough to form two junior teams. Bill said, "Lately, Nasser's really come out of his shell. It happened after Hong Kong. Once he real-ized how much hockey meant to him – *swoosh* – away he went. He doesn't say much, but when he does, boy."

Nasser learned English by hanging out at Al Ain. He spoke hockey. He developed his passion for the sport even though he'd never seen

The real Nasser

an NHL game. "Over here, we get fifteen-second games," he told me, referring to the highlight clips shown on ESPN World. "You see a goal, maybe two, then it's over. You don't know the names of the players. They tell you nothing about the game in our language."

There were about twenty-five, thirty kids circling the rink. It brought back the simple pleasure of moving on skate-blades, of pushing off with the wind licking my face, my ears and cheeks numb with joy, imagining I was a figure from an Edgar Rice Burroughs or Jack London book, a rough-hewn boy set adrift in the northland, moving as if propelled by nature. Even though these kids on this desert rink had never heard of Jack London or Scott Young or Foster Hewitt, had never skated in the snow or cold – most would never feel cold, ever – I could tell that they felt the same things that I had. They skated: face opened, tongue fluttering, legs and hips twisting, arms frugging side to side. One kid's turban became loose and fluttered above the nape of his neck. His feet scraped the rink with every stride, his back hunched. Nasser and I took to the ice and were joined by another UAE player, Turqi, who was wearing white robes and a white turban and looked like a speeding desert prince. We wove a path in between two young skaters who were chopping at the ice, trying to keep up. As I flew past them, they looked over their shoulders at me, startled by the ease and fluidity of my movement. They chopped the ice harder and tried to catch me, but they could not, tumbling on their backsides and snowing their jeans and jackets. I stopped with a *shhhvvvv*, circled backwards, and stood over them. I reached down with my hand and said, "Okay. The first thing you've got to know about hockey is this: you're gonna fall down."

They raised their arms and I hoisted them to their feet. The leather of my Winwells swallowed their hands and, as I pulled them up, I said, "Have you guys signed up for hockey yet?" They said nothing and stared at me. "Go see him," I said, pointing to Nasser. Then I skated away, followed by a *chipchipchip*, the sound of their small blades coming up behind me.

PART THREE

Transylvania

21

WHERE SPEARING COMES FROM

The train moved out of Bucharest, snaking its way north into southern Transylvania. The midday light gave way to dusk as we chugged through the Prahova Valley past old linden and chestnut trees into a dense alpine landscape, where conifers covered the mountains like a great wool sweater. The dark green of the forest made for a sombre setting. Even though dapples of dying sunlight topped the trees like candles on a birthday cake, it was the shadows I watched, the edges of the woods swimming in dim light, revealing the odd stone house or cottage on a farm.

This was exactly how I had imagined Transylvania, which is to say, it was easy to stare into the mysterious woods and imagine Dracula stepping out with his cloak pulled across his face, his eyebrows twitching fiendishly. The top of the mountain range was swirling with fog that was thick as smoke. Half the trees had been touched by the autumnal palette of deep rust-red and yellow-green, the other half was already bare and reached out their branches like long, bony fingers. The Transylvanian Alps reminded me of the Canadian Rockies except that they looked as if they'd spent centuries trying to turn away from the sun rather than climb towards it. As night overcame day, I pressed my hand against the cold window, and remembered that hockey lay at the end of the line.

I hadn't intended to visit Transylvania to play hockey, not initially. But after discovering through the website of an obsessed Swede, Stephan Kreuger, that hockey had long been a favoured game there, it struck me that Dracula's homeland was one of those Eastern European enclaves that had yet to put its name on the international hockey map; it was therefore worth visiting.

The parallels between hockey and Transylvanian myth are striking. For instance, the legend of Vlad Tepes – also known as Dracula or Vlad the Impaler, ruler of Wallachia in the 1500s – is that he dispatched his enemies by driving a stake through their hearts, a manoeuvre not unlike that used by the 1974 Broad Street Bullies to "subdue" the opposing team. Vlad was pretty sadistic. He liked to plunge over-sized toothpicks through his victims' backs without touching a single vital nerve, ensuring at least forty-eight hours of blood-letting and conscious suffering before death. It is purported that Tepes rarely dined without a Turk writhing on a stake in front of him, and while this may seem like a bizarre and unusual ritual, it turns out that he was simply carrying on family tradition; his cousin, Stefan cel Mare, is reported to have "impaled by the navel, diagonally, one on top of each other," 2300 Turkish prisoners in 1473.

It's not unusual to find certain ill-tempered members of the hockey world sharing Vlad's name, though I don't think it's very good luck. Boris Mikhailov, the hard-nosed left winger of Team Russia's '72 Kharlamov line, was called this by the Canadian press, only to see his team lose the Summit Series in the final thirty-four seconds. This Vlad incurred threats from everyone from J.P. Parise to Jesse Palermo, my grandmother – neither of whom I'd mess with. The most recent skater to be called Vlad the Impaler was Detroit's Vladimir Konstantinov, whose dead-eyed toughness, in combination with a skill level unmatched by almost anyone in his line of work, was legendary, until a limousine accident two days after the Wings won the Stanley Cup stuck him in a wheelchair.

Were Vlad Tepes alive today – as some modern Draculian cults would have you believe – there's no doubt in my mind that he'd be a hockey fan. Sure, football is a tough sport, but it's more about broken bones and cracked skulls than blood; basketball is a sport of twisted ankles and tensor wraps; baseball is a game of bent pinkies and torn rotator-cuffs (any sport where a blister can inhibit an athlete's performance deserves a good impaling); and while boxing, under the right conditions, promises a copious amount of the red stuff as well as lots of turned-out flesh, it never goes far enough so that the floodgates are opened; even wrestling has become purely theatrical, depriving sports lovers of sanguine facial spiderwebs. Hockey, on the other hand, still produces buckets of blood fanning across the white ice, splashes of colour that would make even Jackson Pollock blush.

Vlad would have loved ex-Leaf Bobby Baun. There have been two modifications made to the hockey skate as a result of Baun's injuries: the reinforced shell of the toe, and plastic tips on the end of the blade. Baun was perhaps the most-mangled player in the history of hockey (his big toe was broken more than thirty times). Once, in practice, Frank Mahovlich was messing around with a plastic blade. The stick burst upon impact with the puck, exploding into nasty polyvinyl toothpicks, one of which penetrated Baun's skin a quarter-inch from his eye, sliced through the side of his head below his sideburn, and reappeared behind his right ear, streaking blood down the side of his face. In 1961, the Leaf defenceman was involved in another blood epic when he collided with New York's small forward, Camille Henry, and fell to the ice. As he did, the rear tip of Henry's skate accidentally cut into Baun's neck, coming to rest against the underside of his tongue. So much blood spilled from the wound and from Baun's mouth that he thought his jugular had been severed. He headed to the infirmary, a blood-soaked towel plugged against his throat. Upon close inspection, Dr. Kazuo Yanagisawa – hockey's Dr. Nick Riviera – deemed the injury minor, and sent Baun back to the ice with the wound cleaned and stitched. With the exception of a Band-Aid, Baun looked and played in the second period as he had at the beginning of the game but, by the end of the game, he was having trouble breathing. The hole under his tongue had filled with blood and was pressing against his windpipe. As he boarded the team's bus outside old Madison Square Gardens after the game, he went into convulsions when his torn neck muscles began to hemorrhage. Only emergency action by teammate Tim Horton prevented him from swallowing his tongue. He was rushed across the street to Polyclinic Hospital where, upon viewing him, the nurse asked, "Stabbed, huh?" Three blood transfusions and a drain plug in his neck eventually restored his normal breathing pattern, though it was feared that Baun would never play again, or at best, be through for the year. One week later, he was back in uniform.

Janet and I spent the night in Brasov and caught the train the next morning to Miercurea Ciuc. The skies pelted rain and the air grew colder, and through the fogged-up windows, I could just make out that the mountains had given way to lush farmland: the Ciuc Depression with Miercurea Ciuc at its centre. Ciuc (pronounced Chook) was the capital of Szekely (pronounced Saykay) land, the ancestral home of ethnic Hungarians. Ciuc was founded during the reign of Hungarian King Ladislaus I in the early 1000s, and even today eighty-three per cent of its people are of Hungarian descent. But the Szekelys had been pegged throughout Romania as disloyal to the country that governs them, and after the union of Transylvania and Romania in 1918, some 200,000 Hungarians fled, including thousands of Szekelys who feared oppression. As a result, Transylvanians have always kept closer ties to Hungary than to the rest of Romania, outsiders in their own country. Only recently, in early 1996, did Hungary relinquish all territorial claims on Transylvania in exchange for Romania's agreeing to respect the rights of some 1.8 million ethnic Hungarians (the Szekelys) in Romania.

I busied myself during the trip by reading a tabloid called *Pro Sport*, which I'd bought at the train depot for 2,500 lei. After buying the paper, I realized it would take me a while to get used to

Romanian currency. In Brasov, we'd exchanged traveller's cheques at one of Ion Tirac's National banks, which was a little like doing business at Al Arbour's Currency Exchange or John Brophy's Money-Mart. An ex-hockey player, Tirac was the former shaggy-haired tennis coach of Ilie Nastase and Boris Becker. He had been a national-team defenceman who once confronted a pair of Russian forwards by snapping his stick over his knee, wielding the jagged end, and threatening, "Hokay, who iss first? Better to make your mother weep than mine!"

Whenever I hold foreign currency for the first time it always feels like magic beans. Some of the Romanian coins were octagonal, others smaller than my thumbnail, and I knew that, should I find them years later at the bottom of a change drawer, it would be like rediscovering a small, integral detail of a dream. My problem with the lei was that it was traded in the hundreds of thousands. I'd often find myself staring at a chocolate bar and thinking: "Ten thousand bucks for a frigging chocolate bar? What is it, gold plated?" until I realized that it worked out to about forty cents. Still, it hurt my brain trying to convert the currency, so eventually I just stopped. From then on, I was able to enjoy the ridiculous thrill of walking around town with wads of cash in my pocket, which, while it might have bought only a roll of Scotch tape and a cigarette, allowed me to ask my wife, "And how many million should we bring today?" as if we were Rockefellers.

It was just before nightfall when we arrived in Ciuc. The train depot had no platform, so we just threw our stuff onto the tracks, which ran just a few feet from the road that led into town. We caught a taxi to the Hotel Harghita, a two-minute ride. The moment I walked inside the hotel, I felt more like I was in a Communist country (even though I wasn't) than I had in all of China (even though I had been). The lobby was empty and quiet and dark. And, of course, cold. The floors, walls, and ceilings were covered in musty wood panelling that gave way to a glittering, winding staircase leading to an upstairs dining area, which I never saw anyone use. The hotel was ostentatious and grand, and must have looked great in 1970. Smoke hung in the air and curled around the lobby's light fixtures. Opposite the registration desk, a glass-encased kiosk where a bun-haired woman in a red suit sat writing in a ledger and smoking a cigarette, three elevators with utilitarian green arrows belched metal as they arrived, their steel doors roaring open to reveal an interior like one I would imagine in a Soviet submarine. Beyond the registration desk was a long open bar showcasing an array of glittering bottles, under lock and key, in the kind of glass cabinets you'd find in your grandmother's sitting room. The bar's counter was polished and looked rarely used. Above it, a Britney Spears video flickered on a television, an image reflected in the tall, paned windows that looked out onto the town square. That, too, was dark and empty, a sea of brown stone, the centre of nothing.

Our room was as cold as a mine shaft and smelled of tobacco and cheap aftershave. Even though I never saw another person on our floor, I imagined the Leningrad Cowboys lurking outside our door, huffing blunts and swilling quarts of Hai Karate. There were even a few times when, after hearing the elevator stop in the night, I leaped from the room in my pyjamas in hopes of spotting the offending parties. But there was only ever the buzzing of the dim lamps and the stillness of the red-carpeted hallway, a perfect setting for agents in long coats.

After we'd settled into our room, I tried to call Denes Szekely. Denes was the architect of Ciuc's website, and had suggested, via e-mail, that I come to town at this time, the start of the Romanian National League's season, which kicked off with the Romanian Cup. The league comprised eight teams, all from Transylvania, except one – Steaua (pronounced Stawa), the team from Bucharest set up by the now deposed – and dead – Communist dictator, Ceauşescu. But phoning Denes was no easy task, for each time I dialed the hotel operator, my ear was blasted with what appeared to be the screeching cry of a very angry weasel.

After repeated efforts, I finally connected with Karolina Oprea at the sports ministry, with whom I'd also communicated online. Since I hadn't actually spoken to any of these people yet, I had no idea what to expect, and I was a little startled to discover that Karolina was young and spoke good English. We actually had a semblance of a conversation until the screeching weasel cut us off, but we got far enough to decide that I would meet Denes and the coach of the Ciuc kids' team, a man named Ferenc Molnar, in the lobby in half an hour.

When Janet and I descended in the submarine to the main floor, the doors opened to reveal two large smiling men with their hands plugged in their winter coats. Both had beards and were in their mid-forties. We followed them to a table near the bar which, to my surprise, was now fully lit and patronized by groups of men in turtle-necks and great swoops of hair, wearing leather jackets, drinking vodka and beer.

"We are very pleased that you are here," said Denes, for Ferenc spoke no English. "There is a lot to see at this time. There is the Romanian Cup, which is now being played at the rink. All of the teams are here; it is the perfect time to be in Ciuc. We all have hockey on our minds," he said, smiling.

"Does the whole town participate?"

"Of course," he said. "Of the whole town, ninety per cent of us play hockey."

"And they attend the tournament?" asked Janet.

"Yes. During the final, you will see something you have never seen before. You will not believe the crowd reaction. But I . . . I don't want to say . . . you'll see for yourself. People here are very proud of the local Sport Klub."

Ferenc told me, through Denes, that I was welcome to train with the kids' club if I wanted to. I did. He also said that almost everyone involved in Romanian hockey would be in town for the championship and that he would arrange interviews for me. At the end of the tourna-ment, I would get a chance to skate with the Old Boys team.

Ferenc was in charge of athletics for the city of Ciuc, while Denes was responsible for computer technology at City Hall. Denes had created Ciuc's website on his own, without government money, in an effort to enlighten the rest of the world about Ciuc's culture, in particular their love of hockey. It had piqued the interest of Kreuger, the Swede, and now it had brought me to Ciuc.

"You would like to see the town?" asked Denes.

"Well, we're sort of tired from our trip," I confessed.

"Well, it is not a big town. It will take ten minutes," he said, laughing.

"Is there hockey tonight?" asked Janet.

Ferenc spoke.

"No, not now," said Denes, translating. "The games for today have been completed, but there will be more tomorrow. The championship game between the Ciuc Sport Klub and Steaua will take place in two days," said Denes, parting his fingers. "That will be the one to see," he said, nodding his head.

We left the hotel and walked with Denes through the town. Ciuc was small and lacked a main street – Ceauşescu had torn it down, and only a tiny strip remained – but wherever we stood, we could see the countryside, which ringed the town. I was always aware of the low, rolling hilltops that surrounded us; the clouds that wove through them made me feel I was at the bottom of a stewing pot, low and isolated from the rest of the land.

We walked Ciuc's cobblestone strip. We passed a bank, a cinema (which was showing *The Matrix*, as well as *Babe: Cel Mai Curatos Porc Din Lume* and *Inspectorful Gadget*), two department stores, a handful of tiny restaurants, and a smoke-filled café crowded with young people, where the sound of Elvis yelping was blasting from a speaker. Dimly lit shops, run by stooped old women in drooping socks and aprons, showcased tubes of toothpaste, boxes of detergent, and plastic-wrapped cylinders of cookies in their half-draped windows. In a few places, where there should have been a shop there was a cavity, as if whatever had stood there had been cruelly wrenched from the earth. The holes were filled with bags of garbage and industrial detritus, and they served as a playground for dirty-faced children who popped out of the holes like foraging raccoons. At one point, I came across two boys standing next to a gnarled brick wall spray-painted with the words "PRETTY FLY FOR A WHITE BOY."

"Fawk," said the first boy.

"Fok," said the second.

"Fawwwk."

"No. Fok."

"Fouk."

"No! *Fok!*"

"Fok."

"Ah! Fok."

"Fok."

The rest of the town was made up of half-built apartment blocks and the chassis of abandoned buildings, ambitious post-revolution projects that had died for want of capital. Ciuc was suffering from both pre- and post-revolution blues, but nevertheless had a thriving fast-food industry comprising two shiny hot-dog carts, umbrellaed with blue tarp and helmed by sour men with bushy moustaches.

While the hot-dog vendors did steady business, nothing could compare to the new convenience store that had opened the week before we arrived. It was always packed with people. The first time I went in I noticed that most of the folks in the store weren't actually shopping; they were taking in the dazzling array of products the way one might tour a museum exhibit. Shoppers stood back from the items and studied them before carefully handling the strange products: maple syrup, bouillon cubes, bags of candies, jam, Dijon mustard.

At times, Denes could sense our amazement, so he made a point of saying repeatedly, "You know, Ciuc was not always this way."

"It used to be very beautiful and very old," he said, "but Ceauşescu – you know of Ceauşescu?"

We nodded.

"Well, you've noticed our square?" asked Denes.

We told him we could see it from our window.

"He tore down all the buildings in the square. It happened on my wedding day. Except for the piece of the old road, the rest is new, since the 1980s. The new buildings in the square were put up by the Communists, to revitalize the town, or so they hoped. One of the things Ceauşescu wanted to do was to get people from the country to move into the cities, to leave their farms and come and work here. You travelled through the country. You saw this?"

"The villages were empty," said Janet.

"Yes. All old people," said Denes.

"At one point while we were on the train, I looked into a field," Janet said, "and they were all old people, working out there and harvesting by hand. Corn. I didn't see one person under seventy."

"I know. Now there are only old people left to work the land. Romania was once a great agricultural centre, but it has disappeared. We were once the greatest exporter of wheat in Europe, but at present, we are the greatest importer. This is our government," said Denes, holding out his hands.

We continued walking along the old road. "Is there a popular bar or meeting place in town where people get together to watch games?" I asked Denes.

"No. It's not done here," he said. "When the Communist regime was in power, you invited suspicion if you got together with others in groups. Some would end up in jail, possibly worse. You know, we aren't used to assembling in public places; people haven't learned yet how to behave this way and, well, it will take a while to change this mentality."

"What about at hockey games?"

"Yes. See, there it is different, even though the government has always been very suspicious of Ciuc and our players. You know, we are Szekelys, descendants of Hungary. We speak Hungarian, not Romanian. Every summer, thousands of people come back to Ciuc for a festival, Szekelys from all around the world: a pilgrimage. Ciuc, to them, is their homeland. We are independent people from the rest of Romania, even though we are part of Romania, you see? That is why hockey is so important to us. It is our voice, our way of expressing who we are. In the past, whenever Sport Klub played Steaua the government did everything to prevent us from winning. In Ciuc, we produce eighty per cent of the hockey players in Romania – half of the national team comes from this town – and yet we are given only ten per cent of the sports budget from the ministry in Bucharest. We have to recycle equipment because Steaua gets all the money and the best equipment. In the past, we've had to use broken sticks and skates. You will see at the final; the army team has new jerseys and many coaches because the government in Bucharest does not want us to win. When you come to the game, you will understand the situation. The whole town will be there. There will be singing and shouting."

"You'll have to teach us the songs," I said, imagining my shirt stripped off, a giant blue T smeared in paint on my chest, screaming into a megaphone.

"Yes. Well, I won't be seeing too much of you outside of today. I have to work. I've taken three jobs because I have two children. My wife works, too. Things have been very hard in Romania since the so-called revolution. Before, when I worked at the government, I made three times what I make today, even though I've risen to the top of my position. Inflation is very bad and it is hard for the old people, who used to be taken care of, but now have no social support. The only people who seem to do well in the town are the hockey players, both the Old Boys and today's Sport Klub players. It's here that you can see why they are important to us. They draw a salary when the rest of us are working three jobs. But you will see tomorrow. If they beat Steaua, we're happy. Maybe tomorrow you will see a revolution."

22

THE EPIPHANY OF VAKAR LAJOS

"Do you like Boston?" asked Karolina, standing in the lobby.

"I used to."

"I think they are very good."

"You mean Boston, the group, right?"

"Yes. The music. Later, we will take a drive in the boss's car and I will play for you my tape of Boston."

Karolina walked us to the rink through a park. She wore a smart grey coat and had long, black hair pinned high on her head. Karolina was elegant and young and among the brightest of the post-revolution youth. She'd attended seminars in Bucharest, where the most promising of the next generation of Romanians, selected by their schools, assembled to discuss politics and culture. She was Ferenc's assistant and our guide and translator.

It was mid-morning in Ciuc, and the scene was still, the chatter of our voices filling the park. At the top of the grounds was a cenotaph. The sky was cold and grey and I had to pull my hood over my head to stay warm in the frigid wind that swept down the Ciuc Depression.

The arena lay at the bottom of the park; a grey building that looked like a giant concrete accordion, PATINOARUL VAKAR LAJOS JEGPALYA painted in blue on a wooden marquee over the entrance. As we approached it, we passed two sets of statues, both of hockey players. One was a wire-work sculpture of a player positioning himself for a faceoff. It was set flat against a large silver disc rooted in a bed of black-eyed susans. To its right was a much bigger, more impressive rendering: two ten-foot-tall, constructivist metal figures in full stride, their sticks stretched out in pursuit of the puck, eyes peeled, skates kicking out behind them, silver blades knifing the air. They made me think of fearsome Tin Men, their welds like veins through which molten steel was coursing. Their names were engraved on the shafts of their sticks – Czka Istun and Vakar Lajos – and sometimes, when the sun found them, light shot from their elbows, boots, and sticks, bringing the park to life.

Erected in 1975, these were the first statues of hockey players in Europe, predating those in Russia, Sweden, and the Czech Republic. Transylvania, it seemed, had a jump on the rest of the hockey world and, as I passed into the lobby of the Vakar Lajos rink, this became obvious. On one wall of the foyer hung a set of black-and-white photos. It was, more or less, the Vakar Lajos Hall of Fame. Ferenc joined us as we studied the photos and, with Karolina's help, he guided us through Lajos's life, a legacy that includes being quite possibly the first ever European hockey player.

Vakar's stick hung diagonally against the wall. It looked like an old ruler, thin and straight-bladed, with his name pencilled along the shaft. It was this stick, said Ferenc, that changed the face of hockey in Europe.

"This is the one he made for himself, after he saw the Canadians playing hockey. He made it from a tree, so excited to have discovered the game."

"Where did he see the Canadians?" I asked.

"In a film."

"What film?"

"I don't know; no one knows. It was a film before another film."

"Another film?"

"You mean like a newsreel?" asked Janet.

Ferenc and Karolina conferred.

"Yes! There was a ten-second film of Canadians on the ice, playing hockey."

"When was this?"

"1923."

In 1923, Frank Calder was the president of the four-team NHL. Babe Dye of the Toronto St. Pats won the scoring title and Lester Patrick announced his retirement. In a game between the Montreal Canadiens and the Hamilton Tigers, Bert Corbeau attacked Habs goalie (and ex-teammate) Georges Vézina and broke his nose with a punch. The next time the two teams played – for which Vézina dressed despite his broken nose – the Montreal crowd became unruly and littered the ice with lemons, hitting referee Lou Marsh in the face; Marsh attacked his assailant and landed a few blows. In the Stanley Cup final that year, King Clancy of the Senators played every position, including goal, which he was forced to occupy after netminder Clint Benedict received a penalty. In those days, goalies had to serve the full two minutes in the box, so Clancy bravely stepped in and didn't allow a goal.

Teams iced seven men in 1923 and, in March of that year, Foster Hewitt of the *Toronto Star*'s new radio station, CFCA, was assigned to broadcast a game between Kitchener and Parkdale at Mutual Street Arena, his first game behind the microphone. At the beginning of the season, Newsy Lalonde was traded to the Saskatoon team of the Western Hockey League for Aurel Joliat, who would go on to play with Howie Morenz and Black Cat Gagnon for the Montreal Canadiens. The NHL champions in 1923 were the Ottawa Senators, who defeated the Edmonton Eskimos, led by Bullet Joe Simpson, in two games. Frank Nighbor was one of the Senators' stars. Early in the season, he played in six consecutive games without relief, not once coming off the ice. He was supposed to be chased out of Edmonton by rival Duke Keats, but it never happened. Nighbor and the boys took the train back east, bringing with them the Stanley Cup, parading their silverware on the platform of each stop en route. And, in Romania, Vakar Lajos watched them on the flickering screen, thinking to himself, *We can do that.*

It was a staggeringly early beginning for hockey in Europe, and it proved why there was such a deep love and closeness for the game in Ciuc. I studied the photos and was particularly drawn to one of Lajos's team showing some of the players in berets and short pants with knee socks, and others in wool cardigans with striped ties and upturned collars. Lajos himself was a handsome man, with a narrow chin supporting an enormous forehead and crest of wavy hair. But the two goalies who were kneeling at the front of the picture fascinated me the most. One of them wore a flat white cap and a sweater borrowed from the Michelin Man. It was bulky around the middle and ribbed along the arms and shoulders, giving the illusion of a muscular upper body. It looked as if whalebone padding had been sewn into the sweater itself, which is what Cyclone Taylor's mother did back at the turn of the century. She removed the ribbing from her old corsets and sewed it straight into Cy's hockey jersey, revolutionizing the skater's ensemble.

But the team's other goaltender was even more compelling. She was Vakar's wife, Elizabeth. She was the only player smiling in the

Ciuc at the dawn of hockey (Vakar Lajos is sixth from the left)

photo – a beautiful dark smile, at that – and she wore a black toque and over her ribbed sweater was the team's jersey – a black jersey with a white stripe and the team's Transylvanian logo across the middle. But the most astonishing thing about her equipment was her non-catching glove, which had a flat, rectangular panel above her hand: a blocker. Many hockey historians credit Frank "Mr. Zero" Brimsek with inventing the blocker – he was the first to insert bamboo piping into his glove to stop shots with the back of his hand – but he played in the late 1930s. This photo was from the late 1920s. Mrs. Lajos's blocker predates the NHL's by ten years.

Elizabeth Lajos was very important to Sport Klub. Denes told me that, in her retirement, she was "part of the equipment" and occupied a special chair just to the left of the goalie, from where she watched the games. She became something of a good luck charm for the team, and if ever she was late for a game, the Sport Klub would delay the start. Elizabeth and Vakar first met during a pickup game. I imagine him coming in on a breakaway, looking up for an instant and being captivated by her beauty, the puck rolling off his stick. Co-ed hockey games were popular among the Ciuc youth in the 1920s and 1930s and, like teen dances in North America, they were the centre of their social lives.

I moved over to the next wall. There was another set of photos, these more modern and in colour. They were of a junior tournament staged here in 1987. The teams entered were Yugoslavia, Bulgaria, the Czech Republic, Russia, Romania, and North Korea. For years, Romania had been linked, as had China, to the great Soviet hockey program, and there'd been an unofficial arrangement between Communist Bloc nations for their national teams to play each other a certain number of times per year. It's one of the reasons Jin Guang visited here in the 1970s with the Chinese Nats, and had played against the Romanians and others in unofficial tournaments set up to further each other's domestic programs.

Ferenc didn't know too much about the tournament, only that North Korea had finished without a win, and that the Romanians had played an inspired game against the Soviets, but lost. I was about to be led away by Karolina into the rink itself, but something caught my eye. I looked closer, and there he was, a teenager, smaller than the rest, looking in:

Jagr.

There was no Navratilovian mullet to give him away, no earring. But there were his trademark flushed cheeks, his wonky eye, his bubble helmet. Jagr. I recognized a few others, too, but couldn't place their names (Jiri Slegr and Jaroslav Modry were on the team, as well). It was 1987, before the fall of Communism, and Jagr was all of fifteen. He was not yet a glimmer in a scout's eye, three years away from being drafted fifth overall by the Penguins of Pittsburgh, where he would ask for, and be given, the number 68, to remember the year that Soviet tanks crossed the Czech border and seized power. He had not yet grown to tower above the rest of the players, nor were his shoulders as big as they would be when he ascended to the pros. In 1987, his life was spent in tournaments like these, games in small, hockey-crazed towns across Eastern Europe, twenty-four hours from Prague by train. He had rolled through the forest, eating salted meat and bread, withdrawn from the rest of the world, yet looking out, as I had, at the endless trees and dark woods and mountains, wondering what kind of hockey lay ahead, and against whom he'd be playing. At fifteen, he was within reach of the skills that would make him one of the most elegant scorers of his time, eleven years removed from waving his Olympic gold medal from the stage in Prague's Old Town Square. When Jagr took to the ice at Vakar Lajos rink in 1987, could he have imagined that his life would work out the way it did? Or did he just play?

Jagr. A swooping bird.

I moved over to the photo of the Soviet team, and spotted Pavel Bure. Small features and tiny arms, peeking out from behind a defenceman's elbow. A mite, a scamp. Taught the game in Moscow by his father – whom neither he, nor his brother, Valeri, speak to anymore – a disciplinarian. Pavel. Scampering across the pond, his speed coming not from his hips or thighs, but his feet, a zealous wind-up toy, a skittler, waving his hockey stick in front of him. In the 1998 Olympics, he scored five goals against the Finns in the semi-final, then moved on to play Jagr in the gold-medal game, both players the focus of systems designed to make the ice theirs. Bure. Moscow. Saucy, elite; a player whose speed and deft hands were obvious from the beginning. The bus rides were an affront to him. He bit his lip and ploughed through, stopping in places like Ciuc, only to play against North Koreans whose equipment was the worst he'd seen. But also . . . Jagr. They met. The two great stars of the beginning of the twenty-first century skated head-to-head for the first time. It was here, in Vakar Lajos arena, where the future of the game took shape, where the styles of these two players mixed in a form that later gave the game identity and shape after Lemieux and Gretzky passed into history. A game being born. In the final game of the tournament, Bure met Jagr. "It was extraordinary game," one Transylvanian hockey fan told me later. "So fast. So exciting. Tied four to four."

I left the photographs and walked into the rink. Progrym Gheorgheni were playing Ciuc Sport Klub. Karolina led us up to the VIP section ten rows above the ice, where long, purple, upholstered benches fronted by a dark rosewood railing stretched out below the press gallery. It was a little wine-coloured salon in the middle of the rink, which had maybe 2,000 seats, all but a hundred of them empty. There was an old, 1960s-style score-clock at one end, where seconds elapsed in illuminated pixels around the circumference of a circle. Both ends of the rink were protected with floor-to-ceiling webbing that trapped flown pucks. Below them, goal judges sat in steel cages operating a series of lights: green (the play is on), red (a goal is scored), and white (a whistle, or stoppage in play). The rink was evidently well used: the plastic seats were scuffed and the walkways spread with years of grime. A banner for Ciuc Beer hung around the boards, and Karolina told me that Miercurea Ciuc was known throughout Eastern Europe for two exports, hockey and beer. That, I told her, was familiar to Canadians. Under another banner I spotted six soldiers in grey riot helmets and blue-and-white camouflage uniforms, their backs to the game, smoking cigarettes.

Ciuc dominated play for most of the game. Gheorgheni was a town about fifty kilometres from Ciuc, where the players trained and played out of doors, on artificial ice in a closed valley between two mountains (Vakar Lajos and the state rink in Bucharest were the only two indoor rinks in Romania). Though Gheorgheni was one of the few teams in Romania to have city council pay their full wages – it was a staggering notion considering how desperate the local economies were – they didn't have the skill or team play of Sport Klub. The Ciuc attack was driven by two defencemen – number 6, Attila Nagy, and number 5, Jozsef Andordjan. Neither wore a face guard, and both played in the style of a young Randy Carlyle: fast and thick-bodied, rushing whenever they got the puck. I was also drawn to a forward, Istvan Gereb, a sad-faced forty-year-old Ciuc veteran who skated stiffly and with his head down, but possessed just enough Mike Waltonian savvy to stand out from his teammates, most of whom were a lot younger. Among this youthful group was the tiniest of forwards, a little buzz saw of a player who filled the ice with puck-carrying razzmatazz. His slipperiness allowed him to avoid being hit (even though it wasn't a physical game) and when I asked Ferenc who he was, he pointed to the ice and said "Vakar Lajos!" then moved his hand half-way up his chest.

"Laszlo Kovacs," said Karolina, smiling.

"Who?"

"Vakar Lajos' grandson."

Ciuc won the game easily. The crowd was quiet during most of the play, but stirred as a group of players in athletic sweats walked into the rink and stood together between the two benches. Fans on one side of the arena signalled across to the other, who stood up and started shouting and whistling at the players. An old man shook his fist and bellowed "*Kazuku!*" which meant Gypsy, a racist taunt common throughout Romania. The skaters on the ice noticed this and looked around, slowing the action. The unwelcome newcomers moved closer together and formed a cordon. Ferenc shook his head and scoffed while Karolina looked at the floor.

Steaua.

23

THE LAST CANADIAN GAME

Most of our time in Ciuc was spent either at the rink or the hotel. We'd rise early in the day, eat breakfast, then head out with Karolina.

At the rink, Karolina introduced us to a passel of Romanian hockey dignitaries – ex-players, coaches, and broadcasters – who gave us insight into the history and development of the local game. There was only one figure from Romanian hockey I didn't meet, although I spent much of the trip waiting for him to appear. His nickname was Whiskey. The dashing Robin Hood of Romanian hockey, Whiskey was a former player from Hungary turned bank robber. I anticipated a covert meeting with him – maybe in the park after sundown, in a cold flat on the fringe of town, under the rafters during a game – but he never appeared. He was considered public enemy number one by the Hungarian authorities, even though, as Karolina and others liked to point out, "He only steals from banks, never the people. He is also very polite and very gentle. All the people from Ciuc are behind him, especially the fans because he was a player, too. He is very clever, and his actions hurt no one." Whiskey was linked to twenty-seven robberies, in which, along with

Orbin Gbor, a fellow Hungarian player, he'd stolen 140 million Hungarian forints. He was the most wanted man in Hungary, a reputation that no doubt increased his popularity among the hockey fans of Szekely land, and a Barilkoesque legend had developed around it.

There was a rumour that Whiskey would attend the final Ciuc game against Steaua, which organizers had moved up to Saturday afternoon so that it could be broadcast nationally. This was done because the previous year's game had been the second-highest rated sporting event of the year after Romania's first ever soccer victory over Hungary. The pitch of the tournament seemed geared towards the clash between these two teams, and you could feel the tension tighten as the tourney progressed. Both Sport Klub and Steaua disposed of teams from Gheorgheni and Galati, the latter team having ignominiously traded their starting goaltender to Steaua for a bag of second-hand equipment, which they needed to keep their program alive. One of the first people to tell us about the Steaua–Ciuc rivalry was a fellow named Zoltan Becze, a small, garrulous man who pointed his finger at me when he spoke; that is, when he wasn't grabbing my jacket and pulling my face to his. A writer for the local Hungarian-language newspaper, he was proud to call himself a member of the international sports press. Zoltan was Romania's Foster Hewitt. He was both the play-by-play and colour commentator whenever games were televised nationally (usually one or two matches a year). On my last day in Ciuc, he took me to the local television studio and showed me footage of the finals of the Romanian championships from the 1980s, which were played outdoors in Gheorgheni, snow falling as the players scrabbled after the puck, the beautiful Transylvanian Alps rising above the end boards. Zoltan's play-by-play technique was to describe the action in a reserved, bordering on moribund, tone, then screech breathlessly into the microphone whenever a goal was scored. When I told him that Foster Hewitt's gondola in Maple Leaf Gardens used to be considered the Noah's Ark of Canadian radio, he exclaimed, "I too have an ark. From where I sit and tell people the truth!"

Zoltan was a wealth of information. Upon first being introduced to me at the arena, he took me to the Sport Klub's director's lounge, which, besides being the only heated room in Ciuc, was decorated like a '60s party pad. "This is a place for chiefs!" exclaimed Zoltan, calling out the door, at which point the secretary of the Ciuc sports federation came in with a tray of beer and an urn of coffee. As I turned on my tape recorder, Zoltan squeezed my shoulder, and said, "We must start with Steaua."

"What's the history between the two teams?" I asked.

"Well, in hockey, you see, we in Ciuc have demonstrated to Romania that we are the best. We have shown the world that, even though we are a minority, hockey is ours, it is our voice. In seventy years, we have not had one Romanian play for us, only Hungarians. Out of this has evolved a great love for the team, and in 1989 Miercurea Ciuc became the first place in Romania where five thousand men were heard singing in public a song in the Hungarian language! It was our team's hymn – what you'd hear in a church – that had been composed by a very talented local composer and whose text had been written by my father, Anton Becze. You will hear them sing this song tomorrow when we play against Steaua, and millions of people will watch on TV and hear this Hungarian song! They will hear our voices, right across the country!

"We sang this song even though we knew that the rest of Romania did not want to hear it. We sang it in victory and in defeat. Our voices came out, out, out!" he said, putting his hand to his mouth as if pulling out string. "We did this even though we knew that Sport Klub would be prevented from winning by the Communists. It goes back to Ceauşescu, I believe. Ceauşescu liked to think he was a sportsman, so he gave a lot of money for sports, but it was more out of propaganda, like the Third Reich. Steaua got most of the money and became the military's team, Ceauşescu's team, the Communist's team. They were the team from the city, Bucharest. Because we came from a small town and were a Hungarian team, we got very little of this money, still do. They would only support us if we would give away our best players to Steaua. Of course, we would not let them do this, so we suffered, and during Ceauşescu's reign, they did every-thing they could to stop us from winning. The Steaua team trav-elled with soldiers and the Securitate. One time, in 1985, they took away our best player and had him committed to the mad house. They put him away for three days so he could not play. Then they told the rest of the Ciuc team, 'If you do not lose this game, the rest of you will go to the hospital, too!'

"Ceauşescu was afraid, of course. He was worried that if he sent a team with Hungarian names to the European championships, the leaders of other countries would get the wrong idea. He would be embarrassed. So he ordered that the winning team must be Steaua and that the players with Hungarian names would have to change them if they wanted to advance. Could you imagine that? To play for your country, to have to change your name? They threatened and intimidated the referees, and after a while, they didn't even have to do that. The referees knew that if they called a game against Steaua, they would be paid a visit by the Securitate. Perhaps it is hard for you to understand, but it was a matter of life or death."

The Securitate were Ceauşescu's security police, and were all-encompassing in their powers. They were a vast network of informers recruited from the ordinary population, common spies. Citizens were played against each other, and the most loyal were trained to be part of Romania's secret police. They tapped phone lines, intercepted mail, and reported conversations overheard in public places, resulting in, as Denes had told me, a fear of gathering, even in small groups. There were more than a million informers in the Securitate, each of them backed up by a militia responsible for keeping track of those citizens considered unreliable – kids who sang in coffee bars, writers, painters, former activists. Under Ceauşescu's regime, no person was allowed to change dwellings without permission from the militia, and anyone who made a visit of more than twenty-four hours to a town they did not live in had to report to the authorities.

In this political climate, hockey provided one of the few forums for self-expression, a place where citizens could be together in great numbers and form a unified voice. At the rink fans were able to scream and yell and taunt Steaua. Even though some fans were jailed before games – one of them, an old man who'd played in the Lajos era, had been prohibited from going within one hundred feet of the rink – the Ciuc crowd were brave and resilient, and for many years, those who sang their Hungarian freedom hymn from the stands were the most defiant voices heard in all of Romania.

"The government has always resented the Sport Klub fans," said Zoltan, sipping coffee from a small porcelain cup. "This was the case even after Ceauşescu. During one game a few years ago between Steaua and Ciuc, the Steaua team invited their soccer fans to come to a game simply to outnumber the Ciuc fans. These were people who had never seen a hockey game in their lives: hooligans, thugs. They taunted the Ciuc fans, chanting: "*Criminals!*" and "*Out with Hungarians from Romania!*" Since there were no police at the game, the fans fought. Knives were drawn. There was no Plexiglas on the boards, so the hooligans hopped onto the ice and attacked the players from Sport Klub. In the Romanian papers the next day, they talked about how the Ciuc fans were not to be trusted, how they incited violence and were a bad influence and should not be allowed to participate. The papers used this as a tool, or a tactic, to influence opinion; they still do. They told people that it was not safe for Romanians to come here to visit. They tried to get us banned from all games away from Ciuc, going so far as to suggest that no championship be played at Vakar Lajos for fear of the safety of the people. These writers have never been to Ciuc, and still like to think that we live in a Communist country."

We finished our coffee, and the secretary came in and took away our cups. I told Zoltan that his insight was valuable, and his final words were "Be careful of yourself and your wife at the game. You sit in the VIPs, you'll be okay, but beware of the crowd. You just sit, listen, and learn, yes?" With this, he swept me out of the room. I walked down a hallway tacked with finger-paintings of Sport Klub players by children from a nearby school.

From speaking with Zoltan and others, I saw that the Transylvanians were proud and defiant about their culture's voice being so closely linked to their sport. It was refreshing to hear this in light of the changing state of the game in Canada, where fans are becoming ever more uncertain about how the game defines them. Now that pro hockey has traded its grassroots identity for an American-style suit of lights, it's easy to forget that, for decades, hockey was the only brush we used to paint our image. Just as the Ciuc fans encouraged players from their community to fight against the imperialists from Bucharest, there was once a time when the dreams of citizens in Toronto, Montreal, and other Canadian cities were acted out by skaters with whom they shared a heritage, and whose teams wilfully triumphed over the rival Americans.

But times have changed. I never understood that more clearly than I did while hanging around the Vakar Lajos arena. The scene there was a throwback to the days of the NHL when games were more about the clash of societies than the ability of one team to out-spend the others. I was reminded of the night before we left for Transylvania, riding my bicycle to the Air Canada Centre for the Leafs' home opener against Boston. It had been autumn, and the wind had a snap to it, and early on in my ride, I turned around and retreated for gloves and a toque – hoser formal wear for the start of another hockey season, the last of the century.

I listened to my Walkman as I headed east along Bloor Street. I was tuned to Prime Time Sports, where a panel of sportswriters debated the '99 edition of the Montreal Canadiens. They agreed that the current version of the Habs was the worst in franchise history. There wasn't a twenty-goal scorer among them, and their new captain – Saku Koivu, a Finn – had come off his lowest-scoring season ever as a pro. The Leafs had opened the season against the Habs, winning 4–1 in Montreal, but fans had dismissed the easy victory by saying, "Well, no big deal, it was only the Habs." One of the writers couldn't remember there ever being such a reaction in the past. He was astonished that the Canadiens were now regarded as just another team.

Prior to the Leafs–Habs opening-night game, two thousand tickets were left unsold, a number that would stagger anyone raised in the era when these two teams were all that mattered in Canadian sport. But things had changed: the '99 Montreal Alouettes of the CFL employed more French-Canadians than did the Habs. The panel inventoried the Francophones on the hockey team: Patrick Poulin, a fourth-line centre; José Théodore, a back-up goalie; Patrice Brisebois, an injured defenceman; and a rookie named Francis Bouillon, an American whose father was Haitian. No one would ever mistake them for Lemaire, Lapointe, Lafleur, and Savard. The problem had compounded over the years. Montreal was once a haven for Québécois talent, but emerging Francophone stars like Roberto Luongo and Vincent Lecavalier invariably went to American teams that were as steeped in tradition as yesterday's goulash. This exodus of hockey-playing Quebeckers was symbolized by Patrick Roy's trade to Colorado, which handed the Avalanche the '96 Stanley Cup. It was an early sign that things were awry: the Habs as feeder team for a trendy American hockey club.

Some hockey fans relished the demise of the Habs. I know many in Toronto who did, and I must admit I drew a measure of satisfaction in seeing Canadiens supporters suffer from the pain Toronto fans had felt for decades. Habs fans can be the most arrogant of any sport, wearing their twenty-four Stanley Cup banners like a royal seal, pointing to them through good times and bad. Whenever I prodded the tender spot of a Habs fan over a losing streak or playoff loss, their trump card was, "So when's the last time you guys won a Stanley Cup?" No other team in pro sport boasted such consistency and excellence, and until the last few years, they had been the model for success.

The Habs' fall from grace was a slow tumble, made worse by the sheer weight of history that they carried. For years, Habs fans boasted that the Forum was the temple of hockey – of course, I argued that Maple Leaf Gardens was, but had to concede that their rink had been the scene of far greater success than ours – but now that the team had left it, their point was moot. Like the Boston

Garden, the Forum had worked a dark magic upon visiting clubs, giving the puck an extra push when needed, a degree or two here and there. The building spooked those who weren't the beneficiaries of its supernatural hold. You could see it in the opposition's faces when they skated out and looked around at sixteen thousand chanting Québécois. It was a phenomenon worth a handful of points in the standings every year. But the ghosts of the old building had been abandoned. A few weeks after the last game, the Texan – the diner where everyone from Jean Pusie to Toe Blake had filled themselves with dollar pancakes and steak and eggs – burst into flames. The Habs lost their spiritual upper hand. In sport as in life, only a fool would ignore such an omen.

In the Forum, the depth of colours grabbed you: the deep blue and blood-red of the jerseys; the golden froth of the beer; Roger Doucet's flash of silver hair; the silk ties and overcoats and scarves of the patrons, who were just a little more stylish than fans at any other NHL rink; the milky white of the ice; and the grey haze of cigarette smoke that clouded the corridors between periods, when fans lined up for poutine and beer. During play, the crowd sat hushed as if attending a play or an opera. The building demanded a certain dignity from its patrons, and Habs fans carried themselves confidently, with a panache that reflected the success and poise of their franchise. In Toronto, there were a lot of sagging shoulders and old women knitting – losing draws out these humble features – but in Montreal, people held their chins high. Many of us hated them for it, but we would have given our eye teeth just to know how it felt to be a Habs fan.

On Boxing Day '98, the Montreal Canadiens made their final visit to Maple Leaf Gardens. I bought two tickets for Janet and me out of the newspaper for face value. The fellow who sold them to me was a hockey fan from long ago, and when he delivered the tickets, he said, "Listen, I know they're getting five hundred dollars each for these on the street, but it just isn't right to make so much money off something so sad. Pretty soon you or I won't be able to afford to go to any game. Period." He was right. Not only did every new NHL rink boast modern features, but the prices had gone high-style, too. In 1989, the best seat in the Gardens cost $29.

In 1999, it cost $118.

During their last season at the Gardens, the Leafs invited Hall of Famers from visiting teams to take part in ceremonies to mark their final visit. Both Bobby Orr and Gordie Howe dropped pucks, and there was a rumour around the Gardens that Rocket Richard was to appear at the Habs' last stand. Even so, he was the last person we expected to see. He was recovering from abdominal cancer (an affliction that would take him two years later) and was reported to be convalescing near his home in Montreal. At the time of his operation, reporters had written the kind of columns that passed for *faux* obituaries, and in the middle of the year, the NHL minted a new trophy – for most goals scored in the regular season – in the Rocket's name. He was a player adrift in twilight. It seemed that even though Richard was still alive, he had already passed into history.

After both teams warmed up, the lights went down in the Gardens. There is a rare intimacy in sports stadia when thousands of people suddenly find themselves sitting in the dark. They stop bustling, put down their popcorn, and fall silent. Paul Morris, the Leafs' rink announcer, spoke a few words, and then introduced former Leafs captain Teeder Kennedy, whose eyes, like Richard's, now only hinted at the kind of intensity with which he once played. The spotlight swam over him as he walked slowly, out onto the blue foam carpet towards the red line, his gait encumbered by a new hip, which he was still getting used to. The crowd applauded respectfully, then Morris picked up his announcement, "For every franchise to be great, they must have great rivals . . ." We listened as Morris paid tribute to the Habs.

"Over the years, the Montreal Canadiens have been one of sport's greatest teams . . ." The Habs fans in attendance – many of them Torontonians in Montreal jerseys, others having made the trip down Highway 401 for the historic game – started the cheer. There were a few boos among dyed-in-the-wool Leafs fans, but the rest of us joined in. I'd never heard this before at a Leafs–Habs game: rival

fans cheering together. Our voices grew louder, more sonorous. I'd
hated the Habs for years, but now my mind turned to how Montreal
had wrested the sport from the Philly Flyers, whom I hated even
more. I thought of Marcel Bonin, a sword-swallower and circus
strongman in the off-season; of Bob Gainey, who, on the day he
turned eleven, went up to his best friend, Hank Fisher, and said, "I
won't be seeing you any more. From now on, my life is hockey";
and of New Year's Eve 1975, the greatest hockey game ever played
– Montreal Canadiens 3, Soviet Red Army 3. That game is still vivid
in my memory. I watched it lying on my stomach on my grand-
parents' cold living-room floor in front of the TV, the two of them
sitting behind me on the couch, the lights low, the screen flickering
against their faces. I thought of Tretiak, Kharlamov, the Roadrunner.
I'd liked his name.

I thought of the symbiosis of the two teams: two cities, one
country. I cheered knowing that this would be the last time I would
look down upon a hockey rink and feel this close to my country's
past. After Morris finished his ode to Montreal, the Gardens' scoreboard flashed an image of the Rocket, and we were beside ourselves.
People were leaning against the railing and screaming down at the
ice. Dick Beddoes once wrote that the Rocket played with "bursts
of crackling hate," and the picture on the screen reflected this: fero-
cious eyes violating the lens, hands locked on his stick, one skate
stabbing the ice in front of the other. In the photo, he is charging at
the camera like a soldier across a battlefield.

With the Gardens fans in full throat, the Rocket appeared. It
would be his last appearance at the old rink. Ever. You could have
folded Canada's century into that moment: one man who defined
Quebec taking centre ice in a building that defined Canada. The
Rocket stood there for a few seconds, still. Then he lifted his hand
and moved it back and forth. He looked like a man standing dock-
side, waving at an ocean liner as it headed out to sea. The crowd
was darkly lit, but I could feel the shadow of a great vessel passing
over our faces. It was a glorious scene. The Rocket was cast in silvery
blue light, illuminated by flashbulbs crackling from the stands like a
sky of dying stars. I looked down at Janet.

She was crying.

Teeder Kennedy stood beside Richard on the carpet. Teeder used to check the Rocket. They'd gone up against each other countless times and had done unspeakable things to each other on the ice. Teeder had been the Leafs' captain for several years. He'd been invited to stand next to Richard so that those who never saw them play could measure them and imagine. They swayed there for five full minutes before either extended his hand. The Rocket finally did. Kennedy sure as hell wasn't going to.

24

STEAUA WEARS A BLACK HAT

Game Day.

From the minute you wake up, your mind is focussed on the game. You rise feeling connected to thousands of other people you've never met who, like yourself, are turning over in their beds with the same buzz of anticipation, waking up restless, their thoughts drawn to the faceoff. Over the course of the day, every act is carried out with an eye to the game. "This is the food I will eat on the day my team wins (or loses) the Stanley Cup!" you tell your corn flakes. Every gesture, every nuance, becomes symbolic of the game. The baby had a fitful sleep; your car wouldn't start; a bird shit on your shoulder; everywhere you looked, you saw the number 23. All of these things portend what will happen once the puck is set in motion.

In the city, on your street, in your province or country, the game marks everything. Supermarkets are stocked with potato chips, soda pop, and Aspirin; beer stores are busy from the unsnapping of the first dead bolt; there's an extra run on newspapers; feasts are prepared in fretful homes with an eye towards Bacchanalian intermissions and half-times (food barely touched if your team is behind, devoured with a lead); every radio and TV station is filled with babble about the game, including exhaustive pre-game analysis, interviews, and predictions tilted towards the home team; lucky charms are rubbed; socks and underwear with winning records are worn; pennants flown; slogans painted on garages and the sides of vans, frosted across windows, and scribbled on bus shelters. On game day, you feel like an actor performing in the script of your life, conscious that you will remember each event as together they build like a timpani roll to the first note of the game.

Dave Bookman is my most obsessed friend on game day. Chance past his home during a Buffalo Bills game and you find it dark, even on the sunniest of days. His shutters are closed, drapes drawn, and windows sealed. He doesn't answer his phone. There are no visible signs of life. Inside, the only light in his room is cast from his twenty-eight-inch television screen. The sound on the set is on, but he's also listening to two transistor radios – both of them set on distant Buffalo stations with weak and crackling signals – positioned on either side of his sofa, one per ear. *Pro Football Weekly*, *USA Today*, the *Buffalo Daily News*, and the four Toronto dailies are laid out on his table. He is squeezing a nerf football. He is wearing a bathrobe. He will not appear in public until the game has ended.

Those obsessed with sports know that one's behaviour on game day is too important and fragile to mess with. The fan cannot score or coach, but he or she can be mentally prepared so that a collective consciousness is in place should the team require skills beyond their means to tip the game's result. The reason fans have such faith in positive thought is that, at least once in our lives, we've witnessed our team rally from an impossible deficit and believed, unequivocally, that a certain gesture or incantation or thought had something to do with it. When this occurs, it's hard to disassociate yourself from the game's outcome. The two are indelibly linked.

The 1987 Canada Cup. The Rheostatics were driving across the country on our way home after completing our first Canadian tour: two long, difficult months on the road. During the tour, sport became the one thing I could count on – it wouldn't break down, cancel shows, forget to pay us, fail to advertise the gig, neglect to feed us, cancel hotel rooms, or throw a punch at me – and its drama and intrigue were a reprieve from the vagaries of rock-and-roll life on the road. We were in Winnipeg on the eve of Canada's semi-final versus Czechoslovakia.

We spent the afternoon in the company of a veteran blues guitarist by the name of Carlos Johnson. Carlos was in town backing up a singer named Phil Guy, Buddy's brother, whose defining feature was the little toot of smoke that came off the top of his slicked afro, smouldering under the hot lights of the stage. Phil wasn't very good, but Carlos had the stuff. He wore a wide-brimmed hat and sunglasses, and had a moustache like Stanley Clarke's. We sat in his room and listened to him play his vintage 1956 Gibson SG. Minutes stretched into hours and soon the afternoon became evening. We got high on some of the wackiest dope I've ever smoked, and it wasn't until after eight o'clock that I asked him, "Carlos, do you like hockey?"

"What's that shit?" he replied.

I told him that I had to split. I left the hotel where we were staying – the grotty, cursed Royal Albert Arms – and headed into the night. My routine had been thrown off entirely, and I was stoned to boot. I hadn't been given a chance to prepare my head for the game, nor an opportunity to scout the right venue to watch it. I walked down Portage looking for a bar when, just out of earshot, I heard the sound of a crowd and a voice speaking excitedly. I followed the voice and ended up in front of a variety store, where a tiny speaker positioned above the front door was broadcasting the game. It was voice of Joe Bowen, the same person who'd called the 1984 Cup. I stood below the speaker and listened anxiously as he described the furious, end-to-end action. Czechoslovakia had jumped out to a 3–0 lead, and Canada was on the ropes.

Bowen's voice gave way to another: Darryl Sittler. Being far away from home and in a strange, unfamiliar part of Canada, not to mention broke, high, and exhausted, I was pulled in by Sittler's voice. It rushed out of the speaker: "Canada better pick it up, Joe. The Czechs look good. They can't afford to waste another shift." I stood there with my hands in my pockets, listening. The wind picked up and a flag across the street rippled and snapped. A few cars rolled past, but most people were at home, watching the game. I stood in front of the store with my head down, Sittler's voice rooting me to the sidewalk. I thought that, if I held my ground, I could pull together all the circumstances that had conspired to make Canada vulnerable to defeat. I waited until the period was over, then moved on. Eventually, I settled into a pub for the final period, and watched Mario Lemieux, playing on a line with Gretzky and Michel Goulet, score a natural hat trick. Canada went on to win 4–3. I left the place wiping my brow, feeling like a man who'd just missed taking a bullet.

To celebrate game day, Karolina, Ferenc, Janet, and I made a pilgrimage. It seemed like the right thing to do on the afternoon of Ciuc's most important game of the year, so we hopped in Ferenc's car and drove to the top of a hill outside of town, part of the same range I'd admired from the city.

Karolina played her Boston tape. It sounded great, but I don't think it was Boston. I didn't have the heart to tell Karolina.

"Do you like this tape of Boston?" she asked.

"Love it!"

From the top of the hill, I was able to look down at Vakar Lajos arena and think, "There's where the shit's gonna happen." I did this while sitting on a large stone pulpit surrounded by old-growth forest and crosses erected by small villages around the region. It was the ancestral centre of the Szekelys, the site where they gathered by the thousands each year to drink, fight, party, and pray. The pulpit gave way to a steep slope that had been shaved up the middle, a ski run used by Sport Klub members to train.

At the bottom of the hill was a well with water gushing from two spouts. A pair of soot-faced young men drew the water into dirty wine bottles. The water was an offering to those who'd made the pilgrimage to the top of the hill, so Karolina asked us if we'd like to have a drink.

"Try. Try. Is good," said Ferenc.

"Is it safe?" asked Janet.

"Yes. Yes. Very," said Karolina.

We took deep gulps, regretfully. The water was cool and fresh-tasting, but dense with mineral deposits. It was like drinking sand at the bottom of a beach bucket.

On the way back to our car, we bought a chimney cake from a woman who'd baked it over an open hearth that morning. During my correspondence with Denes, he'd told me that Szekely culture was represented by three things: the chimney cake, a drink known as the fence-breaker, and the knife that the Szekely men carry in their pockets. Denes would show me his knife; he would send me home with a bottle of clear, fifty-proof hootch made from the dregs of plum brandy ("They call it fence-breaker because after drinking it, you feel like Mike Tyson. You want to fight, but you can't hit anything with your fists, so you break off part of a fence to better hit someone"); and now, with our chimney cake, we'd partaken of the total Szekely experience. The cake was shaped by wrapping dough around a wooden cylinder. Then it was baked to a crispy brown and coated with sugar. We ate it in the back of the car while listening to the band who wasn't Boston, and taking in the golden hills and deep, brown forest of the Ciuc Depression.

Our next stop was the oldest church in Szekely land, built in the 1600s. When we arrived, they were in the middle of a service: six men in long white robes standing around a pulpit and incanting a Hungarian prayer. The church was one of those beautiful European buildings that you stumble across, oh, once every ten feet. The ceiling was domed, like the underside of a petal, and you could hear the voice of the priest echo around and then fall to the back of the room, where we were standing with our heads down and hands crossed.

"Do they ever mention hockey?" I whispered to Karolina.

"Well, they talk about tradition and the importance of maintaining the identity of the Szekelys. They talk about keeping the old ways. They will not single out hockey, but many people believe this is what they mean."

Our last stop before heading back to the hotel to get ready for the game was to visit the high school where Ferenc, Karolina, and the rest of Miercurea Ciuc had gone. It was an old gothic building built in 1668 with twenty-foot-high stained-glass windows, a glorious limestone exterior, and a beautifully detailed entranceway. Inside, there were great wooden staircases, arched windows overlooking courtyards, an auditorium with a stage where a long honeyed curtain made from silk wound around a wooden frame with stylized turrets, and such beautiful glasswork – orbs of mauve, light blue, yellow – that it gave the hallways and classrooms the feel of a museum. There were massive panels of student photographs from the last forty years lining the hallways, and so we looked for Karolina and Ferenc. Karolina pretty much appeared as she did in person – after all, it had only been a few years since she'd graduated from the school – but Ferenc's photo from the 1970s was a bit of a revelation. He looked like he could have played in Boston, or at least on Karolina's tape.

We stopped at the gymnasium, where a bunch of kids – twelve, maybe thirteen years old – were practising basketball. Ferenc told the coach that we were Canadians visiting Ciuc for the Romanian Cup, and that I had something to give them. The coach came out in his sweats, a whistle around his neck, and I handed him a bag of Team Canada pins that the CAHA had given me for my journey.

As we left, I could hear the coach blow his whistle, then the sound of basketballs being dropped as the kids lined up and held out their hands. One by one, the coach laid the icons into their palms as if he were a priest delivering the host, little gold hockey players set against a black and red maple leaf, glittering stigmata for the sport of their blood.

Before the revolution, there had been a forty-team national league in Romania, but now there were only six teams. After 1989, many Romanian and Hungarian players left the country to play elsewhere, some of them going to Hungary, others to Austria, others to colleges in the United States. Ciuc lost more than fifty men to foreign clubs, depleting Sport Klub as a national power. With the demise of Ceauşescu's national sport program, the Steaua team grew even

stronger relative to teams in Ciuc, Galati, and Gheorgheni. The
benefit of playing for a big-city team that was closely linked to the
sports federation meant a job at a sub-officer's salary, as well as
guaranteed sponsorship. By contrast, only ten per cent of the government's hockey budget went to Ciuc, the result of Romania's
long-standing denial of Hungarian culture, as well as the theory that
putting the lion's share of money towards maintaining one high-
level team was more effective than supporting several middling ones.
Besides, there was only one Hungarian in the Romanian Sports
Federation to fight for Ciuc, and it was only the previous year that
the town had elected their first representative to sit in the Romanian
house of parliament.

It was hard for Sport Klub to keep pace with the Army team.
While Ciuc had been the first champions of Romania in 1949 and
had won six titles altogether (the last coming in 1997), Steaua were
the dominant force, winning a total of twenty-eight championships
from 1963 to 1999. In its own way, Ciuc suffered the small-market
blues, only this was not the result of some greedy owner's power
game or a player flexing his dollar signs, but rather years of political and cultural hardship. That the fans in Ciuc continued to hold
out hope that they would one day rise to their rightful place as
kings of Romanian hockey exposed the North American pro sports
scene for the obnoxious entity that it has become. In Ciuc, fans
showed their devotion to the game by turning out in great numbers
for big games, even though they lived in a country where it was
considered a good year if inflation rose by only fifty per cent, as it
had the previous year. For local fans to spend a handful of lei on a
game they couldn't afford to go to was a show of faith that, with
the exception of a few cities and towns, was rare in North America.
Paying for a ticket in Ciuc was like dropping pennies in hockey's
collection plate.

The last time Steaua and Sport Klub clashed, in Bucharest, Steaua
won 5–3, capturing the Romanian championship. But this was a new
season (the Romanian Cup was played at the beginning of the schedule, the Romanian Championships at the end) and the local fans
were optimistic.

That afternoon, we made our way to the rink. We fell in step with a stream of people and walked through the park, which was filled with families picnicking before the start of the game. The scene around Vakar Lajos arena was no different than that outside old Maple Leaf Gardens. There was a scrum of a few hundred people outside the rink, their voices high with chatter: men with their hands plugged inside their jackets; boys in blue-face; young girls waving flags and pennants; old men sipping coffee; women smoking and talking about the game. A kid with an old fashioned air horn stood in front of the rink going *whaoooonk!* and shouting in Hungarian with his friends, who had blue and white S's and C's drawn on their cheeks. We met Denes under the marquee and I asked him what they were saying.

"'Go back to Romania,'" he said, rubbing his hands.

"For Steaua or their fans?"

"Steaua have no fans!" he said, laughing.

"What do you mean?"

"If they had fans, they would travel here. They would come and watch the games like the supporters of Ciuc. But they don't. They are afraid," he said.

I showed my pass to a rumple-faced man with a bushy moustache, handing him my accreditation – a white greeting card that had been stamped and signed by the organizer of the local sports federation – and he held it in front of him, eyeing me suspiciously as if I were a local nogoodnik trying to bust my way into the rink.

I complimented him on the hat he was wearing.

He grunted and handed my papers back.

In the lobby, Sandor Gal, a former player whom I'd met briefly, called Karolina over and asked her to clarify a point he'd made to me in an interview I'd done the day before. Sandor was the assistant trainer of Ciuc and had played for Romania in the world championships in Vienna, Austria, in 1978.

He waved his hands when he spoke, breathlessly rattling off the details of a trip to Vienna in 1977, when Romania had defeated the USA 4–3. "The trainer remembers," said Karolina, looking at Sandor, "that in 1977, the teams were the Soviet Union,

Czechoslovakia, Canada, Sweden, the USA, Finland, and Germany."
With each country, Sandor nodded and said: "Ya. Ya."

"He remembers playing with Espo . . . Espo . . . Espo . . ."

"Espo-sito!" said Sandor.

"Yes, Esposito," repeated Karolina. "Phil Esposito?"

"Ya. Ya."

"Phil Esposito."

"I know him," I said.

"Oh! You know this Esposito?" asked Karolina.

"No. Not know. I mean, I've heard of him."

"Well, the trainer says that he remembers Esposito because he
was the biggest player. He had the biggest head of hair, too. There
was another one, Tony, his brother. The Romanian team was very
excited, nervous, to be playing his team, but Esposito was relaxed.
He met Esposito and he has a photo."

"A photo?"

"Yes. A picture. Trainer says he will bring it."

"Thank you, thank you," I told him, shaking his hand.

"Ya!" he said, turning away into the rink.

The arena was stuffed with fans. And riot police, hundreds of
them. They'd fastened heavy Plexiglas visors to their helmets and
were carrying billy clubs. The crowd was already singing the
Hungarian freedom song for which Zoltan's father had written the
words. It was a great, throaty anthem. Fans locked arms and swayed
when they sang, calling out for one side of the stands to join the
other. Janet and I settled in a section above the purple benches, which
were occupied by invited guests: a Hungarian MP, sports writers from
Bucharest, the head of the Romanian sports federation, and local
hockey cognoscenti. Around us, fans cracked the sunflower seeds
sold in paper cones, nervously snapping and chewing as the rosters
were announced over a scratchy public-address system. Denes gave
me a sheet of paper with a hand-written starting lineup, which he'd
got from one of the local writers. He circled the names of the players
from Steaua who were born or bred around Ciuc. They were Andras
Kodstandi and Laszlo Bazilidesz – both members of the top line – as
well as Ioan Timaru, raised just thirty kilometres outside of Ciuc,

who would prove to be Steaua's most effective, and nastiest, forward, a Kenny "the Rat" Linseman of Eastern Europe.

Once the Ciuc lineup was announced, Denes realized that Sport Klub was missing some of its better players. One of them, Kolozsi Lorant, was in jail for having beaten up someone outside a night-club. Three or four others had decided to skate for the Gheorgheni team, while a couple of Ciuc-born forwards were away playing in the Hungarian league. It was a depleted squad but, Denes said, "Not bad. We'll only see what this will mean to Sport Klub once the game begins. At this point, it is hard to tell. Before the game, anything is possible." The referees skated out to the ice, and the crowd readied itself for the appearance of Steaua.

Steaua wore national team jerseys: ROMANIA written in red across royal blue. This was an immediate affront to the crowd. It would be like the Toronto Maple Leafs playing against Montreal in the seventh game of the Stanley Cup finals in Team Canada jerseys. The Steaua sweaters said to the crowd, "We don't even acknowledge you; you don't exist." It would be revealed a few days later that the Romanian Sports Minister had given Steaua the sweaters to help boost their confidence and defeat Ciuc.

The crowd wailed, louder still. Clusters of fans shook their fists and sang the freedom song. There was a veil of smoke hanging over the rink. Toothless old men wearing fedoras and smoking cigarettes cried *"Hungaria!"* and *"Freedom!"* If I hadn't known better, I could have sworn I was at the Felt Forum, circa 1942. Although the section in which we were sitting was mostly occupied by middle-aged men, the crowd was all ages. In the stands nearest to the home side, young men waved blue and white Sport Klub flags. Janet went to photo-graph them, and when she returned, she reported seeing a tiny girl wearing little pink gloves who thrust her middle finger furiously at Steaua when they hit the ice.

While Steaua warmed up their goalie – he was tiny and quick, like Arturs Irbe – Sport Klub skated out to great applause and, of course, more singing. I'd never heard such singing from a crowd. I couldn't tell where one anthem started and where the other ended. There were fans in each section who stood in the front row and

Sport Klub fans

directed the tune in whatever direction they saw fit. They were like conductors in sweats, calling up tunes among the supporters. This resulted in a great, booming wall of sound, a mad sports opera that, once it kicked into high gear with the faceoff, shook me to the bone.

Sport Klub's jerseys were a crazy billboard of logos. Compared to Steaua's – which were new and perfect and had only one name, Gillette, stitched below the crest – Sport Klub's looked like Bobby Unser's bumper. The faces of the players were different, too. Steaua had quite a few clean-shaven, square-shouldered forwards whose physiques showed their training regimen, while the Ciuc players were more individual, scruff-faced, and lumpen. Sport Klub was young and old, big and small, and instead of looking like they'd been equipped by the same outfitter, some of them – like Istvan Gereb, the forty-six-year-old veteran – wore gloves that they might have had since childhood, while Laszlo Kovacs, Vakar's grandson, had modern equipment untouched by time.

I looked across at the Steaua bench and saw that the fellow with the air horn had taken a seat just above the players. He hung the horn over the railing until it was a few feet above the coach's ear, then began pumping it. *Whaoooonk! Whaoooonk!* The coach, a grim-looking man, waved his hand above his head like a man swatting bees. *Whaooook! Whaooook!* The referees called the players to centre ice, where a Finlandia vodka logo bled across the middle of the rink. Ciuc iced a starting five that included Attila Nagy, the visorless defencemen and Ciuc captain. Nagy skated back to his goalie, put his hand on the back of his head and whispered something to him. The goalie nodded and Nagy drifted, stick across his knees to the blue line. As he did this, the antagonist from Steaua, Timaru, stood in the faceoff circle with his hand on his hip. Nagy gestured to the ref and the game began.

The game started slick and exciting and, with the crowd charged the way it was, it had all the drama of a Stanley Cup final. Gereb had Ciuc's best chance early, but he was called for an offside. As the whistle sounded, he floated over the blue line and fired a shot that zoomed just past the head of the Steaua goalie, Viorel Radu. It looked like Gereb couldn't stop his shot in time but, considering the history of these two teams, one couldn't know for sure. As Gereb circled behind the net, Radu shot his stick out, catching the Ciuc veteran just under the shoulder. Gereb spun around and skated backwards outside the zone, glaring at the little Army goalie.

There was more hitting in this game than I'd seen the previous afternoon, but it wasn't the kind of open-ice stuff you'd find at home (or used to find). Instead, collisions happened along the boards and in the corners. Neither team played a physical game, but whenever they had a chance to get a stick or a leg on an opponent, they did. Steaua had two rangy defencemen who did this well. Their first goal came when one of them stole the puck from a Ciuc forward trying to avoid a check. The defenceman stepped over the line like Larry Robinson or Rob Blake and beat the Ciuc goalie, Ladai, with a slap-shot low along the ice. If you'd asked him, Ladai probably would have told you that it was the kind of shot that he usually stops in practice. But, like the rest of us, his nerves were crawling along a knife's edge. The crowd let out a groan, but soon resumed its chanting. I looked over at Denes, who was shaking his head and smiling.

"What're they saying?" I asked.

"Steaua player's mother is a pig gypsy scoundrel!"

"What about that guy?" I asked, pointing to an enormous, bearded fellow dressed like a woodsman who was clapping his hands above his head and shouting in a deep, growling baritone.

"He is talking about possible urination on the head of the player from Steaua!"

"And him?" I asked, gesturing to another fan.

"Gypsy pig traitor!"

There was one Ciuc supporter, as imposing as Sasquatch, who spent the period leaning into our section and giving the sports federation rep from Bucharest the what-for. To his credit, the rep stared straight ahead despite the visceral verbal assault. I was reminded of the night of the Richard riots, when Clarence Campbell was approached by a fan with a program asking for an autograph. Campbell responded implacably, writing his name. The fellow looked at the signature, then raised the magazine and brought it down over the president's head. After that: smoke bombs and busted windows. Campbell's assailant was a little wraith of a man, but the Ciuc fan who was giving the federation rep an earful looked big enough to pick him up and hurl him over the stands to the ice. And we were only ten minutes into the game.

About five minutes after their first goal, Steaua scored again. This time, when the players arrived at their bench, they taunted the fans with their sticks, poking them into the air. They waved their hands and made gestures of strength like posing bodybuilders.

"The idiots from Steaua!"

"*Traitor!*"

"*Hungareeeeaaaaa!*"

The guy with the air horn went mental, sounding it for the whole of the next shift, which resulted in a goal by Ciuc. While this narrowed the score to 2–1, provoking more singing and cheers from the crowd, it also meant that Mr. Air Horn was convinced that his instrument had been the cause of the goal, meaning that the rest of the game featured the kind of air horn solo usually reserved for sax players falling through the circles of hell. The crowd picked up a new chant, so I poked Denes and asked him.

"*The idiots from Steaua!*" he screamed, his voice barely heard over the din.

The period ended 2–1, and so did the noise. The crowd caught its breath. We made our way out to the concourse, where people were milling around, some wandering into the sunshine, others cruising the concession stands, which were two long tables manned by a team of young women. Denes, Ferenc, and I talked about the game and the consensus was that, while Ciuc were still in the game, they had to play better to match Steaua's skill. But in sudden-death games, anything was possible. Besides, if anybody could run Steaua out of the rink, Mr. Air Horn had as good a chance as anyone.

Ciuc perked up in the second period. Kovacs, the heir to the Lajos legacy, buzzed around the Steaua zone, wreaking havoc in the goal crease. He skated like Cliff Ronning, snowing the goalie, poking after loose pucks, and burrowing like a beetle under Radu's skin. Radu was petulant, and Ciuc played this to their advantage. They followed Kovac's lead and pressed on his doorstep until the little goalie took to flailing his stick like an egg beater whenever anyone came close, often putting himself out of position. Still, no matter how hard Sport Klub ran him, he was able to command the game in his end. My sense was that if Ciuc had any real chance of getting back into the game, the second period was the only time. Many of the Steaua players were preoccupied with jibing the crowd, leaving room for Nagy to rush the puck, which he did often and effectively.

Over the course of the period, Radu's behaviour worsened and the tension between the two teams mounted. Tiramu, the little devil, had a chance in close, but he was stopped by the Ciuc goalie, Ladai, whom he promptly punched in the neck. There was a frenetic scrum around the goal with players hanging on to each other, but the referees skated in and broke it up. No penalty was called on Tiramu – "*Gypsy! Traitor!*" – which the gritty Army forward took as a moral victory. This appeared to energize his team and, on the following shift, Steaua scored their third goal, which they celebrated at great length, hugging and jumping and skating as a group back to the bench. It was an obnoxious display of mock joy.

As well as sounding his contraption, Mr. Air Horn leaned over the
railing and screamed insults at the players. There was shuffling
throughout the crowd and I noticed the first sign of activity among
the riot police, who shuttled from one side of the rink to the other,
thickening on the top level above the taunting fans.

The crowd chanted, *"It's now or never!"*

Whaooooonk!

The mantle of smoke on the ceiling was beginning to spread out
into the crowd, and the game took on an ethereal quality, as if I was
watching it through the foggy rear window of a car. Tiramu skated
to the faceoff circle and waved his hand at the crowd, prodding them
like a relentless insult comic. But the veterans Gereb and Nagy, realizing the threat, led their team up-ice. They pinned Steaua in their
zone until they scored, making it 3–2. It was enthralling hockey.
During Ciuc's play, the Hungarian fans threw their shoulders against
each other, arms flailing, necks pulled back, hands gripping their
faces. They'd willed Sport Klub to find the net, the puck popping in
from a seemingly impossible angle. After the goal, Radu lay prone in
his crease like a snow angel. The kids directly above him leaned over
the railing and yowled. Tiramu stood next to him, tapping his pads
and looking worriedly up into the stands.

After the second period, the score 3–2 for Steaua, Karolina
asked if I wanted to interview a former Romanian national team
member in the Sport Klub's lounge. I said that I did, and so we
descended into the bowels of the rink. We were taken to the president's quarters, a small drawing room with pennants of obscure
international teams pinned to the wall: Nederlander Ijshockey
Bond, Ice Hockey Federation of Slovenia, CSSLH, Sg Dynamo,
Trebic, and others. There was also a glass cabinet filled with the
vases, cups, trophies, plates, goblets, urns, and chalices won by
Ciuc over the years.

I took a chair across from Istvan Takacs. He was a gentle, frosty-
haired fellow who had played for the Romanian Nats in the 1959
World Championships in Geneva, and then in 1963 in Stockholm.
He answered my questions slowly, but in Hungarian, as if speaking

deliberately would help me understand him better. Karolina translated. I asked him why he started playing.

"It was in 1946," he said. "I started because, really, it is what all of us did, and still do. It is our way of life, the way it is for you in Canada. My philosophy is: hockey is life. What you learn on the ice, you take to your home, your office. Nothing that you accomplish on the ice is unnecessary."

"What are some of the things hockey has taught you?"

"So much about life, about other people, and getting along with them," he said. "Through hockey, you learn to respect life and to value people. You learn to listen to your coach, and to your heart. You learn how to let your mind speak with your body, because the two become close after playing all these years," he sighed, building a house with his fingers.

"Did you ever play under circumstances like today's game?" I asked.

"It wasn't quite the same for me. My greatest games were international, when I competed around the world. The Olympic ideal was enforced, to play only for the game and my country, never for money."

"Did you ever play against Canada?"

"Yes, many times."

"Can you remember one particular player?"

The old-timer paused. He looked over my shoulder and narrowed his eyes. They became misty as he stared off into the distance, pausing a long time.

"Yes, I remember one."

"Who?" I asked.

"Jules Berry," he said.

The old-timer's eyes grew wet.

"Jules Berry," he repeated, shaking his head.

The room was quiet. I could hear the sounds of fans outside, smoking and drinking and arguing about hockey. The old-timer repeated the name: "Jules Berry."

I have no idea who Jules Berry is. When I returned to Canada, I dug through the pro, minor pro and national team records, but

Berry's name did not appear anywhere. No one in Canadian hockey had heard of him. To Ivan Takacs, however, the memory of Jules Berry was clear as a bell. His name had sent him into a sweet, sad trance. This phantom Canadian Nat represented a time in Takacs' life when he'd crossed the European continent by train and visited two of Europe's great cities, playing out of doors with his countrymen on torchlit rinks in front of hearty crowds of men in scarves and fur hats, children packed in wool, and girls with alabaster skin and golden hair, their voices soft as snowflakes. Discotheques, cobblestones, cafés, raisin buns, reporters with great whooshing cameras, automobiles snorting black smoke, mountain slopes and ski runs, salted fish, sweet beer.

In the world of international hockey, players steal memories from each other. They mark each other's lives without ever being aware of it. International hockey shrinks the world so that two people who come from places on opposite sides of the earth are allowed to skate their names on the insides of each other's hearts. Their lives are tilted simply by playing together, by crossing paths in a game. During the 1987 Canada Cup in Hamilton, Wayne Gretzky invited members of the Soviet Union National team to his parents' home in Brantford for a barbecue. They talked hockey and ate burgers and two days later played one of the most beautiful exhibitions of hockey ever – passing their lives back and forth just as Jules Berry and Ivan Takacs, Sandor Gal and Espo once had.

"I will try to find Jules Berry," I told the old man.

"Thank you," he said, unfolding his hands.

"Death to the fucking federation!"

The third period started with more smoke and more police. The Sasquatch was now standing a few feet from the Romanian hockey rep, pointing at him. Steaua were the first to score, making it 4–2 with about fifteen minutes left to play. What happened next came in such a flurry that it's difficult to remember the sequence of events.

I only know that it came in a flash and set wildfire to what, until then, had been an intense, well-played game.

Timaru was at the centre of what eventually set Ciuc's blood to boil. This was a shame because, as easy as it was to despise his behaviour, he was clearly the best skater on the ice. But I suppose it was his arrogance that had led him in the first place to play for the Army team instead of his home club in Gheorgheni. Timaru's best hockey came in the third period. He was so involved with the play that the Ciuc players did everything they could to try and take the puck off him, resulting in more incidental contact than we'd seen up until that point. Finally, Nagy hit Timaru with his hip and he went down in the corner. The referee hurried in with one hand raised above his head as Nagy stood over the fallen Timaru, poking his foot with his stick, trying to get him to rise. The ref grabbed Nagy around the waist and pushed him away. The Steaua team skated over to Nagy, insulting him:

"*Pig!*"

"*Outsider!*"

"*Go back to Hungary, pig!*"

Nagy, to his credit, said nothing. He allowed himself to be led to the penalty box. Timaru lay still until the Ciuc captain was removed, then he rose to his feet, shaking his head as if emerging from a nightmare. The first thing he did was try to spear the Sport Klub player closest to him. The crowd hollered at Timaru, calling for his blood as he prowled the ice before lining up for the faceoff. He skated around the ice trying to run at the entire team, but he was on the bench when Steaua scored on the power play, making it 5–2. Captain Nagy came out of the box, and you could see him talking to the players on the bench, telling them, "This game isn't over! Don't let them goad you!"

After their three-goal lead, Steaua tried to slow the action. They fell on the puck whenever they could and lagged it through the neutral zone, spinning back in their own end to kill the clock and diving to the ice whenever a Ciuc player skated near. This did not discourage the home team, however, because they came back with pressure, peppering Radu with shots from every spot on the ice, each volley a gesture of defiance. But the little goalie turned them away easily and kept a lid on his temper until, with about three minutes left to go, all hell broke loose at Vakar Lajos.

There was a goalmouth scramble in front of Radu followed by a whistle and some slashing between players. One of the Army players took exception and cross-checked the veteran Gereb. The veteran stood his ground and hacked him across the arm, crumpling the player to the ice. The Steaua team exploded off the bench. Radu, wielding his blocker, punched the Ciuc player nearest to him, Jozsef Andorjan. Jozsef grabbed the back of the goalie's helmet and tried to pull it off his head. Radu windmilled his arms and caught three different players – including one of his own – with clobbering shots. With this, Ladai sprinted from the other end of the ice and was met at the blue line by Tiramu, who pulled him to the ice, obliging the Ciuc coach to release his players, who jumped from the boards and headed straight for the Steaua Rat.

One of the Army players headed to the bench and started swinging his stick at the crowd. Fans were leaning over the railing, their arms and legs draped over the sides, faces wide with panic. The player thrashed up at Mr. Air Horn, whacking the sides of the contraption while the fan pumped frantically *Whaoooonk*! I could hear the rumbling of boots and, before I knew it, the cops had reached the bottom of the stands to, as it turned out, protect Mr. Air Horn from the player. Kids with blue faces stood up and pelted the visiting team with cups. One of the Steaua players turned around on the ice and landed a haymaker on the Ciuc trainer, sending him sprawling to the ice. Bottles exploded like firecrackers as the crowd sang:

"*Hungareeaaaa!*"

The police gathered near where we were sitting. They stationed themselves in front of the VIPs, and I looked down at the Romanian sports rep and the Hungarian MP. Their faces were frozen. Sasquatch was screaming from behind the cops, snaking his arms over their shoulders to get at the Romanian hockey emissary. On the ice, a Steaua player, Robert Mihai, skated over to where we were sitting. He looked up into the stands and pointed at the Hungarian MP. The player held out his finger until the crowd knew exactly at whom he was pointing. Then brought his stick over his shoulder and steadied it there as if aiming a rifle. He leaned his head against the wood, and paused. Then fired a blast that rocked him back on his skates.

25

THE RETURN OF ESPO

After the game, the rink emptied quickly. There were other matches scheduled for the evening between student teams, so I hung around and studied the photos in the lobby, mulling over the events of the day. As I was doing this, Sandor Gal came running into the room, calling "Ey! Ey! Ey!" I turned around and he gave me the stop sign with his hand. He ruffled through the pockets of his sweat suit and handed me a piece of paper. It was a photograph.

"Thanks," I said.

"Espo-sito," he said.

The photo was creased along the middle. It showed Sandor and Espo at the World Championships in Geneva. When he first told me about it, I thought it would be the two of them with their arms around each other, standing outside the rink like tourists on a junket. But it was nothing of the sort. Instead, there was Espo, towering over the defenceman and whomping his fist at Sandor's head, at which the diminutive Transylvanian laid a cross-check into his ribs – the two of them, sweater to sweater, close like brothers.

Espo eats Sandor's wood

26

THE TROPIC OF HOCKEY

After the final, I arranged with Ferenc to play with the Old Boys later that night.

Just before 9:30 p.m. I set off for the rink. I could see my breath against the inky sky, the hills lurking like sentinels on the horizon. I moved meditatively through the grounds, my hood pulled over my head, distancing all sounds save the leaves underfoot that had crisped with the evening's cold. I came upon the steel sculptures, their bodies drawn in moonlight. These figures poised in full-thrust personified the enduring promise of sport. Even though thousands of fans had paraded past them, downcast, after's Ciuc's loss to Steaua, the tin players continued to push stubbornly against the air. While the home team's loss was now in the books – the Sport Klub players had long ago showered, changed, and greeted their families; trainers had collected the equipment and stowed it away; seats and benches had been swept of paper cups, cigarette butts, and candy wrappers; and Steaua had left town victorious in their old, white bus – still the steel figures of Vakar Lajos and Czka Istun remained, their sticks reaching out to spear the night. I looked up at them, reminding myself that even though we frame sport as singular events, it exists in a realm of perpetual play. Wins become losses that become victories. The score is inconsequential as long as you keep playing.

Ferenc arrived shortly after me, and I followed to my private dressing room (I would have preferred changing with the team, but was flattered to be given a room of my own). It was filled with kids' hockey equipment. The juniors had had a practice earlier that day and left their jerseys hanging to dry – Sweden Hockey Camp, Junior Red Wings, Sport Klub, Gheorgheni, New York Rangers. An old wooden blackboard on a wall bore two logos scratched in chalk: NHL and MTV. These were the dreams of Transylvanian kids – to be a rock star or hockey player – no different from what I'd find at home.

It felt good to be pulling on my equipment after a time away from the game and, even though I was fighting a cold, I was able to banish feeling sick once I hit the ice. Invariably, after those first few strides, my mind is thrown open like a screen door in the wind, physical pain and tension and the complications of life giving way to a freedom of thought, an elemental state, light but not empty. Many times over the course of my journey I was astonished by where I was and could think of nothing other than the strangeness of my environs, but there were as many moments while skating when I felt that I was nowhere, anywhere, because I'd glided into that space:

Hockey.

I walked from the dressing room along an old rubber runway under the stands, passing a long, unframed black-and-white photograph of Romania playing the Central Red Army, taken during a tournament in 1972. The Russians had used this game as a tune-up before crossing the ocean to play Canada in the first summit series. As I emerged from the runway into the rink, I saw that the stands had been drained of all the drama and peril – and smoke – of the cup final. It was now a rink like any other, and I, just a player, conscious of only the *snik snik snik* and *krrrrr* of my skates as they carved the ice. I was joined by a few skaters, then a few more. Some wore old yellow and blue Sport Klub jerseys, while others had newer black sweaters with red flames spiking up from the hem, *Old Boys* printed in a zigzag across the chest. Once the whole crew had stepped onto the ice, I asked Ferenc to identify the Olympians. Two of the skaters – Dezso Vargha and Elod Antal – had played on the 1980 Romanian Olympic team in Lake Placid. As with many old-timers, they didn't look fit enough to take the bus let alone score goals. Dez had a pendulous belly that swung when he skated. His head was shaved and he had a friendly moon-shaped face. He was among the first of the Old Boys to skate over and greet me, paddling the ass of my pants with his stick. The other Olympian, Elod, was tall and fragile. The defining feature of his equipment was a mouthguard made of moulded bits of white plastic. It was attached to the side of his square, Red Berenson-style helmet below his chin-strap and, because he was thin and gaunt, it lent him the appearance of a skeleton showing you its teeth.

We separated into two sides and started playing. I soon discovered that the level of hockey was beyond me. The Old Boys whirled and spun around the ice, passing hard and deft through the lanes, using the whole of the ice. They unloaded slapshots with such force that I could feel the gust of their wind-up and follow-through when I stood near. I tried desperately to keep pace, but was forced to take quick shifts to stop my heart from exploding. I was hyperventilating on the bench when Dez sat beside me.

"You. Olympics?" I huffed.

"Ya," he said.

"Romania?"

He nodded.

"1980?"

"Ya."

"Sweden. Third . . ." I said, holding up three fingers.

"Ya."

"Russia. Second," I said.

He nodded.

"USA. One . . ."

"Ya."

"How?" I asked.

He shrugged.

"You. USA?" he asked.

"No," I said. "Canada."

"Ahhh. Canada. Six," he smiled, jumping over the boards.

I took my next shift and peeled onto the ice, determined to touch the puck. As it had in Harbin, it took me a while to adjust to the wide surface, but once I discovered that the key was to try to out-skate the other player, I simplified my game. Which isn't to say that I out-skated anyone, it's just that I had a better idea of what I would have done, had I been able to do it. I caught a pass and broke over the blue line unleashing a wrist shot that had all the power of a wind-blown plastic bag. But it was a start. I handled the puck a little more, and did my usual muck and dig routine, winning the odd battle in the corners, hitting the tape with passes.

After about twenty minutes, I was standing at the edge of the crease when Elod dashed for the puck in the corner. As he picked it up, I shouted "*Ho! Ho!*" and, without looking at me, he turned and fired it towards the net. The puck found my stick and bounced in the air.

Elod's pass was a latitude, a tropic, that crossed many points in the world of hockey. It started on the tape of a player who'd played against Kharlamov, Tretiak, and the rest of the Central Red Army, players who'd trained right here at Vakar Lajos before leaving for Canada in 1972, where they crept across our country, showcasing a style born in a society that would one day give rise to Ceauşescu, who would, in turn, build a team to keep the Transylvanians down, to make sure that the world never heard of Vakar or Elizabeth Lajos. In Lake Placid, Elod had faced-off against the American Miracle on Ice team, and between the Americans and the Russians, the old-timer's hockey career had wound like a thread around the two teams that had made Canadians realize that hockey had become a game of the world, had flown the coops of the Sault, Delisle, and Flin Flon.

I squared to the puck, thinking of Jagr and Bure, two players who'd also skated in Ciuc, who had fought for the puck in the spot where I now stood. They, too, had gone on to do things on the ice that would give pause to those who'd seen Orr, Hull, and Béliveau, inventing a new game after countless bus rides around the Socialist gulag. Then, I thought of Roman Lebedev, the bulbous Russian who'd played for Spartak with Pavel's brother, and how Nasser,

Ahmed, and Kareem had watched him from the stands in Al Ain, their heads on their arms, imagining themselves playing the way the dexterous Russian did. I thought of Espo, the Swiss kids, Sandor Gal. I thought of Jin Guang, the Chinese goaltender. He'd made his comeback here, in China's first tournament after the Cultural Revolution. He'd prepared for the game in the same damp change room where I'd pulled on a CCM helmet made by workers in the factories of Guangzhuo. He'd also pulled a cage over his face and listened to the sound of his own breath as he carved the ice in the very spot where I now twirled to face Dez, who was floating towards me from the blue line, pointing with his old glove at the puck. It had spanked my stick, spun for a second in the air, and fallen into the net.

I remember the goal in slow motion, like a traffic accident, or a first kiss. I remember the puck fluttering in the air like a black butterfly; the toe of the goalie's boot moving across the crease; the puck bouncing once, twice, a third time, then spinning on the ice like a penny; the goalie falling to one knee, his arm sweeping the air; and finally, my hands raised to the sky, howling the howl I was born with. I felt like grooving a flag on the mark where my skates had cut the ice. I was jubilant as Dez put his big arm around me. The puck lay behind the goaltender, and when one of the players went to fish it out, I bent under the crossbar and picked it up, turning it over in my hand.

I skated across the ice to the bench knowing that I was gliding through a confluence of hockey. I'd taken to the road in spring and travelled thousands of miles in search of such a place – a rink in the coldest town in Romania, home to a mosaic of players' lives and events as significant as any in the sporting world, from the newsreel that inspired Vakar Lajos to learn Canada's game to the technique that young Jagr and Bure had perfected so that hockey could move into the twenty-first century. This realization made me feel reverence for where I was, so I let the puck fall from my hand, where it was snatched by a stick and shot away, rising about a foot off the ice, a lovely black curve cruising the air, returning to its place on the tropic of hockey.

ACKNOWLEDGEMENTS

One more story for the road.

On our last day in Romania, walking the streets of Bucharest, we passed a row of clapboard stalls selling used books for a dime apiece. Most of the titles were old and dog-eared and appeared to be Romanian translations of the classics. After spending the afternoon navigating the city by foot – and being dissuaded at every turn from visiting museums, concert halls, and libraries by truculent Romanians – I passed these same stalls on the way back to our hotel. Glancing over my shoulder, I noticed a book that was a little larger than the rest with a blurred white and blue photo on the cover. Then I saw it was *Hockey: The Sports Playbook*, Red Kelly with Martin Lader.

Astonished, I flipped it open to a photo of goalie Ed Giacomin and the words: "This is a game, I discovered, that prepares you for life." I didn't venture to consider how a book about hockey published by Doubleday in 1976 had managed to find its way under the former Iron Curtain and onto the streets of Bucharest, nor did I think too long about how I had been there to rescue it. I handed my hundred lei to the old, aproned woman standing behind the stall and walked away, finally understanding what Harvey Bennett had hinted at years ago in the darkness of that weird Southern night: if you believe in hockey, it will find you.

The Red Kelly book was symbolic of the many literary discoveries I made while researching this project. While it's a popular lament that hockey writing doesn't match baseball's prose when it comes to both quantity and quality, there are numerous hockey titles which I'd count among my favourite sports books. Over the course of my work, I was turned on to Dick Beddoes (*The Greatest Hockey Stories Ever* and *Pal Hal*), Stan Fischler (*Slapshot!* and *Those Were the Days*) and Andy O'Brien (*Rocket Richard* and *Young Hockey Champions*); revisited classic texts by Trent Frayne, Jim Hunt, Jack Ludwig, Hugh Hood, Doug Beardsley, Earl McRae, Roy MacGregor, Jack Batten, Charles L. Coleman, Scott Young, and Bill Roche; and devoured biographies of Turk Sanderson, Vern Buffey, Bill Chadwick, Dave Schultz, Fred Shero, Don Cherry, Tiger Williams, John Bucyk, Stan Mikita, and quite possibly the best hockey book ever written, the autobiography *They Call Me Gump*, by Lorne Worsley and Tim Moriarty. I'd also like to note the stirring work of Jeff Z. Klein and Karl-Eric Reif, whose *Village Voice* columns in the 1980s I consider a benchmark for all modern hockey prose, as well as a few anthologies – David Gowdey's *Riding on the Roar of the Crowd*, Dan Diamond's *Total Hockey*, and Stephen Cole's *Slapshots*. This is not to overlook countless back issues of the *Hockey News*, *Hockey Pictorial*, and *Hockey World*, which never failed to wrest my interest. And I'd be remiss not to mention esteemed poets Richard Harrison, John B. Lee, Mark Cochrane, and, of course, Al Purdy, who died during the writing of this book, a few months before the Rocket joined him on that slippery oval in the sky.

Janet and I would like to thank Herb and Joanne Shoveller, Tom Barnes, the Essex Hunt Club Foxes, Wang Lu, Team Beijing, Nasser and Mohammed, Steve Conniff, Chris Reynolds, and Denes, Ferenc, and Karolina for showing us fathomless warmth and goodwill. I'd also like to note those who helped in the conception, execution, and creation of this book: Kimmo Leinonen, Brad Pascall, James Duplacey, Dan Diamond, Stu Hackl, Dave King, Brian MacFarlane, Ken Dryden, Dave Maloney (who visited

Ciuc in 1977 as a twenty-year-old), Curt Bennett (Harvey's son), Paul Tough, Steve Hubbard, Pat Houda, Stefan Kreuger, Birgen Nordmark, Bob Mackin, Dick Irvin, Steve Cherwonak, Jim Gregory, Pat Flatley, Tom Hayden, Dave Bookman, Steve Stanley, the staff at Toronto Hockey Repair, Matt Cowley, Peter Oliva, Gord Downie, Brian Pickell, Ken Elliott, Warren Campbell, Bruce Dowbiggin, Paul Steenheusin, Craig Taylor, Mark Sadgrove, Nick Hornby, Aurora Browne, and the Rheostatics. I reserve special thanks for my editor and teacher, Dinah Forbes, as well as the team at M&S, and Dave Johnston, the mightiest of agents.

I'm grateful for the efforts made by those who enlightened me about hockey in countries that I wanted to visit, but could not – Scotland, Wales, France, South Africa, Mongolia, England, New Zealand, Australia, and India – and to my Irish friends – Sean, Mary, John, Dolores, Roddy, Belinda, and Mary. I indeed visited Ireland and had the good fortune of playing with the Republic's only hockey team – the Dublin Flyers – where I met Cliff Saunders and Mark Bowes, who will one day bring honour to Irish hockey once they trade in their carpet-dragging tractor for a proper Zamboni. Cheers as well to Tommy Hull and the staff at the Dundonald Ice Bowl in Belfast, where I had the game of my life. I ran out of room to tell the Irish story.

Finally, I would not have written this book were it not for the players with whom I share ice in Toronto, from the fellows in UIC, who started Sunday-night hockey back in 1986 when it was neither popular nor profitable, to my Morningstar teammates, each of whom I love and respect dearly.

If I've learned anything from this book, it's that the world of hockey is terribly intimate, so I really shouldn't have been surprised when I arrived home from my journey to find Billy, McCormick's rumpled rink attendant, underwhelmed with news of my travels. "There was a rink in Hong Kong," I told him excitedly, "with a yellow roller-coaster track running above it!"

"Hong Kong, eh?" he said, leaning on his broom. "That's kinda funny."

"Funny, why?" I asked.

"Because the Koreans were here last week. They took photos of the rink and dressing rooms; they even photographed the 'Emergency Eye Wash' sign. It was weird. They said they're building a replica of our rink back home."

Dave Bidini
June 2000

Please write:
PO Box 616
Station C
Toronto, Ontario, Canada
M6J 3R9